The Encyclopedia Yiddishanica

A Compendium of Jewish Memorabilia

An anthology of Jewish history, culture, religion, language, idioms, colloquialisms and teachings

by
ENDEL MARKOWITZ

Printed in the United States of America
I.S.B.N. 0-933910-02-9
Library of Congress Catalog Number: 79-89973

Unless otherwise noted, all photographs published are through the courtesy of B'nai Brith International

CONTENTS

''from Egypt even until now''
(NUM. 14:19)

The Encyclopedia Yiddishanica

Preface

The *Encyclopedia Yiddishanica* is a comprehensive volume of facts designed to be a source of information for those who wish to have a basic familiarity with things Jewish. Hopefully, it will serve as an incentive to its readers to study further Jewish culture and tradition, for it contains the basic fundamentals of the vast panorama of what we know to be Yiddishkeit. For the young and the student, it avails unto them a vast aggregation of historical facts, religious liturgies, colloquialisms, two dictionaries and numerous pleasureable expressions. To the old and the experienced, it will bring back memorable personal reminders of the Jewishness they once knew as children.

The purpose of the Encyclopedia Yiddishanica is to present a montage of Jewish trivia, facts and folklore. Through this presentation of colloquial expressions, commonly used idioms, historical data, religious rites and functions, a profound sense of wonder will be created as the reader begins to appreciate the scope and complexity of Yiddish significance. Utilizing the Torah and the Talmud as its foundation, Judaism has, in its framework, a multitude of ceremonial and ritualistic experiences embodying the deepest feelings of reverence. Each one has its own symbolism, its peculiar rite and its exclusive purpose and intent. Its performance is testimony to the awe and esteem in which a Jew holds his Creator.

Although there is a massive amount of information included in this manuscript, care has been taken to present the facts in a clear and concise manner. I have focused on information which should be useful to the layman, keeping esoteric and technical data to a minimum. All of the information presented has been compiled with the desire to eliminate confusion and undue complexity.

Basically, the material in this encyclopedia is intended to dispel the enigma of Judaism. To try to define, with written words, the Jewish presence on earth is like unraveling the universe and placing in sequence, all the stars in the heavens. From its origin, more than 5000 years ago, until the present day, the Jews have run the gauntlet of every form of physical, spiritual and emotional extremism. From the time when they first emerged as the adherents of one God, they have been the victims of reaction from those who misunderstood and feared this presence, and retaliated with recrimination and abuse.

—How then do we analyze and define the Jew? How do we arrive at the final equation that explains who and what he is? To find the answer, one must first find the solution to the following questions.

—What is it that enabled him to survive through aeons of time against all odds, extreme recriminations and devastating persecutions?

—What is the mysterious force within him that can find the strength to withstand all forms of torture and find solace in his destruction simply by whispering certain prayers?

—Where did he reach, within himself, to find the ability to laugh at himself in the midst of his misfortunes?

—How did he, out of this historical morass, produce the thousands of intellectuals, scientists, writers and doctors who have enriched the world with their knowledge?

—Comprising a mere fraction of the worlds population, how have Jews managed to survive, through the ages, against the worst acts of man?

The continued presence and steadfast adherence of Jews to their faith is a source of wonder and incredulity. Forced to survive by using their wits, they created self-protective measures to thwart their adversaries and, with the passing of time, their ability to cope against their aggressors took on new dimensions. It asserted itself in many forms; a refusal to turn the other cheek, pride in their religion and the ever-present hope of achieving a homeland which was finally accomplished.

Today, for the first time in their long and torturous past, the Jews have achieved respect and admiration in the world community. In Israel, a true democracy exists and the Jew has found a home where, never again, will he be persecuted for the God he believes in. The primary benefits of this 'Moment of Peace', which has proven so elusive in their long and bitter history, has always produced a wide range of scholarly, ethical and cultural accomplishments. In their

Golden Ages, during short respites from abuse and recrimination, their wisdom and brilliance shone through, only to be thrown back under the heels of their oppressors.

The lesson should be clear. Suffering has instilled in the Jewish people a unique perspective on life which when offered to the world, may well bring about a new Golden Age of love and humanity for mankind.

Dedicated to
Mama and Papa
who taught us,
as young children,
this beautiful and
expressive
Yiddish language.

Introduction

Every man has a story to tell. The writing of books, particularly glossaries, biographies, anthologies, compendiums and the like, have no end. Adding this manuscript to the others would be completely pointless except for two basic reasons, 1- the numerous requests for information relating to Jews, Yiddish, Judaism and other related facts pertaining to Yiddishkeit and, 2- that we have broken new ground in offering the layman a comprehensive encyclopedia involving many phases of Judaism and presented in a manner that is neither overly complex nor confusing.

The Enclyclopedia Yiddishanica is not intended to be a source of comprehensive information for the Yeshiva 'bauchehrs' who are searching for an answer to the complex mysteries of the Mishna or Gemara. The material between its covers is merely meant to inform the Americanized youngster or oldster, whose parents, grand-parents and ancestors were part and parcel of that remarkable group of people whose lives were touched by the hand of God, and who have the desire, the craving and the curiosity to learn of their unconquerable Jewish tradition.

The greatest problem confronting me as I began compiling this information was the inexhaustable amount of relevant material available. A difficult decision had to be made in deciding what to include and what to delete, for the further I delved into Jewish history, the more pertinent everything became. Confronted with this dilemma, I had to evaluate this vast amount of material and select the information which I believed the reader would be most interested in and would readily enjoy and understand. For this reason I have excluded all but minute reference to Jewish esoteric writings, the mystical Caballah, the theosophical works, the metaphysical, exegesis, astronomy, medicine and geography. Without these, however, there is still a mountain of material as can be seen in the Table of Contents.

If this compendium is useful in revealing even a very small part of the qualities that make up Judaism, in all its intracacies, I shall consider this undertaking a success.

The proverbs of Solomon, the son of David, king of Israel;
That men may gain wisdom and instruction,
May understand words of intelligence;
That they may receive instruction in wise conduct,
In rectitude, justice, and honesty;
That sense may be imparted to the simple,
Knowledge and discretion to the inexperienced—
The wise man also may hear and increase his learning,
The man of intelligence acquire sound principles—
That they may understand proverb and parable,
The words of the wise and their epigrams. . . . . . .

EXHORTATIONS
From the Old Testament.

The Origin of Yiddish

Throughout its early history, due to amalgamation and the interrelationships of Jews with alien cultures and nationalities, Hebrew, the sacred tongue of Judaism, was forced to co-exist with an assortment of other languages which gradually drove it completely out of common usage. At the time of the Second Temple, the common language of the Jews, in their daily conversation, was Aramaic; those living in Palestine spoke Greek and for hundreds of years, the Jews in North Africa and the Near East spoke Arabic. Centuries later, during the Golden Age in Spain, a conglomerized language with a Spanish base, called Ladino, was adopted by the Marrano Jews of that area.

At the end of the 15th Century in Spain, driven by persecution and forced to seek haven in other countries, they fled across Europe, settling in Germany, Poland, Russia and other Eastern European countries. It was here, among the Ashkenazims, that Yiddish blossomed into the colorful language that we are familiar with today.

The origin of Yiddish can be traced back to the 11th Century in Germany where, adapting the guttural German tongue to fit in with their needs and purposes, the Jews gradually developed a language within a language. Consisting primarily of German words reproduced into Hebrew characters, it gradually underwent changes in pronunciation and meaning. Adding to this transliteration, Hebrew terms were included to inject their religious and cultural committment.

As Jewish migration to Eastern Europe continued and large bodies of Jews moved to Poland, Russia and Lithuania, their desire to maintain relations with one another infused the Yiddish language with Slavic expressions which gradually transformed their daily speech into a blending of German, Hebrew and Slavic. Because of the environment and their confinement to ghettos and small Jewish shtet'ls, additional idioms, colloquialisms and vocabulary were created to reflect their unusual individual existence.

In the 13th Century, the Yiddish language had become the common speech across the entire Diaspora, serving as a necessary substitute to Hebrew although never replacing the sacred tongue in the liturgy of the synagogues. This dual bilingualism continued well into the 20th Century, being brought over to America on their flight from Eastern Europe to escape recrimination. In the United States, the Yiddish language flourished and was again complemented by the inclusion of many English expressions.

During their entire existence in the Diaspora of Eastern Europe, the pressure of living under adverse conditions necessitated the use of a practical language to fulfill the need for daily communication. Though linked together under a common bond, Hebrew and Yiddish, creating complications in dialogue, served their separate purposes. Hebrew was necessarily confined to the Sabbath and the synagogues, while Yiddish continued to be used in daily conversation. It was through this procedure, that Hebrew was preserved and consecrated through the centuries.

In the 18th Century, traditional Yiddish literature blossomed. With the rise of Hasidism, a tremendous resurgency of Yiddish literary accomplishments occurred and borrowing heavily from their folk lore and history, the Hasidim prepared the way by raising Yiddish to a level of esteem never before attained. Hasidic writers elevated Yiddish story telling, prose and poetry to the highest levels of literary achievement through the unique use of parables and allegorical expressions, and by the latter part of the century, Yiddish literature had reached such a pinnacle that it drew the acclaim of the entire Jewish community.

Towards the end of the 19th Century, the advancement of Yiddish literature was basically the result of a disagreement between the traditionalism of Eastern European Jews and the Enlightenment movement; the two opposite factions of the Haskalah and the Hasidim, which, while creating chaos in traditional Jewish life, nevertheless served as a preservative for Yiddish culture. It was the Haskalah, advocating secularism and worldliness, which convinced Jewish writers and poets that Yiddish culture consisted of more than the traditional orthodoxy of its faith. The reaction of the traditionalists was immediately critical. They claimed that secularism would eventually destroy the sanctification of Jewish faith and tradition and their endeavors succeeded in creating a wide breach in the Jewish community. This fissure in the two schools of thought unwittingly brought about an interval of creative excellence in the fields of literary endeavor. Though locked in a battle of ideals, the opposing factions of orthodoxy and secularism shared a common heritage which resulted in the consolidation of 'Yiddishkeit', the essence of Jewish culture.

It must be emphasized that the foundation of Yiddish literature is based on the long and tortuous road of Jewish history. With the Bible as its source of information, drawing from its rich background of folk lore, and with blood ties to the past, Yiddish poets and writers were able to grasp and delineate the moral philosophies of a people who, throughout history, existed in a world apart from all other people.

Foreword

Mamaloshen (Yiddish) is the fascinating, nostalgic language (Shprach) of our parents and grandparents, brought over to America on the decks of ships which carried them from the heartlands of Poland and Russia. They came to America (the Goldeneh Medine), the land of milk and honey and with them came their culture, their dreams and most importantly, their Yiddish language, their mother-tongue, their Mamaloshen.

In many instances, which are not readily translatable into English, this language of our fathers (Tahtis) and our mothers (Mahmes) is an outpouring of intense Jewish feeling and emotion. There are innumerable examples where an expression's literal translation is meaningless but its real meaning comes from the hearts and souls of East European Jewish culture. A few examples follow:

HOCK MIR NIT KAIN TCHYNICK

Literal translation:	Stop banging the teakettle.
English Meaning:	Cut out the nonsense.

AH KIYE UND AH SHPIYE

Literal translation:	A chew and spit.
English meaning:	It doesn't mean a thing.

DU ZOLST LEBEN AHZOY LAHNG

Literal translation:	You should live so long.
English meaning:	You're dead wrong.

AH NECHTEGEN TAUG.

Literal translation:	A nightly day.
English meaning:	Impossible.

GAY COCKIN AHFFEN YOM.

Literal translation:	Go defecate on the ocean.
English meaning:	Get away from me.

Yiddish, like those who spoke it, is a wild, windswept, provocative tongue. In it is ingrained the deepest emotions of a people, who throughout history, have struggled merely to survive. In all their sorrows and trepidations, their mother tongue contains the humor, the pathos, the wit and the grief of a people who refused to resign themselves to their tragic circumstances but continued to find a strange, fatalistic solace and hope in their sufferings; in the ability to laugh at themselves.

This was their indestructability. The language, like the people, has a latent survival source which continued to exist regardless of the forces and pressures against it. Many adjectives can be used to describe Yiddish; colorful, wild, ridiculous, rootless, warm; to name a few. It pulls at your heartstrings and can embarrass your neighbor but it can never be described as dull and colorless.

In Israel today, Yiddish is a language that is being pushed into oblivion. A reminder of the Nazi holocaust (with its German background), Yiddish, the language of their parents who succumbed to their persecutors, is being ignored by the new breed of Jew. Replaced by Hebrew, their national tongue, Yiddish is rarely heard in the Jewish homeland except in one or two small areas.

Endel Markowitz

The following prayer, written in the early 1940's, was the result of the tragic turn of political events in the world. The Reform Judaism movement, having advocated radical changes in the traditional practices of synagogue ritual, was thrown back on its heels by the traumatic experiences of the Nazi Holocaust. The prayer clearly expresses the stamina, durability and elasticity shown by the Jewish people throughout their history and their ability to withstand attacks against them, and still continue to flourish. It is a testimony of man's ability to endure. It clearly emphasizes that there is something within us, perhaps akin to a mystical, omnipotent force, that can overcome any extreme of torture and abuse.

Hear, O Israel

Brethren, let us bethink ourselves of our past, of our common heritage as children of Israel. A strange folk have we been all these years, a riddle and bewilderment to men. Through centuries without end we have wandered about on Earth, fleeing from eternal Egypt through a shoreless Red Sea. We have seen far-flung empires crack and crumble, and mighty peoples dwindle to naught. Armies beyond counting have marched by us in pomp and glory; with kings and priests, with tyrants and princelings, have they marched by us in pride. Yet of them all is no sign left, for they fell and died by the roadside.

But we, the Jews, still march on. Obstinately we fight off Time and Man, contending at each step with a thousand foes, yet ever marching, marching on.

O may there be sense in our persistence, and reason in our tenacity. May our constancy as Jews not be deemed an end in itself, but solely a way and a means. May we live our lives as Jews only to keep alive our heritage, to keep ablaze the fires our Prophets lit. May we, like our fathers, still stand out against the multitude, protesting with all our might against its follies and its fears. May a divine discontent give color to our dreams, and a passion for holy heresy set the tone of our thoughts. May the soul of the rebel still throb in us as it throbbed in our forefathers, that today and forever we may still be a light unto those who stumble in the darkness.

The Jewish section in Eastside, London in the early 1900's

Trivia

At the conclusion of Saturday night services (Myriff) in the synagogue, a final prayer is intoned. The chazen (cantor) lights a candle, usually a long, red and white twisted candle with two wicks, and fills a goblet of wine. As he recites the prayer for a healthy new week to come, the congregation, holding both hands closed in front of them, slowly begins to open their fists by straightening out their fingers, permitting the light of the temple to penetrate into their palms. This symbolizes their hope for light to overcome darkness in the week ahead. This intonation, in Jewish liturgy, is called 'Havdallah'.

YIDDISH

The Yiddish language can only be described as a conglomeration of ageless, paradoxical sentiment transfused into emotional reaction due to the constant pressure and recrimination heaped upon the Jews through the centuries. Steeped in irony and sarcasm; stained and spattered by bitterness and despair, the poignant Jewish existence, painfully accepted as their destiny, reveals itself through the subtlety of sardonic expressions, which strangely enough, enabled them to retain their sanity and continue to survive. It is incredible how the ingenuity of the Yiddish language was capable of creating, evolving and unfolding the complex design that manifested the phenomena of human consciousness and behaviour.

Oblivious of criticism, devoid of authoritative grammar norms, alien in structure to any other language, Yiddish impishly incorporates legalized brigandry by its inclusion of ribald and slang expressions covering every facet of satire, fantasy, cursing, sex and parts of the body. It reflects the release from tension, the escape from ostracism of a people shunned and deprived of the acceptance by others and for this reason, the language, emphasizing their ability to laugh at themselves and their circumstances, was designed to fulfill their need. Its abstruseness, which differentiates Yiddish from other languages, is its unique interpretation of life with all its ramifications.

The fascination of Yiddish lies in its imaginative creation of subtle variations related to life and human behaviour. It reaches into the entire perspectum of mans existence by its esoteric collection of words, phrases, nuances and colloquialisms which were birthed in despair, engendered through resignation, propagated by anger and multiplied by ironic derision. In retrospect, the Yiddish language, like its creators, is a montage of an emotionally charged existence endeavoring to cope with a world who, through the centuries, tried to destroy them.

YIDDISH GRAMMAR AND PRONUNCIATION

YIDDISH GRAMMAR AND PRONUNCIATION

The transliteration of Yiddish words into English has been simplified for easy reading. The reader who knows no Yiddish would find a more complex transposition confusing, and for this reason, we have attempted to avoid strange spellings for the Yiddish word.

Double vowels are used to accent unfamiliar Yiddish sounds: The CH runs throughout the text (the Hebrew letter 'CHAUF') always being pronounced as in the German 'ach', e.g. BACH.

The TZ (denoting the Hebrew letter 'TZAHDIK' is pronounced as the TS in the word 'nuts'.

The letter R, corresponding to the Hebrew letter 'RAYSH' is trilled by placing the tongue against the roof of the mouth. It has a guttural sound starting deep in the throat.

Another sound in Yiddish which has no English equivalent is the ZH (the Hebrew letter SHINN) which is pronounced as the DG in the word 'FUDGE'.

Basis for Yiddish pronunciation

Although there are no written Hebrew words in this glossary, it won't hurt you to know (DOS VETT DIR NIT SHAHTTEN) what the Yiddish and Hebrew alphabet consists of:

	Comparable English letter		Comparable English letter
AHLEF	A	VAUV	V
BAZE	B	ZIEYEN	Z
VAZE	V	*CH*ESS	(none)
GEEMIL	G	TESS	T
DAHLED	D	YOOD	Y
HAY	H	KAWF	C

*CH*AWF	(none)	FAY	F
LAHMED	L	TZAHDICK	(none)
MEM	M	KOOF	K
NOON	N	RAYSH	RR (trilled)
SAHMA*CH*	S	SHINN	(none)
EIYEN	E	SIN	S
PAY	P	TAWF	T
		SAWF	S

The spelling of Yiddish words transliterated into English has many variations depending upon an authors place of birth, his dialect and his method of transposing one language, with an alien alphabet, into another language. I have endeavored to spell the English equivalent in the clearest manner possible for the readers interpretation. If you learn the four unfamiliar sounds, that have no English equivalent, there should be no difficulty in pronouncing the Yiddish words.

VOWELS:

The vowels in Yiddish have several pronunciations. Each is clarified with an additional letter for simplified reading.

LETTER	TRAN-SCRIBED	ENGLISH EXAMPLE	YIDDISH EXAMPLE
A	AH	M*A*MA	M*AH*NDLIN
A	AW	*AU*TO	H*AU*B
A	AY	H*AY*	PL*AY*TZEH
A	UH	MAM*A*	NISHAUM*A*
E	EE	*EA*STER	M*EE*S
E	EH	H*EA*D	L*EH*RER
I	IY	*YE*E	B*IY*TL
I	I	W*I*TH	M*I*TTEN
O	AH	M*O*COW	LAHTKE
O	O	PH*O*BIA	G*O*LDEH
O	OO	S*OO*N	SH*OO*L
O	OY	BU*OY*	GR*OY*
U	U	PUNY	*OO*NTEHR
Y	Y	*Y*ELLOW	*Y*OONG

CONJUGATION OF THE VERB 'TO BE' (Tzu Zyne)

Present Tense:

I am .... Ich bin
You are .... Du bist
He is .... Ehr iz
She is .... Zie iz
We are .... Mir zahnen
They are .... Zey zahnen

Past Tense:

I was .... Ich bin gevehn
You were .... Du bist gevehn
He was .... Ehr iz gevehn
She was .... Zie iz gevehn
We were .... Mir zenen gevehn
They were .... Zey zenen gevehn

Future Tense:

I will be .... Ich vel zyne
You will be .... Du vest zyne
He will be .... Ehr vet zyne
She will be .... Zie vet zyne
We will be .... Mir vellen zyne
They will be .... Zey vellen zyne

Conditional:

I could be .... Ich ken zyne
You could be .... Du kenst zyne
He could be .... Ehr ken zyne
She could be .... Zie ken zyne
We could be .... Mir kennen zyne
They could be .... Zey kennen zyne

I have to be .... Ich darff zyne
You have to be .... Du darfst zyne
He has to be .... Ehr darff zyne
She has to be .... Zie darff zyne
We have to be .... Mir darfn zyne
They have to be .... Zey darfn zyne

I might be .... Ich meg zyne
You might be .... Du megst zyne
He might be .... Ehr meg zyne
She might be .... Zie meg zyne
We might be .... Mir meggen zyne
They might be .... Zey meggen zyne.

Pronouns:

I	Ich.	YOU	Du, Ir.
HE	Ehr.	SHE	Zie, Eer.
WE	Meer.	THEY ...	Zey.
OUR	Oonzehr.	THEIR ..	Zeyer.
US	Oonz.	ME	Meer.
HIM	Ehm.		

On Learning (From the Talmud)

All beginnings are difficult.

Mekilta to Jethro 19:5

A man cannot forget in twenty years what he has learned in two.

Abot d'R Nathan 24:6

A man who has gold but no knowledge . . . what has he?

Kohelet Rabbah, 1,6

He who understands the why and wherefore of what he learns does not forget it quickly.

The Talmud 5:1

He who studies and does not learn his lessons is as one who plants and does not enjoy the fruit.

Sanhedrin, 90

If thou lackest knowledge, what has thou acquired? If thou acquirest knowledge, what dost thou lack?

Bedidbar Rabbah.

If you do not teach the ox to plow in his youth, it will be difficult to teach him when he is grown.

Midrash Mishle, 22

Take fast hold of instruction; let her not go: Keep her; for she is thy life.

Proverbs 4:13

A TREASURY OF JEWISH PROVERBS, MAXIMS, FOLKSAYINGS, QUOTATIONS AND ANECDOTES

A TREASURY OF JEWISH PROVERBS, MAXIMS, FOLKSAYINGS, QUOTATIONS AND ANECDOTES

Among those who stand, do not sit; among those who sit, do not stand; among those who laugh, do not weep; among those who weep, do not laugh.

Hillel

We must not appoint a leader over the community without first consulting the people.

Berakoth, 55a

Where men truly wish to go, there their feet will manage to take them.

Sukkah, 53a

Without experience there can be little wisdom.

Ecclesiasticus

The man who thinks he can live without others is mistaken; the man who thinks others can't live without him is more mistaken.

Hassidim

The life of the mother takes priority over the unborn child.

Ohalot, 7:6

What is the sign of a foolish man? He talks too much.

Zohar

Wine is an unreliable messenger: I sent it down to my stomach and it went up to my head.

Tahkemoni

Not to teach your son to work is like teaching him to steal.

Kiddushin, 29a

There is a time to love, and a time to hate.

Ecclesiastes, 3:8

In teaching, do not favor the children of the rich; and teach the children of the poor without compensation.

Ta'anith, 24a

Don't run too far; you will have to return the same distance.

Ecclesiates Rabbah, II;9

A woman will uncover her neighbor's pots in order to see what's cooking.

Taharoth, 8

Poverty is the ornament of the Jew.

Hagigah, 9b

A Jew answers a question with another question.

The deeper the sorrow, the less voice it has.

If you have nothing to say, say nothing.

Even when a man is a Rabbi, when his father enters, the son must rise.

Horayot, 13b

The righteous man who says he is righteous—is not righteous.

When you add to the truth, you subtract from it.

Sanhedrin, 29a

Blessed is the son who studies with his father, and blessed is the father who teaches the son.

Talmud

When the smart talk to the stupid, both act like fools.

A bad wife is like a dreary, rainy day.

Yebamoth, 63

The death of a woman is felt by no one so much as her husband.

Sanhedrin, 22

An ugly face is the only effective guardian of a woman's virtue.

Mahberot

If you want to live in this world, equip yourself with a heart that can endure suffering.

Leviticus Rabbah, 30

To shame a man in public is like shedding his blood.

Baba Mezi'a, 68b

To avoid all sorrows, just cut off your head.

Wisdom is to the soul as food is to the body.

Abraham ibn Ezra

The shofar is a prayer without words

Lieberman

Sympathy is medicine to soothe the ache in another's heart.

The less you talk, the healthier.

The best synagogue is the heart.

Those who talk a great deal usually talk about themselves.

A second wife is like a wooden leg.

The mercy of the wicked is cruel.

Book of Proverbs, 12;10

No man is as ugly as the man who is self-satisfied.

Hassidism

The most effective defense against temptation is to shut your eyes.

Ibn Gabirol

If you want to see your best friend, look into the mirror.

Life is a dream for the wise, a game for the fool, a comedy for the rich, a tragedy for the poor.

Sholem Aleichem

Evil is a two edged sword.

The love of gold leads to madness.

The borrower is the servant of the lender.

Book of Proverbs, 28; I

Experience is the name we give our mistakes.

The best charity is good will.

The man who is destined to drown will drown in a glass of water.

The greater the man, the greater his potential for evil.

Sukkah, 52a

Half an answer also tells you something.

Honor is more precious than glory.

The hardest work of all is to stay idle.

A true Jew is distinguished by three characteristics: sympathy, modesty, benevolence.

Sayings of the Fathers, 5:22

It is worse to learn nothing than to know nothing.

Where love is, no room is too small.

The fear of misfortune is worse than the misfortune.

Beauty wanes, but a name endures.

Ahikar, 2:49

Thought is a universe of freedom.

God first looks at a mans heart, then at his mind.

Wisdom increases with the years, but so does folly.

One word can be cancelled by another

Talmud

There is no cloth so fine that moths are unable to eat it.

Of what use is wisdom that is not taught.

Ecclesiasticus, 20:30

God could not be everywhere so he created mothers.

Hope for a miracle—but don't depend on one.

Megillah, 7b

At times even liars speak the truth.

Shirat Yisrael

A lack of accomplishment is the greatest suffering.

The rich eat when they want to, the poor when they can.

Necessity can break iron.

A little sin is big when a big man commits it.

Genesis, 32:9

The summit of intelligence is reached in humility.

Ibn Gabirol

Fish die out of water; men die without law and order.

Abodah Zarah, 4a

Children without a childhood are tragic.

Sefarim

Poverty shows first on ones face.

When a scholar makes a mistake it is a big one.

A big blow from a stranger hurts less than a small blow from a friend.

Better a young widow than an old maid.

You can't put a 'Thank you' in your pocket.

Where there is no vision, the people perish.

Proverbs 29:18

It is cruel not to forgive one who begs for forgiveness.

Rashi

Better be ridiculed than shamed.

The truth lights but money warms.

Only one kind of worry is proper: to worry because you worry too much.

Trees bend only when young.

The man who accepts tradition without examining it with his own intelligence, is like a blind man led by others.

Bahya ibn Paquda

The capacity to sympathize raises man above the animals.

Adam was the luckiest man: he had no mother-in-law.

Sholem Aleichem

A man looks to you the way you look at him.

I trust you completely, but please send cash.

Even the mercy of the wicked is cruel.

The prayers of the poor are heard by God ahead of all others.

Zohar

Some scholars study so much they don't leave themselves time to think.

As long as words are in your mouth, you are their lord: once you utter them, you are their slave.

Ibn Gabirol

A parable from a fool is worthless because he tells it at the wrong time.

Ecclesiasticus, 20:20

To have bad luck, one still must have luck.

If you can't endure the bad, you won't live long enough to enjoy the good.

No one knows the sorrows of another.

The world is new to us every morning—that is God's gift, and a man should believe he is reborn each day.

Baal Shem Tov

A woman can argue even with the Angel of Death.

Suffering creates ailments: happiness cures them.

A convert is neither a Jew nor a Gentile.

The deeper the grief, the less words can express it.

A slave is a free man if he is content with his lot; a free man is a slave if he seeks more than he needs.

Love and hunger cannot live together.

Whoever is able to write a book and does not, is as if he has lost a child.

Nachman

The road to a cemetery is paved with suffering.

If you live with a devil, you become a devil.

The man who has no money to lend friends makes no enemies.

When you pour out your heart, it feels lighter.

A drowning man will grab even the point of a sword.

Those who consider a thing proved simply because it is in print are fools.

Maimonides

The greatest of worries do not pay the smallest of debts.

A clown may be first in the kingdom of heaven, if he has helped lessen the sadness of life.

Talmud

If the rich could hire the poor to die for them, the poor would make a very good living.

Include yourself in any reproof.

When you turn proud, remember that a flea preceded you in order of divine creation.

Sanhedrin

Charity with a smile shows the donor's character.

Nachman

It is not wise to borrow from a poor man—or kiss an ugly girl.

A fool if rich is treated like a lord.

If you lie with dogs, you rise with fleas.

Of the making of books, there is no end.

Ecclesiastes, 12

The masses aren't asses.

A fool dreams foolish dreams.

A guilty man runs when no one is chasing him.

When things are not as you like, like them as they are.

Do not dishonor the old; we shall all be numbered among them.

Ecclesiasticus, 8:6

If men knew what one thought of another, they would kill each other.

The poor man thinks, the rich man laughs.

You can't pull two hides off one ox.

An informer should be hanged by his tongue.

A fool measures water with a sieve.

It's better to be dead drunk than dead hungry.

Lust and reason are enemies.
Ibn Gabirol

God loves the poor but helps the rich.

A carpenter without tools is no carpenter.
Exodus Rabbah, 40:I

Usury is a form of murder.

If you can't have what you want, want what you can have.
Ibn Gabirol

Never beat or inflict pain on any animal, beast or insect.
Sefer Hasidim

If you betray your cause, you support the other's.

If you open a shop, stock up on charm.

Borsht is as sweet to the poor as caviar is to the rich.

We laugh alone and we weep alone.

Dear God, help me get up: I can fall down by myself.

Gamblers show no mercy when gambling.

If you don't plow in the summer, what will you eat in the winter?
Midrash

Yesterday is your past; today is your future—because tomorrow is unknown.

A saloonkeeper may love a drunkard, but won't let him marry his daughter.

God has no riches of his own: it's what he takes from one that he gives to another.

The just way is always the right way.

A peace which comes from fear is the opposite of peace.
Gersonides

Paupers need no guards, and fear no thieves.

Weep for the man who does not know his good fortune.
Sanhedrin, 103a

Humble yourself here, and you won't be humbled hereafter.
Exodus Rabbah, 30:19

The man who seeks a faultless friend will remain friendless.

When you start thinking of death, you are no longer certain of life.

If fire strikes the wet, what chance have the dry?

You can catch flies better with honey than with vinegar.

If you don't eat garlic, you won't smell.

There is no one more lonely than those who love only themselves.

What the daughter does, the mother did.

Where many walk, no grass will grow.

Where men truly wish to go, their feet will take them.

Sukkah, 53a

Those who can't love, flatter.

When bribery increased, the span of life decreased.

Sotah, 47b

Adam would never have taken a wife if he hadn't been put to sleep first.

For children, we tear the world apart.

The Angel of Death doesn't look at calendars.

When one link snaps, the whole chain collapses.

It is good to look at the fair; and live with the wise.

God saw that heaven and earth were jealous of each other, so He created man out of earth; and his soul out of heaven.

A pretty face costs money.

A learned bastard stands higher than an ignorant priest.

Numbers Rabbah 6:I

The homeliest life is better than the prettiest death.

He who has nothing to lose can try anything.

Of God's purpose, one should not ask questions.

The tongue is a dangerous enemy.

New brooms sweep cleaner.

The rich have heirs, not children.

Some scholars are both wise and handsome—and would be still wiser were they less handsome.

Talmud.

Without luck nothing happens right.

Be very humble for man's destiny is the worm.

Sayings of the Fathers, 4:4

Gossip is silenced with gold.

Don't question God, for He may reply, "If you're so anxious for answers, come up here."

The man who gives little with a smile gives more than the man who gives much with a frown.

He who seeks the daughter flatters the mother.

Fools see men's clothes; wise men see men's spirits.

To die, you don't need a calendar.

Conquerors here are conquered in the hereafter.

Sefer Hasidim

One man can't eat with two mouths.

Envy is hatred without a cure.

Kad ha-Kemah

Glory avoids those who chase after it, and is endowed on many who did not try to pursue it.

In the public baths, all men are equal.

Every bride is beautiful.

Kethuboth, 17a

Man is not even called man until he is united with woman.

Zohar

When the stomach is empty, so is the brain.

If there were fewer swine, there would be fewer bastards.

The eye is small but devours all.

How odd is death: the old often survive the young.

If charity cost nothing, the world would be full of philanthropists.

If you don't want to get old, hang yourself while young.

When drink enters, judgement leaves.

Fortunate are those who actually enjoy old age.

Corn can't grow on the ceiling.

Gray hair is a sign of age, not wisdom.

If you can't do what you want, do what you can.

Two things that never come together—contentment and envy.

Ibn Gabirol

In dreams, fools get rich easily.

All colors look alike in the dark.

The greatest charity is to enable the poor to earn a living.

Shabbath, 63a

He who seeks to know everything grows old quickly.

Good men need no monuments: their acts remain their shrines.
Mishneh Shekalim, 5:2

The good is remembered; the bad is felt.

What soap is for the body, tears are for the soul.

As man acts, God reacts.
Bal Shem Tov

My friend is one who will tell me my faults in private.
Ibn Gabirol

Where there is honey, there are flies.

What can't be avoided can be welcomed.

He is the kind of man who first prepares the bandage, then inflicts the wound.
Megillah, 13a

Only the ignorant are really poor.

Naked a man comes into the world, and naked he leaves it; he carries away nothing except the deeds he leaves behind.
Rashi

It is better to beg for bread than be dependent on ones son.

Men worry about the loss of their possessions, not over the loss of their years—which never return.

Someone else's cloak won't keep you warm.

The tongue has no bones, so it is very loose.

The jealousy of scribes helps increase wisdom.

Talmud

One word can start a war.

Good manners will open any door.

It is no challenge to die like a Jew; the real challenge is to live like a Jew.

Chofetz Chaim

People usually hate what they do not understand.

Shirat Yisrael

Your best friend is a friend who does not expect anything.

A man is what he is, not what he used to be.

Money goes to money.

A mother understands what a child does not say.

The only whole heart is the one that has been broken.

Chofetz Chaim

There are bones without meat, but no meat without bones.

Not every heart that laughs is cheerful.

Ears are the gates to the mind.

Shirat Yisrael

Some of the most traveled roads lead nowhere.

Don't rely on IF and PERHAPS.

Bachya ibn Paquda

If you don't climb too high, you won't have far to fall.

When a bachelor dies, girls are avenged.

If you eat your bagel, you'll have nothing left but the hole.

Ropes drawn too taut break.

Spit in a whore's face and she'll say "It's raining."

Gluttons dig their graves with their teeth.

Too much is unhealthy.

Some things smell sweet but taste bitter.

Dogs fight over a bone, mourners over a will.

Jews are like everyone else—only more so.

Joy and sadness are as close as day and night.
Hayyim of Volozhin

Don't try to fill a sack that's full of holes.

Every answer raises a new question.

Learning requires a talent for sitting.

When luxuries grow, so do necessities.

Better a bad peace than a good war.

The heaviest weight in the world is an empty pocket.

A poor man is tempted by a slice of bread.

The less you talk, the healthier.

Words should be weighed, not counted.

The world is like a ladder: one man goes up while another goes down.

Numbers, 49

Worms eat you when you are dead; worry eats you up alive.

If you're going to do something wrong, at least enjoy it.

The rich swell up with pride, the poor from hunger.

Sholem Aleichem

Man can forget anything except when to eat.

Whoever fears God is afraid of nothing.

Ecclesiasticus, 34:14

Most bastards have a just complaint.

Kiddushin, 4; II

Love can't take advice, and lovers won't.

YIDDISH COLLOQUIALISMS AND IDIOMATIC EXPRESSIONS

YIDDISH COLLOQUIALISMS AND IDIOMATIC EXPRESSIONS

The most colorful aspect of Yiddish is its flair for metaphorical comparisons. In the majority of cases, the expression itself is so far removed from its basic meaning that it hinges on the absurd. For example: when one wishes to say "It doesn't mean a thing", the Yiddish expression is "*Ah Kiye Un Ah Shpiye*", which literally translates into "A chew and a spit." This expression is not used in rare instances. In any Yiddish conversation, if someone is informed of a situation that he or she believes to be trivial and unimportant, their reply would be, "Dos iz nawr ah kiye un ah shpiye."
And so, let us proceed:

AH KLAYNEH GELECHTER

Literally .... A small laugh.
Translation ..... It's a tragic situation.

GAY COCKIN AUF DEM YAHM

Literally .... Go move your bowels on the ocean.
Translation ..... Stop bothering me.

HOCK MIR NIT KAYN TCHIYNICK

Literally .... Stop banging the teakettle.
Translation ..... Stop talking nonsense.

AH KONAUHORRAH
Literally .... Warding off a jinx or evil eye.
Situation .... After a prediction.

MEHRTCHISHEM
Literally .... If God so wills.
Situation .... When one hopes for something good to happen

AH KILLEH IN BOYCH
Literally .... A rupture in your stomach.
Situation .... Putting a curse on someone.

AH LEBIDIKEH VELDT
Literally .... A lively world.
Translation ..... Having a hilarious time.

AH MOCHISHAYFEH.
Literally .... A mean, devilish woman
Translation ..... A female trouble maker.

DU ZOLST LEBEN AHZAY LAHNG.
Literally .... You should live so long.
Translation ..... Who are you trying to fool?

AH NECHTIGEHR TAUG.
Literally .... A yesterday's day.
Translation ..... Can't be done—unbelievable.

AH LAUCH IN KAUP.
Literally .... A hole in the head.
Translation ..... What do I need it for?

ICH DARFF DOS VIE TAYTEH BAHNKES.
Literally .... I need it like a dead person needs suction cups.
Translation ..... It is absolutely useless to me.

DU ZOLST LEBEN BIZ A HOONDERT UN TZVANTZIK YAWR.

Literally .... You should live until 120 years.
Situation .... Wishing someone well.

MEESSEH MESHUNEH.

Literally .... An ugly end
Situation .... Cursing someone; to die a violent death.

GORNISHT MIT GORNISHT.

Literally .... Nothing with nothing
Translation ..... It's worthless.

AH SHVARTZ YAWR

Literally .... A black year.
Translation ..... A catastrophe.

KLOP ZICH KAWP IN VANDT

Literally .... Hit your head against the wall.
Translation ..... You're wasting your time.

AH FRAHSK IN PISK.

Literally .... A smack in the face.
Translation ..... A slap.

FINSTER IN DIE EIYGEN.

Literally .... It's dark in the eyes.
Translation ..... Horrible to look at.

COCK EM AWN.

Literally .... Move your bowels on him
Translation ..... The hell with him.

AH SHTIK DRECK.

Literally .... A piece of body stool.
Translation ..... He's nothing but a bum.

AH GRAWBEHR YOONG.

Literally .... A fat young man.
Translation ..... A stupid and ignorant youth.

AH GOLDENEH MEDINA.

Literally .... A golden Utopia.
Translation ..... A land of milk and honey (i.e., America)

GEFOONENEH GELT.

Literally .... Found money.
Translation ..... An unexpected gift.

OYF MIR GEZUGT.

Literally .... On me it should be said.
Translation ..... It should happen to me.

SHVEHR UN SHITTEHR

Literally .... Heavy and loose.
Translation ..... A lot of nothing.

TAUCHIS AUFEN TISH

Literally .... Your rump on the table.
Translation ..... Put up or shut up.

AH BAWBEH MYSEH.

Literally .... A grandmothers tale.
Translation ..... An untrue story; a lie.

GAY KEBENYI MAHTRI.

Literally .... Get out of here; go away!
Translation ..... Get out of my life.

YENTEH TELEBENDE.

Literally .... A character created in a Jewish newspaper by the writer, Jacob Adler.
Meaning .... A gossip; a vulgar woman.

KRICH ARIYN IN DI BAYNER.

Literally .... Creep into the bones.
Translation ..... To intrude into someone's life.

ALTEHR KOCKER.

Literally .... An old defecator
Translation ..... A useless, fussy old man.

CHAIM YIYNKEL.

Literally .... Two common Jewish names.
Meaning .... A plain, ordinary man.

IN MITTEN DERINNEN.

Literally .... In the middle of something.
Meaning .... Suddenly; interrupting for no reason.

MOISHE KAPOIR.

Literally .... The name Moses; and the word for 'backwards'.
Meaning .... A contrary person who does things backwards.

AHFEN GONIFF BRENT DEHR HITTEL

Literally .... A thief's hat is on fire.
Meaning .... To a thief, everyone else is a thief.

AHN OICH UN VEY

Literally .... A grunt and a pain
Meaning .... It's just too bad.

Commonly Used Expressions	English translation
BEHRYEH	A capable woman
BAWBI MYSEH	A fairy tale
CHOZZERAI	Junk food
CHUTZPA	Brazen nerve
FARBLUNDJET	Strayed or lost
FARPOTCHKET	Messed up
FARMISHED	Mixed up
EINREDINISH	Imaginary ailment or idea
DRAYKOPP	A con man; restive person.
CHAUCHEM	A smart man; man of wisdom.
ALEVIY	If only
KIPTZIN	A pauper
KIBBITZIN	Fooling around
L'CHAIM	To your health
LAHNGEHR LUKSH	A tall, slim person
GAHNTZEHR K'NOCKER	A big shot.
NEBBECH	How unfortunate; a pity.
NO GOODNIK	A low life.
PASKUDNYAK	A nasty person, scoundrel.
SHLIMAZEL	An unlucky guy.
SHMIGEGGEE	A dolt; blockhead.
TZUDRAYT	Mixed up.
TZETUMMELT	Bewildered
EFSHEHR	Could be; perhaps.
MISHOOGENEHR	A crazy person.
KATCHALOPPI	A sloppy person
BALMALOCHEH	A craftsman
CHALEHRYEH	A curse
SHPAHTZIRIN	A casual stroll
PAHVAULLYEH	Take it easy.

Tongue Twisters (Tzoong Fardrayinish)

Yiddish	English Translation
*EIN*GEMEHNEERTEH	Marinated
SHPAHT*TZIR*EN	Relaxing; a slow walk
*TOO*MILDIK	Bedlam
*OYS*GEMAHTERT	Exhausted
ENT*SHOOL*DIKT	Pardon
FAR*MISHT*	Mixed up
KAUTSHI*LAH*PEH	Nincompoop
FAR*BLUND*JET	Lost
MAHLACHA*MAU*VES	Angel of death
MAHKA*SHAY*FEH	An evil woman
FAHR*TSHEP*INISH	A snag, catch
GE*PRAY*GELTEH	Fried
MACHA*TAYN*ISTEH	Daughter in laws mother.
AH*REIN*TZUGEYN	To enter
AH*RIEN*GHENG	Entrance
VAH*NET*ZIMEHR	Bathroom
PERL*GROY*PN	Barley
GE*BOY*RENTAUG	Birthday
*TZU*KERKEH	Candy
OO*GHEH*RKIS	Cucumbers
PAHR*VAUL*YEH	Careful
AH*ROYS*GAHNGG	Exit
*SHAH*TZOONG	Estimate
*OYS*BLAHNKEEREN	Fade
*SHPIZ*KRAUM	Grocery
*EYZN*VAHRG	Hardware
KAWREE*DAWR*	Corridor
*OON*TERHEYBEHR	A jack

Yiddish	**English Translation**
*IBER*LAUZIN	To leave over
ME*KHAN*IKEHR	Mechanic
TZAY*TOON*GEN	Newspapers
BRAYREH	Option; choice
*SHPIZ*KAHMEHR	Pantry
*REHRIN*SHLAUSEHR	Plumber
DEHRLOYBENISH	Permission
*EN*TZL	Retail
*VIS*INSHAHTLEHR	Scientist
*OONTER*SHRIBN	Signature
GEH*SHVAU*LLN	Swollen
*TEK*NEEKEHR	Technician
TZUZ*AH*MEN	Together
VA*KAHT*ZYEH	Vacation
VE*LEESH*EH NIS	Walnuts
BALMA*LOCH*EH	Craftsman
KATCHA*LOPP*I	A sloppy one
TZU*MISH*INISH	Confusion
*KLAY*DEHRBAHRSHT	Whisk broom
ZAHL	Hall
FAHR*SHPRAY*TOONG	Spread

ATLAS OF JEWISH HISTORY

A CHRONOLOGICAL ATLAS OF JEWISH HISTORY

A CHRONOLOGICAL CHART OF JEWISH HISTORY

The Wilderness period	
The Patriarchal Age	Prehistory
The Exodus	
Moses and Joshua	1325 - 1250
The Monarchy	1250 - 1002
David (Hebron period)	1002 - 995
Solomon	962 - 922
ISRAEL The Divided Kingdom	
Jeroboam	922 - 901
Nadab	901 - 900
Baasha	900 - 877
Elah	877 - 876
Omri	876 - 869
Ahab	869 - 850
Ahaziah	850 - 849
Joram	849 - 842
Jehu	842 - 815
Joahaz	815 - 801
Joash	801 - 786
Jeroboam	786 - 746
Menahem	745 - 738
Shallum	738 - 737
Pekahiah	737 - 732
Pekah	732 - 724

Hoshea	722 - 721
Final Assyrian Conquest	
JUDAH	
Rehoboam	922 - 915
Abijam	915 - 913
Asa	913 - 873
Jehosaphat	873 - 849
Joram	849 - 842
Ahaziah	842
Athaliah	842 - 837
Jehoash	837 - 800
Amaziah	800 - 783
Ussiah	783 - 742
Jotham	742 - 735
Ahaz	735 - 715
Hezekiah	715 - 687
Manasseh	687 - 642
Amon	642 - 640
Josiah	640 - 608
Jehoiakim	608 - 597
Zedekiah	596 - 586
Final Babylonian Conquest	586
Babylonian Exile	586 - 520
Fall of Jerusalem	485
Final Greek Conquest	320
Maccabean Revolt	168 - 165

Israel—Its creation—From the Hebrew; "Striven with God."

Israel is the name given to Jacob as the figurative designated ancestor of the Hebrews, the chosen people of God. Its twelve tribes were named for the ten sons of Jacob:—Reuben, Simeon, Judah, Zebulun, Issachar, Dan, Gad, Asher, Naphtali and Benjamin:—and the two sons of Jacob's son, Joseph:—Ephraim and Manasseh. The 13th tribe, Levi (from Jacob's third son), was set apart and had no portion of its own. After the break in the Hebrew kingdom under Rehoboam, the northern Kingdom, consisting of all but the tribes of Judah and Benjamin, and many Levites, was called Israel. The southern Kingdom remained known as Judah. This event occurred in 922 B.C.E.

THE FLIGHT OF THE JEWS THROUGH THE WILDERNESS

1. Moses leads the Jews from Egypt pursued by Pharaoh.
2. The Jews camp at Mt. Sinai where Moses receives the Ten Commandments.
3. The Hebrews wander in the wilderness for 40 years.
4. The Canaanites attack from Hormah and are defeated.
5. The Hebrews defeat the Amorites, Moabites and Midianites and enter the Promised Land.

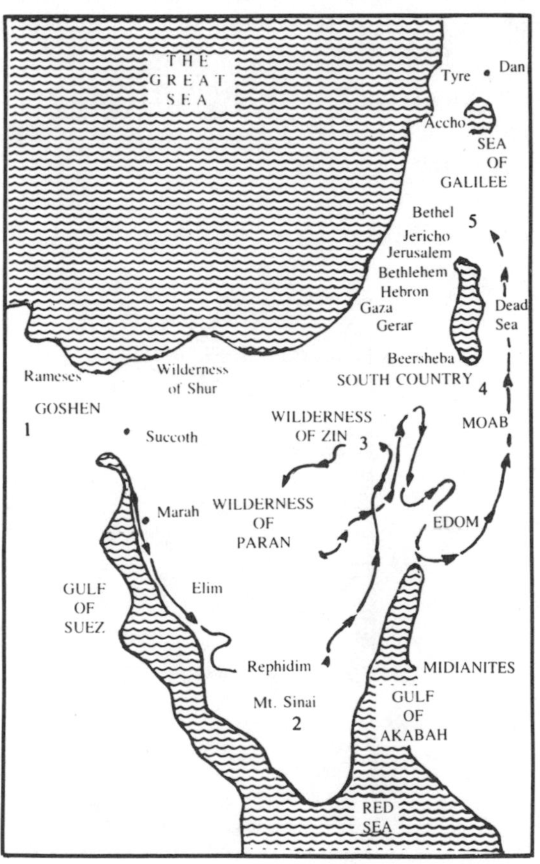

JOSHUA'S CONQUEST OF CANAAN —DEUTERONOMY: CHAPTERS 1 - 12 - 22

Upon the death of Moses, Joshua assumed command of the Israelites. They crossed the Jordan, whose swollen waters were miraculous dried up with God's intervention then proceeded to attack Jericho, whose walls crumbled, enabling an easy victory. Heading North, after conquering the South country, Joshua ordered a forced march to the waters of Merom.

At Merom, Joshua completely defeated the enemy and immediately proceeded to MISREPOTH MAIM, on the Great Sea then headed back to HAZOR, the bastion of the opposing forces and reduced the city to ashes.

After this great victory, Joshua portioned out various lands to the twelve tribes of Israel, all except to the Levites who were dedicated to religious obligations.

ISRAEL AND JUDAH AFTER THE DIVISION OF THE MONARCHY

Israel consisted of the Ten Tribes with the tribe of Ephraim dominant.
Israel's first capital was first at Shechem, then Tirzah and finally at Samaria.

The Southern kingdom was primarily Judah plus the small tribe of Benjamin.

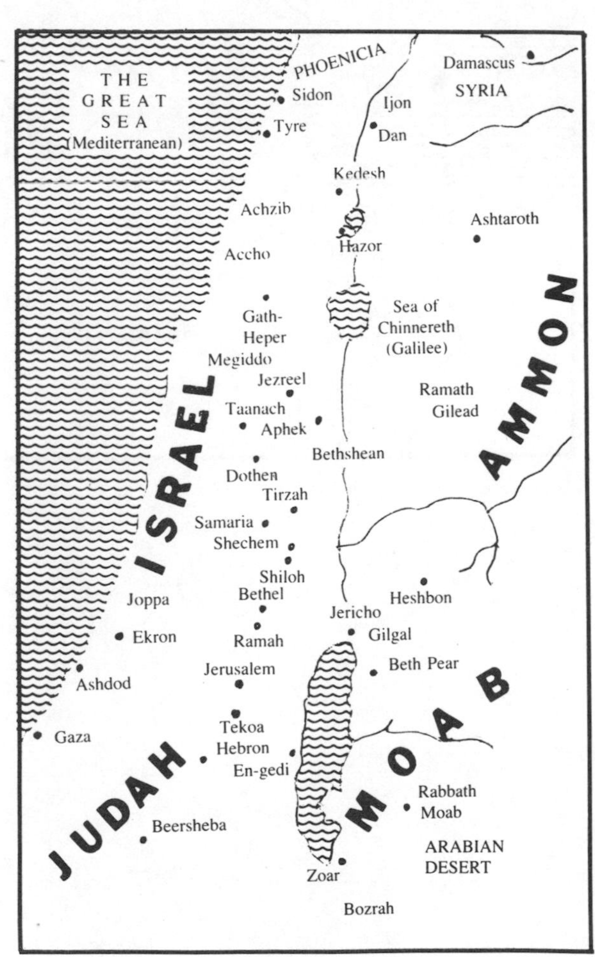

THE ANCIENT NEAR EAST

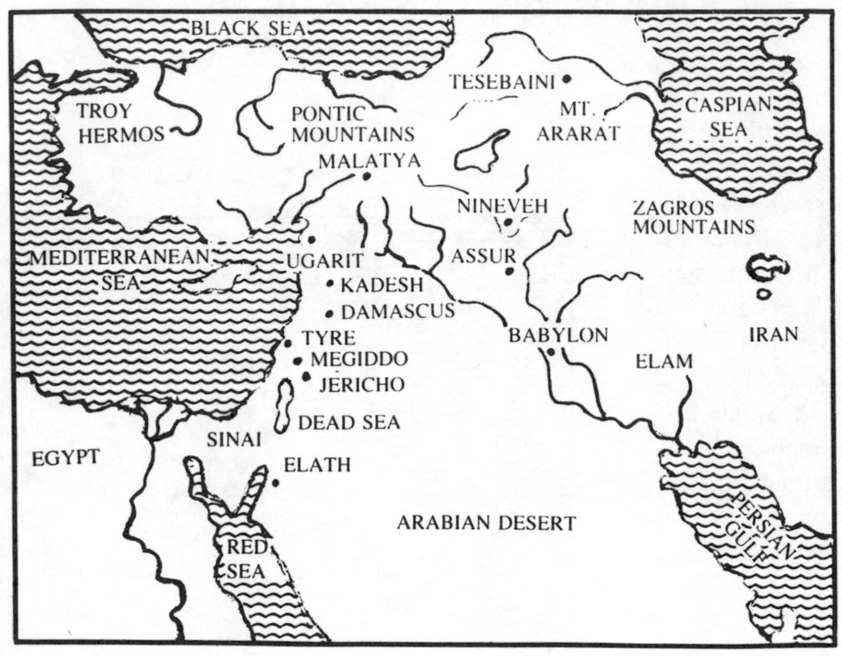

THE ANCIENT LAND OF CANAAN

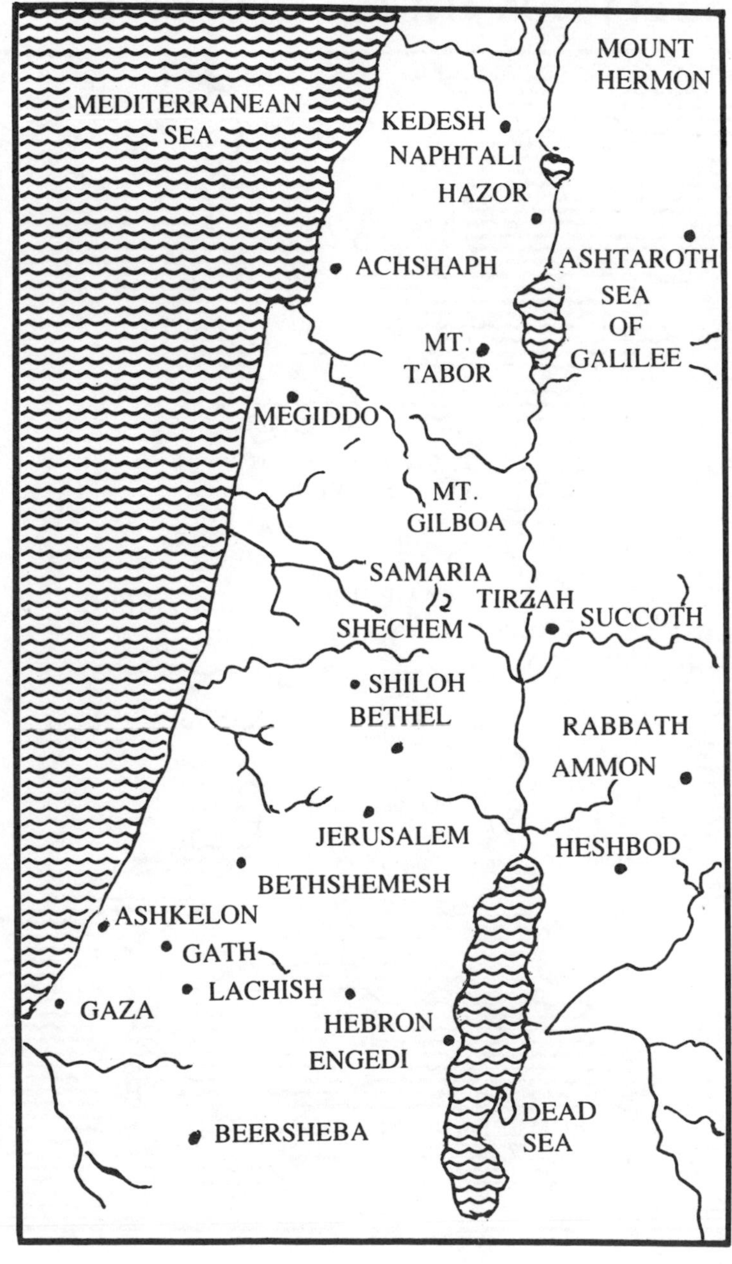

FRANCE—GERMANY: THE AGE OF PERSECUTION 4TH TO 8TH CENTURY A.D.

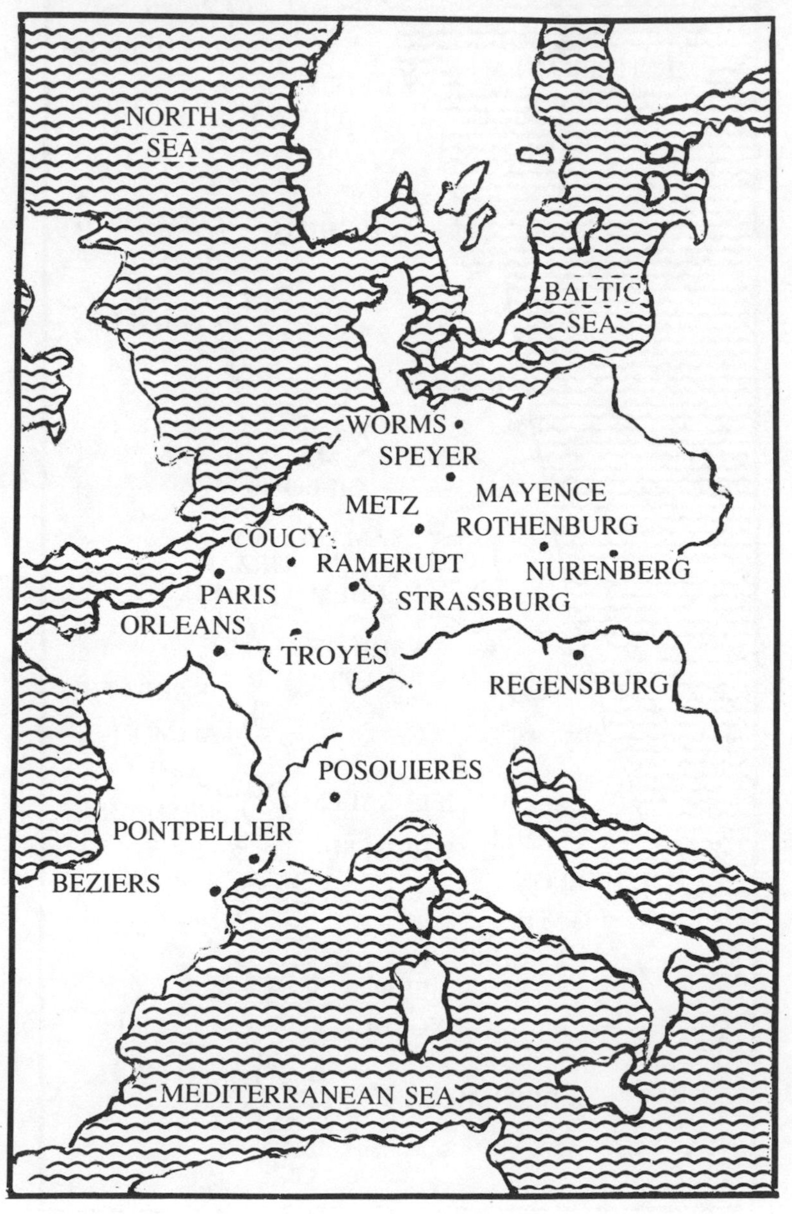

THE AGE OF REFORMATION—1796-1873

The Renaissance

France
Austria
Sweden
Denmark
Greece
England
Germany
Italy

Continued Discrimination

Russia
Roumania

JEWISH FACTS AND ARTIFACTS

JEWISH FACTS AND ARTIFACTS

From the time of creation, through the historical maze of mankind, amazing tales of unbelievable proportions have occurred involving Jews and their neighbors. How a microscopic portion of the world's population could have had such a profound impact on world civilization is unbelievable yet, it is safe to say that the Jews have made vital contributions in virtually all areas of human endeavor whether they be religion, the complex fields of science, the mysteries of the universe, the academic heights in the fields of art, medicine, literature, sports, finance, music, the theatre or politics.

The following catalogue of personalities and events is but a small portion of the many Jews who arose from the colony of man to record their names in the annals of mankind.

ACTORS AND ACTRESSES: STAGE AND SCREEN

Luther Adler:	Stage and screen actor
Stella Adler:	New York Stage—Little Theatre Group
Woody Allen:	(Allen Konigsberg) Writer, actor, director and producer.
Alan Arkin:	Motion pictures and TV.
Lauren Bacall:	Motion Pictures and Broadway; Wife of Humphrey Bogart.
Carrol Baker:	Motion Pictures; (Convert)
Martin Balsam:	Motion Pictures.
Theda Bara:	(Theda Goodman) Most famous vamp in silent pictures.

Binnie Barnes:	Motion Picutres.
Richard Benjamin:	Motion Pictures.
Mel Blanc:	Radio.
Geraldine Brooks:	Motion Pictures and Stage.
Red Buttons:	Motion Pictures and TV.
James Caan:	Motion Pictures.
Dyan Cannon:	(Diane Friesen) Motion Pictures; Former Wife of Cary Grant.
Jeff Chandler:	Motion Pictures.
Lee J. Cobb:	Motion Pictures.
Tony Curtis:	(Bernard Schwartz) Motion Pictures.
Howard Da Silva:	(Howard Silverblatt) Motion Pictures.
Kirk Douglas:	(Issur Demsky) Motion Pictures.
Melvyn Douglas:	Motion Pictures; Married to Helen Gahagan Douglas.
Richard Dreyfuss:	Motion Pictures.
Marty Feldman:	Motion Pictures.
Carrie Fisher:	Motion Pictures; Daughter of Eddie Fisher and Debbie Reynolds.
John Garfield:	(Julius Garfinkle) Motion Pictures.
Paulette Goddard:	Motion Pictures; Married to Charles Chaplin.

Elliot Gould:	(Elliot Goldstein) Motion Pictures.
Leo Gorcey:	Motion Pictures.
Lee Grant:	(Lyova Rosenthal) Motion Pictures.
Laurence Harvey:	Motion Pictures.
Goldie Hawn:	Motion Pictures.
Dustin Hoffman:	Motion Pictures.
Judy Holliday:	Motion Pictures.
Oscar Homolka:	Motion Pictures.
Leslie Howard:	(Leslie Stainer) Motion Pictures.
Sam Jaffe:	Stage and Motion Pictures.
Carolyn Jones:	(convert) Married to Aaron Spelling. Motion Pictures.
Danny Kaye:	(Danny Kaminsky) Radio, Motion Pictures.
Stubby Kaye:	Motion Pictures.
Abbe Lane:	Singer: former wife of Xavier Cugat.
Sam Levene:	Stage and Motion Pictures.
Jerry Lewis:	Motion Pictures and TV.

Peter Lorre:	Motion Pictures.
Paul Lukas:	Motion Pictures.
Hank Mann:	Star of silent films.
Marx Bros:	Motion Pictures.
Walter Matthau:	Motion Pictures.
Marilyn Monroe:	(Convert) Motion Pictures.
Yves Montand:	(Ivo Levi) Motion Pictures.
Paul Muni:	(Muni Weisenfreund) Motion Pictures.
Alla Nazimova:	Motion Pictures.
Anthony Newley:	Motion Pictures.
Paul Newman:	Motion Pictures.
Lilli Palmer:	Motion Pictures.
Eleanor Parker:	Motion Pictures.
Larry Parks:	Motion Pictures.
Nehemiah Persoff:	Stage and Motion Pictures.
Louise Rainer:	Motion Pictures.
Edward G. Robinson:	Motion Pictures.
Jill St. John:	Motion Pictures.
George Segal:	Motion Pictures.

Peter Sellers:	Motion Pictures.
Sylvia Sidney:	Motion Pictures.
Rod Steiger:	Motion Pictures.
Barbra Streisand:	Motion Pictures.
Elizabeth Taylor:	Motion Pictures; (Convert)
Topol:	Motion Pictures.
Eli Wallach:	Motion Pictures.
Cornel Wilde:	Motion Pictures.
Gene Wilder:	Motion Pictures.
Shelley Winters:	Motion Pictures.

TELEVISION:

Jack Albertson	(Chico and the Man)
Edward Asner	(Mary Tyler Moore Show)
John Banner	(Hogan's Heroes)
Gene Barry	(Bat Masterson)
Milton Berle	(Mr. Television)
Joyce Brothers	(Talk shows)
Kitty Carlisle	(To Tell the Truth)
Sid Caesar	(Show of Shows)

Michael Douglas	(Streets of San Francisco)
Peter Falk	(Columbo)
Allen Funt	(Candid Camera)
Virginia Graham	(Talk Show)
Lorne Green	(Bonanza)
Monty Hall	(Let's Make a Deal)
Gabe Kaplan	(Welcome Back Kotter)
Werner Klemperer	(Hogan's Heroes)
Jack Klugman	(Odd Couple)
Harvey Korman	(Carol Burnett Show)
Martin Landau	(Mission Impossible)
Michael Landon	(Little House on the Prairie)
Louise Lasser	(Mary Hartman)
Hal Linden	(Barney Miller)
Peggy Lipton	(The Mod Squad)
Tina Louise	(Gilligan's Island)
Ross Martin	(The Wild, Wild West)
Leonard Nimoy	(Star Trek)
Rob Reiner	(All in the Family)

William Shatner	(Star Trek)
Dinah Shore	(Talk Show)
Phil Silvers	(Comedian)
David Susskind	(Talk Show)
Abe Vigoda	(Fish)
Henry Winkler	(Happy Days)

THEATRE:

Herschel Bernardi

Sarah Bernhardt

Fanny Brice

Morris Carnovsky

Anna Held

Eugenie Leontovich

Zero Mostel

Paul Muni

Rudolf Schildkraut

COMEDIANS: RADIO, TV, and NIGHTCLUBS

Joey Adams	Nightclubs
Morey Amsterdam	TV
Jack Benny	Radio, TV

Shelly Berman	Nightclubs
Theodore Bikel	Stage and Screen
Joey Bishop	TV
Victor Borge	TV
David Brenner	Nightclubs
Lenny Bruce	Nightclubs
George Burns	Radio, TV
Eddie Cantor	Stage and Screen
Jack Carter	TV, Nightclubs
Myron Cohen	Nightclubs
Bill Dana	TV
Rodney Dangerfield	TV, Nightclubs
Totie Fields	TV, Nightclubs
Larry Fine	One of the Three Stooges
Buddy Hackett	Nightclubs
Curly Howard	One of the Three Stooges
George Jessel	Radio, TV
Al Jolson	Radio, Screen and Nightclubs
Alan King	Nightclubs

Pinky Lee	Nightclubs
Jack E. Leonard	Nightclubs
Ted Lewis	Nightclubs
Sam Levenson	TV
Jackie Mason	Nightclubs
Jan Murray	Nightclubs
Carl Reiner	TV
Don Rickles	TV, Nightclubs
Ritz Bros.	Motion Pictures
Joan Rivers	Nightclubs, TV
Mort Sahl	TV
Soupy Sales	TV
Dick Shawn	TV, Nightclubs
Allan Sherman	Nightclubs
David Steinberg	Nightclubs
Sophie Tucker	Nightclubs
Ed Wynn	Radio
Henny Youngman	Nightclubs, TV

STUDIO AND FILM EXECUTIVES:

Barney Balaban	President of Paramount Studios, 1936
Harry Cohn	Head of Columbia Studios, 1940's
Edward Feldman	President of Filmways
William Fox	One of the pioneers in motion pictures. Head of 20th Century Fox.
Samuel Goldwyn	Head of Goldwyn Productions; The Goldwyn in Metro-Goldwyn-Mayer.
Leo Jaffe	Chief Executive Officer of Columbia Pictures Industries.
Jay Kanter	Vice President at Columbia Pictures.
Norman B. Katz	Chief Executive Officer at Warner Bros.
Arthur B. Krim	President of United Artists.
Howard W. Koch	Vice President in Charge of Production at Paramount Studios.
Carl Laemmle	Founder of Universal Studios.
Jesse L. Lasky	The pioneer of all studio executives.
Marcus Loew	Owner of Loew's theaters and head of M.G.M.
Louis B. Mayer	Head of M.G.M. The Mayer in Metro-Goldwyn-Mayer.
Irving G. Thalberg	Chief of production at M.G.M. Married to Norma Sheaarer.

Warner Bros.	Heads of Warner Bros. Studios. They started the talkies with ''The Jass Singer.''
Adolph Zukor	The founder of Paramount Studios.

PRODUCERS AND DIRECTORS:

Buddy Adler	Produced ''From Here to Eternity'' and many others.
Irwin Allen	Produced ''The Towering Inferno'' and ''The Poseidon Adventure.''
Samuel Z. Arkoff	Executive Producer and founder of American-International Pictures.
Pandro S. Berman	Produced all the Fred Astaire-Ginger Rogers films. Also the ''Hunchback of Notre Dame''.
Julian Blaustein	Produced ''Bell, Book and Candle'', ''The Day the Earth Stood Still.''
Mel Brooks	Producer and director of numerous comedy films.
Richard Brooks	Produced ''Elmer Gantry'' for which he received an Academy Award.
George Cukor	Produced and directed ''A Star is Born'', Directed ''My Fair Lady'' and ''Camille''
Jules Dassin	Directed ''Naked City'' and ''Never on Sunday''.
Samuel Engel	Produced ''Boy on a Dolphin''.
Charles K. Feldman	Produced ''Red River.''

Max Fleischer	Producer of animated cartoons. ''Popeye the Sailor.''
William Friedkin	Directed ''The French Connection'' and ''The Exorcist.''
Arthur Freed	Producer and songwriter. ''On the Town'', ''Singing in the Rain'' and ''An American in Paris.''
Harold Hecht	Produced ''Trapeze'', ''Cat Ballou.''
Sam Katzman	Early pi oneer producer. ''The Hopalong Cassidys.''
Sir Alexander Korda	Produced ''Catherine the Great.''
Garson Kanin	Famous writer and director.
Stanley Kramer	Independent producer; ''Death of a Salesman'', ''Home of the Brave'', ''High Noon''
Lew Landers	Directed many low budget films.
Mervyn LeRoy	Produced ''The Wizard of Oz'', ''Quo Vadis''
Sol Lesser	Producer of the Tarzan films.
Joseph E. Levine	Produced ''Harlow'', ''The Carpetbaggers''
Anatole Litvak	Producer and director
Ernst Lubitsch	Produced ''Ninotchka'', ''The Merry Widow''

Martin Melcher	Produced all Doris Day films
The Mirisch Brothers	Produced many notable films
Sam Newfeld	Directed many B films.
Joe Pasternak	Produced "The Great Caruso", "One Hundred Men and a Girl"
William Perlberg	Produced "Forever Amber", "The Song of the Bernadette."
Irving Pichel	Directed "A Medal for Benny".
Robert Rossen	Producer and director; "The Hustler", "Body and Soul."
Dore Schary	Produced many hundreds of films. Also a fine screen writer.
David O. Selznick	Produced "Dual in the Sun", "Gone With the Wind." "King Kong."
Sol C. Siegel	Produced many films
Sam Spiegal	Produced many famous successful films. "The African Queen", "On The Waterfront", "The Bridge over the River Kwai."
Erich Von Stroheim	Directed "Sunset Boulevard"
Mike Todd	Producer; Married to Elizabeth Taylor.
Billy Wilder	One of the most talented producers. directors and writers.
Fred Zinnemann	Academy Award director; "From Here to Eternity", "High Noon"

MEDICINE:

Lajos Adam 1879-1946	A famous Hungarian physician: Made tremendous progress in the field of anesthesia.
Isidor Albu 1837-1903	A leading German ophthalmologist: became personal physician to the Shah of Persia.
Heinrich Banberger 1826-1888	A leading Czechoslovakian heart surgeon
Simon Baruch 1840-1921	Performed the first appendectomy
Isaac Berenblum 1903-	One of the leading authorities in the field of cancer. He is now at the Weizmann Institute in Israel.
David Bodian 1910-	A member of the National Academy of Sciences.
Leo Buerger 1880-1940	An Austrian who became a famous pathologist (Buerger's disease)
Burrill B. Crohn 1884-	Specialized in regional ileitus (Crohn's disease)
Leo M. Davidoff 1898-	The doctor on the Byrd expedition to the Arctic in 1925
David de Leon	Surgeon General of the Southern Confederacy during the Civil War.
Ludwig Edinger 1855-1918	Famous German cardiologist (Dressler syndrome)

Paul Ehrlich	A biochemist who discovered a cure for syphilis (Salvarsan or 606)
Morris Fishbein 1889-1976	Head of the American Medical Association.
Casimir Funk 1884-1967	Famous Polish biochemist: Discoverer of a pill, later to be developed into a vitamin which was used in the cure of beriberi.
Joseph Goldberger 1874-1929	Isolated the disease known as pellagra
Isaac Hays 1796-1879	An ophthalmologist and founder of the American Medical Association. He was a leading researcher in the field of color blindness.
Phineas J. Horwitz 1822-1904	Director of the U.S. Bureau of Medicine and Surgery
Abraham Jacobi 1830-1899	The first recognized pediatrician in the United States.
Henry D. Janowitz 1915-	President of the American Gastroenterological Association.
Ephraim Katchalski 1916-	A famous biochemist: Member of the National Academy of Sciences.
Paul Klemperer 1887-1964	A foremost expert on the spleen.
Abraham Levinson 1888-1955	A leading expert on meningitis

Hermann Oppenheim 1858-1919	One of the world's foremost experts on brain tumors.
Samuel Rosen 1897-	A famous otologist who cured many thousands of people.
Albert B. Sabin 1906-	He developed the oral polio vaccine that has saved many lives.
Jonas Salk 1914-	The famous epidemiologist who developed the polio-vaccine. (Salk vaccine)
Bela Schick 1877-1967	He developed the Schick Test for diphtheria.
Felix Simon 1849-1921	Personal physician to King Edward VII of England.
August Von Wasserman 1866-1925	Discovered the test which detects syphilis. It has proven so reliable that it is used exclusively to this day. (Wasserman Test)
Selman Waksman	Discovered the antibiotic streptomycin used against infections
Israel Wechsler	A foremost expert on epilepsy: President of the American Neurological Association.

JUDGES:

Louis D. Brandeis 1856-1941	U.S. Supreme Court
Benjamin N. Cardozo 1870-1938	U.S. Supreme Court

Abe Fortas 1910-	U.S. Supreme Court: Attorney for President Lyndon B. Johnson
Jerome Frank	Judge on the U.S. Court of Appeals.
Felix Frankfurter 1882-1965	U.S. Supreme Court: Received the Medal of Freedom
Stanley H. Fuld 1903-	Chief Judge of the New York Court of Appeals
Harry A. Hollzer 1880-1946	Judge of the U.S. District Court.
Theodore Levin 1897-1971	Chief Federal Judge for the Eastern District of Michigan.
Charles E. Wyzanski Jr.	Federal District Judge for the District of Massachusetts.

MEMBERS OF CONGRESS:

Bella Abzug	New York
Anthony C. Beilenson	California
Sol Bloom	New York
Emanuel Celler	New York
Earl Chudoff	Pennsylvania
William M. Citron	Connecticut
Samuel Dickstein	New York
Morris Edelstein	New York

Joshua Eilberg	Pennsylvania
Nathan Frank	Missouri
Martin Frost	Texas
Elizabeth Holtzman	New York
Julius Houseman	Michigan
Charles S. Joelson	New Jersey
Florence Kahn	California
Edward I. Koch	New York
John Krebs	California
Fiorello H. La Guardia	New York
Elliott H. Levitas	Georgia
Marc L. Marks	Pennsylvania
Nathan D. Perlman	New York
Benjamin S. Rosenthal	New York

SENATORS:

Ernest H. Gruening	Alaska
Simon Guggenheim	Colorado
Jacob K. Javits	New York
Herbert H. Lehman	New York
Howard Metzenbaum	Ohio

Abraham A. Ribicoff	Connecticut
Edward Zorinsky	Nebraska

PUBLIC FIGURES:

Bernard Baruch	Adviser to many presidents
August Belmont	Chairman of the Democratic National Committee; Belmont Park named after him.
Murray Chotiner	Adviser to President Nixon.
Benjamin V. Cohen	A member of President Roosevelt's Brain Trust.
Samuel Dash	Chief Counsel during the Watergate Trials.
Max M. Fisher	Special Adviser to President Nixon.
Arthur Goldberg	Secretary of Labor, Supreme Court Justice and Ambassador to U.N.
Louis Harris	Director of the Harris Poll
Louis J. Lefkowitz	Attorney General of New York.
Mortiz Pinner	One of the founders of the Republican Party.
Maxwell M. Rabb	President Eisenhower's attorney.
Samuel I. Rosenman	President Roosevelt's adviser. Created the phrase 'New Deal'

BUSINESS:

Benjamin Altman	Founder of B. Altman and Co.
Louis V. Aronson	Founder of Ronson Lighter Corporation.
Jules S. Bache	Head of Bache and Co.
Louis Bamberger	Head of Bamberger and Company.
Marcus S. Bearsted	Founder of the Shell Oil Co.
Jacob Blaustein	Founder of the American Oil Co.
Bloomingdale Bros.	Founders of Bloomingdale's Dept Stores.
Alfred S. Bloomingdale	Founder of the Diners Club.
Charles G. Bluhdorn	Chairman of the Board of Gulf-Western
August Brentano	Founder of Brentano Book Stores
Samuel Bronfman	Head of Seagrams Limited
Andre G. Citroen	Head of Citroen Automobile Industry in France.
Henry Crown	Former owner of the Empire State Bldg.
Max Factor	Max Factor Cosmetics
Abraham Feinberg	Head of Kayser-Roth
Joseph Fels	Founder of Fels-Naphtha Company
Lincoln Filene	Filene's Dept Store
Lee K. Frankel	Vice-President of Metropolitan Life Insurancc Co.

Adam Gimbel	Founder of Gimbel's and Saks Fifth Avenue.
Marcus Goldman	Founder of Goldman, Sachs and Co.
Armand Hammer	Developer of Occidental Petroleum
Herman W. Hellman	Founder of the Merchants National Bank
Harry B. Henshel	President of Bulova Watch Co.
Lena Himmelstein	Founder of the Lane Bryant chain.
Nathan S. Jonas	Head of the Manufacturers Trust Co.
David N. Judelson	Head of Gulf & Western Industries
Harold Krensky	Head of the Federated Department Stores.
Abraham Kuhn	Founder of Kuhn, Loeb and Co.
Albert D. Lasker	Developer of Lord and Thomas
Fred Lazarus Jr.	President of Federated Department Stores.
Robert Lehman	Head of Lehman Brothers Banking House.
Frederick Lewisohn	Founder of Anaconda Copper Co.
Sol M. Linowitz	Chairman of the Board of Xerox; U.S. Ambassador to the OAS.
Solomon Loeb	Founder of Kuhn, Loeb and Co.
Stanley Marcus	Head of Neiman-Marcus
Israel Matz	Founder of Ex-Lax Co.

Abraham Mazer	Founder of Hudson Pulp and Paper Corp.
Andre Meyer	Head of Lazard Freres Banking
Nathan Ohrbach	Founder of Ohrbach's Dept. Store
Adriano Olivetti	Head of Olivetti-Underwood Typewriters
Alfred E. Perlman	Head of the New York Central Railroad.
Charles H. Revson	Founder of Revlon
Meshulam Riklis	Head of the Rapid American conglomerate
Julius Rosenwald	President of Sears-Roebuck
Samuel Rubin	Founder of Faberge Perfumeries
Helena Rubinstein	Head of the company in her name.
Irving S. Shapiro	Chairman of the Board of E.I. du Pont and Co.
Herbert J. Siegel	Head of ChrisCraft Industries.
Norton Simon	Head of Norton Simon Industries
Alfred P. Slaner	President of Kayser-Roth
Isidor Straus	Head of Macy Department Store.
Levi Strauss	Founder of Levi's jeans
Gerald Swope	President of International General Electric

Laurence A. Tisch	Head of Loew's Corporation
James D. Zellerbach	Head of Crown Zellerbach Corp.

SPORTS:

Lyle Alzado	Football; All-Pro defensive end for the Denver Broncos
Abe Attell	Boxing: World Featherweight Champion.
Red Auerbach	Basketball: Head coach of the Boston Celtics.
Max Baer	Boxing: Heavyweight champ of the world.
'Bo' Belinsky	Baseball: Pitched a no-hitter for the California Angels.
Rod Carew	(Convert) Six time American League batting champion.
Andy Cohen	Baseball: Infielder with the New York Giants
Herbert Flam	Tennis: Number Two in the U.S. 1956 and 1957
Bennie Friedman	Football: All-Pro Quarterback 1927-1931
Sid Gilman	Head coach of the Rams, Chargers and Oilers.
Marshall Goldberg	Football: First Team All-American 1937-1938
Brian Gottfried	Tennis: Wimbledon Doubles Champion in 1976

Hank Greenberg	Baseball: Most valuable player in the American League two times. Member of the Hall of Fame.
Nat Holman	Basketball: Member of Original Celtics. One of the greatest of all time.
Ken Holtzman	Baseball: He won four World Series games.
Red Holzman	Basketball: One of the finest professional coaches in history.
Joe Jacobs	Boxing: Managed champion Max Schmeling
Irving Jaffee	Skating: Won two gold medals in the 1932 Olympics
Kid Kaplan	Boxing: Featherweight Champ of the world. Won 101 fights.
Sandy Koufax	Baseball: Los Angeles Dodger great. Pitched four no-hitters.
Nancy Leiberman	Basketball: Top woman basketball player in college.
Benny Leonard	Boxing: Lightweight champ of the world, 1917-1925. Considered one of the greatest lightweights in history.
Battling Levinsky	Boxing: Light Heavyweight Champ of the world 1916-1920.
Ted Lewis	Boxing: Welterweight Champ of the world. 1915-1919.

Sid Luckman	Football: All-Pro with the Chicago Bears 1941-1942-1943. In the Hall of Fame.
Ron Mix	Football: All-Pro with the San Diego Chargers.
Tom Okker	Tennis: Fourth in professional ranking in 1969.
Al Rosen	Baseball: One of the greatest to ever play pro ball. Led the A.L. in homers and was Most Valuable Player in 1953.
Carroll Rosenbloom	Football: Owner of the Los Angeles Rams.
Maxie Rosenbloom	Boxing: Light Heavyweight Champ of the world 1930-1934.
Barney Ross	Boxing: One of the greatest welter-weights. Held titles in two divisions.
Mark Roth	Bowling: Leading bowler in the world in the 1970's
Larry Sherry	Baseball: Ace Los Angeles Dodger pitcher in the 1960's
Al Singer	Boxing: Lightweight Champ of the world in 1930
Harold Solomon	Tennis: Famous pro-tennis player
Mark Spitz	Swimming: Won seven gold medals in the 1972 Olympics.
Lew Tendler	Boxing: One of the great lightweights in history.

THE ABSOLUTENESS OF THE TORAH.

Judaism's greatest gift to mankind is the Torah. As the Romans and Greeks found satisfaction and fulfillment in philosophy and idol worship, so the Jews found their peace of mind in a transcript that offered them a deep and true morality. The Torah deals with human life in all its dimensions. Its laws regulate relationships between man and God, God and man, and man and man.

Extreme pains are taken to insure the authenticity of a text which has served as the final authority for the Jewish people for more than five millenia. To prevent changes and alterations, the Torah scrolls, which are read in the synagogue, must be tediously handwritten by thoroughly trained religious Jewish scribes with particular attention given to the slightest details. Rigid rules, prescribed by sages long gone, are fastidiously observed. They are as follows:

Each Torah consists of fifty seven parchments sewn together, with a definite number of columns on each sheet, a definite number of letters to the line, and so many words to the section. Should a Torah scroll be found to have an error, though it may be one letter or part of a letter, it is considered 'invalid' and unfit for use. The ink used in its construction is made from an ancient formula utilizing a copper wash that turns black when mixed with water.

Upon the completion of the Torah, the final test is yet to come. As the reader in the synagogue reads from the scroll aloud, he is carefully listened to by the congregation. At the slightest deviation or error, the congregation immediately notifies the reader, who must not continue until a correction is made.

It is in this manner, throughout the history of the Jewish religion, that the Torah has retained its original thesis that every letter has a distinct purpose which must not be deleted or tampered with so as not to change the essence of its meaning.

****

The Talmud states that not only are marriages made in Heaven but that forty days before the birth of a child, his or hers future spouse is fore-ordained.

****

The three people considered to have made the greatest impact on civilization in the past hundred years are Sigmund Freud, Albert Einstein and Karl Marx, all Jews.

ISRAEL (Graphic Portrayal)

Israel proper contains 7992 square miles (20,700 sq. km.); population in 1979 was 3,760,000 people; located in S.W.Asia on the Mediterranean Sea. The area is based on the 1949 Armistice Agreement and does not include the territories occupied after the Jordanian, Syrian and Egyptian wars in 1967 and 1973. The capital of Israel is Jerusalem.

Israel is a narrow, ragged shaped strip of land bounded in the North by Lebanon, on the East by Syria and Jordan, and on the Southwest by Egypt. It consists of four principal regions; the coastal plain which runs along the Mediterranean Sea, the mountains East of the plain, the Negev desert which includes the Southern part of the country and the Great Rift valley which is part of the Jordan valley and lies North of the Negev.

Israel's climate consists of long, hot summers and short, rainy winters. The Negev region has less than 10 inches of rainfall a year thus making it a semi-arid country. Israel's scientists have been working on a desalination process to solve this water shortage wherein an inexpensive solution would solve the urgent water problem by increasing development and encouraging population growth.

The largest river in Israel is the Jordan. Other bodies of water are the Sea of Galilee, the Dead Sea, and smaller rivers such as the Yarkon, the Yarmuk and the Kishon. The highest point in Israel is Mount Meron (3,692 ft. high). The lowest point is the Dead Sea (1,292 ft. below sea level); which is also the lowest point on Earth.

Since 1948, more than 100,000,000 trees have been planted in an intensive reforestation program. The economy of Israel is based on both state and private ownership. Although handicapped by adverse land and weather conditions, farming and agriculture has been developed to a degree comparable to the most advanced nations.

Sufficient poultry, eggs, fruit, vegetables, milk and dairy products are produced to supply all domestic needs. Much of the arid land has been irrigated and the cultivation of the soil has been extensively increased. The basic products produced in over 500,000 acres of land are citrus fruit, melons, bananas, peaches, sugar beets, peanuts, cotton, egg plant and many exotic species of flowers.

CHRISTOPHER COLUMBUS

Although general agreement of Christopher Columbus' roots has never been accomplished, conjecture as to his ancestry has been discussed and debated for many years. The concurrent events surrounding his life are too numerous to be discarded as pure coincidence. Let us enumerate:

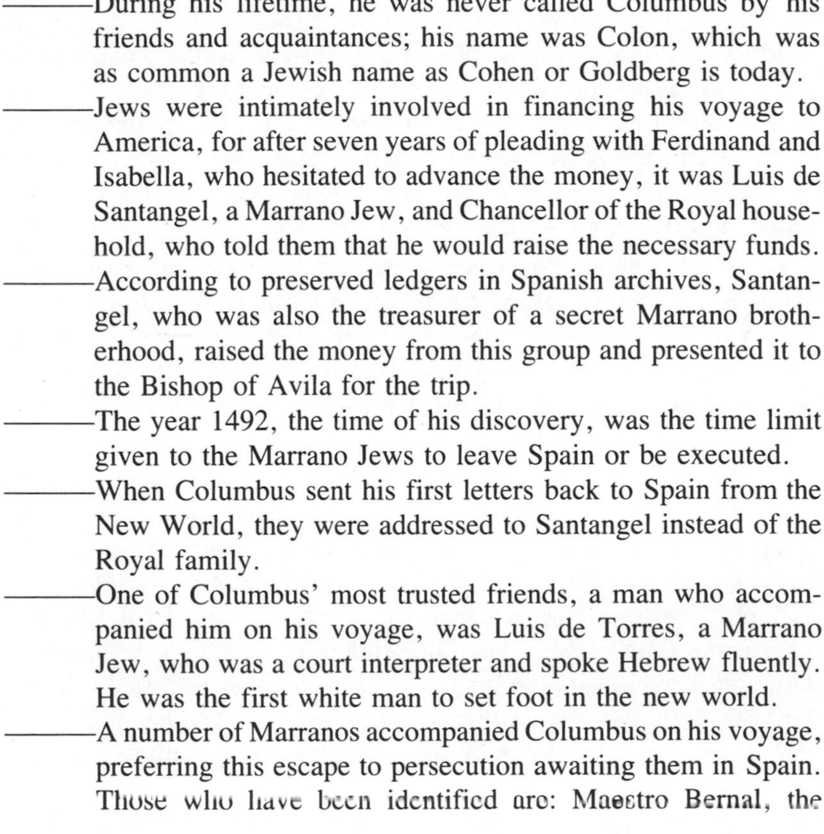

———During his lifetime, he was never called Columbus by his friends and acquaintances; his name was Colon, which was as common a Jewish name as Cohen or Goldberg is today.

———Jews were intimately involved in financing his voyage to America, for after seven years of pleading with Ferdinand and Isabella, who hesitated to advance the money, it was Luis de Santangel, a Marrano Jew, and Chancellor of the Royal household, who told them that he would raise the necessary funds.

———According to preserved ledgers in Spanish archives, Santangel, who was also the treasurer of a secret Marrano brotherhood, raised the money from this group and presented it to the Bishop of Avila for the trip.

———The year 1492, the time of his discovery, was the time limit given to the Marrano Jews to leave Spain or be executed.

———When Columbus sent his first letters back to Spain from the New World, they were addressed to Santangel instead of the Royal family.

———One of Columbus' most trusted friends, a man who accompanied him on his voyage, was Luis de Torres, a Marrano Jew, who was a court interpreter and spoke Hebrew fluently. He was the first white man to set foot in the new world.

———A number of Marranos accompanied Columbus on his voyage, preferring this escape to persecution awaiting them in Spain. Those who have been identified are: Maestro Bernal, the ship's surgeon; Rodrego de Triana, a deck hand; Marco, a cook; Luis de Torres; and Rodrego Sanchez, who was sent along to watch the investment.

****

At the beginning of 1979, its 31st year of statehood, the Israeli population is estimated to be 3,760,000 people, of which 3,158,000 are Jews and 600,000 are non-Jews. In 1948, at its inception, there were 716,000 Jews and 150,000 non-Jews residing in Israel.

A JEWISH POPE

In the year 1130 in Rome, the amazing saga of the Jews added another bizarre chapter to its already complicated history by having a man with Jewish blood elected Pope.

Anacletus II, the great grandson of a Jewish businessman, named Baruch, who lived in the Jewish quarter of the city, despite bitter opposition from anti-Semitic forces, was elected to the papacy and ruled as the Pope for eight years until his death in 1138.

****

In the long course of history, the city of Jerusalem, sacred to the world's three major religions, has been conquered and ruled over by fifteen different peoples: The Canaanites, Israelites, Egyptians, Assyrians, Babylonians, Persians, Greeks, Romans, Byzantines, Saracens, Arabs, the Crusaders, Turks, British and presently, once again, the Jews.

****

The Italians can go back to their ancestors, the Romans, over 2000 years ago, as being the creators of their favorite food, the pizza, when they placed Italian salami, cheese and olive oil on Jewish matzos for the first time.

The Diaspora

Beginning with the eviction of Adam from the Garden of Eden, it appears that God's great design for the Jews was their dispersion to every corner of the earth. Perhaps a deeper motive may have been involved in His thinking, for wherever they assembled a profound effect on the institutional processes of that country came to pass. These amalgamations inevitably brought about diversified reactions stemming from their involvement; a continuous cycle of uncertainty and recrimination, which in many cases, resulted in persecution and exile. Many of these events, individually tragic and in many cases, overwhelming, must lead us to one conclusion: that without the Diaspora and the unshakeable faith of the Jews in their religion, their civilization, and their entity as one people, they would never have survived.

Listed below are the more notable experiences of Jewish scattering and dispersion:

1. In 586 B.C., with the destruction of the First Temple by the Babylonians, practically all of the Jewish population was taken captive to Babylonia (now known as Iraq). Seventy years later, when the Babylonians were defeated by the Persians, the Jews were permitted to return to Israel. However, during those seventy years in Babylon, the Jews rose to great heights, building many colleges and becoming international traders. Great prophets arose in their midst and it was at this time that the greatest document ever written was assembled. This was the Babylonian Talmud, known throughout history, up to the present day, as the definitive explanation of the Bible.
2. Many other Jews, during this era, responding to the broadmindedness of Alexander the Great, moved with the tide to other countries. When Alexandria, Egypt was first colonized by that warrior, there is massive evidence to support the fact that it was accomplished with the help of the Jews, for during the destruction of the Second Temple, over a quarter of a million Israelites were residing in Alexandria.
3. The Roman conquest of Jerusalem in 485 is remembered for its almost complete annihilation of the Israeli people. For sheer cruelty, even the Nazi Holocaust does not compare to the sadism involved. In besieging the city, the Romans built a high earthen barricade to prevent escape. All Jews who were captured were crucified on the

spot, as many as 500 a day. Then, the Romans initiated a planned siege to create starvation. According to Josephus, who recorded the event, he wrote that a famine raged inside the walls with people dying by the thousands. Eventually, when the Romans entered the city, they set fire to the Temple and in time, the entire city was aflame. In the end, thousands of captives were taken who were then forced to fight gladiatorial contests until the death. However, it took three years for the Romans to finally capture the Masada, the last stronghold of the Jews.

4. There have been many individual cases in Jewish history where historical figures were ordered to leave their abodes. Abraham was ordered by God to leave his home and to start a new life in Canaan. Isaac had to travel to another country. Jacob and his family were ordered to go to Egypt. Moses and the Israelites had to flee Egypt to wander for 40 years in the wilderness. It is from this instance, when God ordered Abraham to move, that the word 'Hebrew', from the word 'Ivri' was first used. It means 'someone from the other side'.

5. Another tragic chapter in the Jewish caravan is the Spanish and Portuguese Inquisition where thousands of Jews, under pain of death, were forced to convert to Catholicism. This situation created many strange occurrences wherein Jews entered the clergy to avoid detection and rose to the ranks of bishops and cardinals. When the ruse was finally discovered, practically every person who was executed was a member of the clergy. In Portugal, in a period of seven years, from 1619 to 1626, 231 Marrano Jews were put to death. Among them were 44 nuns, 15 clergymen and 7 canons. It was during this time, at the height of the Inquisition, that the background of Christopher Columbus came under scrutiny as having been a Jew.

6. The Nazi holocaust is but another example of Jewish persecution and exile. In this episode of Jewish helplessness, over 6,000,000 Jews were slaughtered, but for the first time in over 2000 years, their suffering helped lead to the establishment of a Jewish homeland.

The strange paradox of Jewish persecutions is that of all the nations involved, none remain. Babylonia is forgotten, the Roman Empire was destroyed, Spain and Portugal have never recovered from the expulsion of the Jews, and the Third Reich of Adolf Hitler was completely defeated. Of the ancient people, the Romans, the Greeks and the Egyptians of that era, have vanished. Only the Jews remain with a steadfast link between their ancient people and their modern descendants.

The Diaspora has enabled the Jew to remain alive. For over 2000 years, he has been driven and scattered from one country to another. More than seventy nations have considerable Jewish populations and, to date, Israel has received immigrants from over 100 different countries. There are Jews of every color; black and yellow, as well as white. Jewish communities thrive in India, China, Mexico, Ethiopia, Cuba, Japan, Chile, Bolivia, Afghanistan and many others. When Australia, Bolivia, Afghanistan and even the United States were founded, there were Jews among the explorers.

****

TRIVIA

Yiddish Exclamations:

AHAH!	That's it!
EYE, EYE, EYE!	That's good!
OY VAY!	Terrible!
FEH!	No good!
GEVALT!	Help!
HOO HAH!	Oh boy!
NU?	Well?
NU, NU.	C'mon, speed it up.
NUUUUU. . . .?	What's keeping you?
TZU, TZU, TZU.	Tsk, tsk, tsk.
GAY IN DREHRD.	Go to hell—drop dead.

THE 9TH OF AV (July-August)

This date of the Hebrew calendar, marking the memorial day of Tishe B'Ov, is observed as a day of fasting and mourning for it commemorates numerous tragedies that strangely have befallen the Jews on that particular day in history. Tishe B'Ov has such monumental meaning that during the services in the synagogue, the worshippers sit on the floor or on low stools as an expression of their grief. Part of the liturgy is the reading of the Book of Lamentations.

By some strange coincidence, the following catastrophies have occurred on this particular date:

1. The destruction of the First Temple in 586 B.C., by the Babylonians.
2. Six hundred years later, the Second Temple was destroyed by the Romans on the same day.
3. The defeat of Bar Kochba and the destruction of the Bethar fortress in the year 135, 65 years after the destruction of the Second Temple.
4. The Jews were expelled from England in the year 1290 on that date.
5. The expulsion deadline for the exile of Jews from Spain in 1492 was the ninth of Av.
6. Hadrian's complete destruction of Jerusalem fell in that time period.
7. The execution of Rabbi Akiba.
8. In 1555, the Jews were ordered into a ghetto in Rome during Tishe B'Ov.
9. The final solution of the 'Jewish problem' was ordered in Germany on Tishe B'Ov.

ISRAEL—ITS UNIQUE INHERITANCE

Considering the TACHTONIM, the creatures who inhabit the earth, or the human race, according to the genealogical table in Genesis X, the world consisted of seventy nations who spoke seventy languages. In literature written by Jews, it is but natural to find prominence given to the people of Israel. It was also stated, in no implicit terms, that the people of Israel were the Chosen People. This is, of course, a Biblical doctrine but it receives the greatest amplification by the Rabbis. The Talmud reiterates, over and over again, the unique relationship which existed between God and His people. Its importance lies in the fact that it was exclaimed when the Jews had gone through an overwhelmning crisis. The Temple had been destroyed, the State broken up, and the population dispersed into alien lands. In this terrible situation, many must have felt that their God had deserted them. Consequently, in the schools and synagogues, the comforting message was preached that Israel was still God's people and His guardianship over them had not ceased.

So close is the relationship between them that the treatment accorded to Israel on earth is reflected upon God in heaven. "Whoever rises up against Israel is as though he rose against the Holy One, blessed be He." (Mech. to XV. 7; 39a) "Whoever hates Israel is like one who hates Him." (Sifre Num. 84: 22b)

If, however, Israelites are the Chosen People, it is not for the purpose of receiving special favoritism from God. Far from being in a better position than other people, the Jew, from the material point of view, does not receive special benefits. As a result of this choice, he bears a heavy responsibility and his liability to punishment is greater. The main responsibility of Israel is the protection of the Torah, the Divine Revelation. Since the purpose of the world's creation was the glorification of God's name through the medium of the Torah, with Israel its recipient, it follows that Israel was in God's thought before the creation of the Universe.

It was said that God offered the Torah to all nations but only Israel agreed to accept the responsibility. If there had been no nation to accept the Revelation, the purpose of Creation would have failed and the entire population of the world would have been blotted out. Israel, too, would have perished in the wilderness after the exodus from Egypt if they had rejected the Revelation. The Holy One, blessed be he, inverted Mount Sinai over them like a huge vessel and declared, "If you accept the Torah, well and good; if not, here shall be your sepulchre." (Shab. 88a)

It is obvious in the opinion of the Rabbis that the Jews possessed no inherent superiority for which they merited this distinction and also that this special status would immediately come to an end if they abandoned their commitment. On the contrary, it was destined for all mankind, and hope is great that the day will come when all nations shall accept it. It is said, "This is the law of mankind, Lord God." (Sam. vii 19)

It is not written that, "This is the law of the priests, or the Levites, or of Israel, but the law of mankind." The ideal of the religion of the Rabbis was the extension of God's Kingship over all the peoples of the world, and the Jews were constantly reminded of this. It follows that the doors could not be bolted against any Gentile who desired admittance from pure motives. Genuine converts were welcomed and highly esteemed. Proselytes are dear to God, for they are described in the same terms as the Israelites.

When a proselyte came in to be accepted as a convert, he was asked, "Do you not know that Israel is now afflicted, persecuted, humbled, distracted, and suffering chastisements?" If he replies, "I know and am unworthy.", he is accepted forthwith and instructed in some of the minor and more important precepts, as well as in the penalties which are attached to them. He is told, "You must know that before taking the step, you partook of forbidden fat and profaned the Sabbath without incurring punishment; but henceforward, if you do these things dire penalties will befall you." In the same way that he was informed of the punishments attached to the precepts, he is like-wise informed of the rewards. He is told, "You must know that the World to Come is reserved for the righteous, and Israel at the present time is unable to accept the abundance of good or the abundance of punishment." If he still accepts the responsibility, he is circumcised forthwith. After he is healed, he is ritually immersed and two disciples of the Sages stand by him and instruct him in some of the minor and more important precepts. When he has immersed himself and ascended from the water, he is an Israelite in every respect. (Jeb. 47a, b)

The sacred obligation regarding the preservation of the Torah is contained in the Mishna, included in the Tractate "Pirke Auvoth" (The Sayings of the Fathers). They were the pioneers of the Talmud whose labors ushered in an era that led to devoted study from generation to generation. Here are a few extracts to enable the reader to understand and appreciate the cumulative effect of their work:

Upon three things the world is based: upon the Torah, upon divine worship, and upon acts of benevolence. (I. 2)

Whoso engages in much gossip with women brings evil upon himself, neglects the study of the Torah, and will in the end inherit Gehenim.

Provide yourself with a teacher of the Torah, and get yourself a companion, and judge all men on the scale of merit. (I. 6)

The more Torah, the more life. . .He who has acquired for himself words of the Torah has acquired for himself life in the World to Come.

If you have learnt much Torah, ascribe not any merit to yourself, for thereunto were you created. (II. 17)

Qualify yourself for the study of the Torah, since it does not come to you as an inheritance, and let all your deeds be done for the sake of heaven. (II. 17)

It is not your duty to complete the work, but neither are you free to desist from it. If you have studied much Torah, much reward will be given you; and faithful is your Employer to pay you the reward of your labour; and know that the grant of reward unto the Righteous will be in the Hereafter. (II. 21)

Where there is no Torah, there are no manners; where there are no manners, there is no Torah. Where there is no wisdom, there is no fear of God; where there is no fear of God, there is no wisdom. Where there is no knowledge, there is no understanding; where there is no understanding, there is no knowledge. (III. 21)

CABALLAH—(its origin)

The word 'Caballah', in Hebrew, means 'Tradition'. Since the beginning of time, due to recrimination and persecution, segments of the Jewish community had been infused with a mystical experience that offered them a refuge; a shelter wherein they found relief from the abuses heaped upon them. From its origin, this method of supplication had remained secret. Fearful of retaliation from outside the Jewish community, they juxtaposed their religious experience by creating complex and distorted texts in order to confuse their enemies.

In the 11th Century, a Spanish philosopher named Ibn Gabirol, labeled these mystical symbols 'Caballah' and its tradition was passed down 'orally' from generation to generation, from teacher to pupil, thus assuring its truthfulness and continuity. Two centuries later, recorded in a book called 'ZOHAR' (Book of Splendor), much of the Caballah's practices and teachings were revealed.

Unlike the Talmud which clearly and explicitly defines Jewish Law and practices, Caballah necessitates the involvement of ones mystical, spiritual and emotional self. Its strict requirements demand the complete withdrawal and elimination of one's ego which is transported into an existence consisting of all matter, both real and ethereal.

Caballah is literally a mystical application of Jewish belief, entirely reliant on Judaic principles, integrated with Judaism and completely dependent upon the Torah. The mystical practices of Caballah would be impossible without an understanding and knowledge of Hebrew, in which lanaguage the Torah is written. Each word, in fact each letter of each word in the Torah, is the subject for deep contemplation, analysis and juxtaposition. So shrouded in mystery and so interwoven in the multi-faceted schools of thought in the lifeline of Judaic fundamental conduct, Caballah, as expounded by Caballistic masters, is still misunderstood among the vast majority of world Jewry.

Every age brought about new masters who in turn brought forth new theories and guide lines. Different teachers initiated new interpretations and with the dispersion of the Jews creating constant obstacles, it became impossible to establish a consistent pattern of mystical practice for the entire Jewish community. Despite the antipathies of alien environments, it is amazing that the mystical applications of Cabbalistic practices remained so closely allied.

Caballah has thrived, in different stages, on different levels and in different interpretations for over 5000 years. It is so interwoven in the basic structure of Jewish culture that its elusiveness remains like a thin veil—unnoticed and accepted. Its understanding is completely based on the explication and teachings of its masters. A few indications of its mystical attachments expoused by Caballistic masters are herewith illustrated:

———A man should actually detach his ego from his body until he has passed through all the worlds and becomes one with God; till he disappears entirely out of the bodiless world.

Maggid of Mezerich

———When the Torah enters the soul, light comes with it like a sun's rays entering a house. Even more, it is truly firelike . . . because all its words and letters are like coals seemingly extinguished, but when anyone begins to work on it, a great many-colored flame arises from every one of its letters. That is the knowledge hidden in each letter.

Moses Luzzatto

———Truly all that God does in the world is an emblem of the divine Wisdom . . . Further, all the works of God are the ways of the Torah . . . and no single word is contained in it but is an indication of ever so many ways and paths and mysteries of divine Wisdom . . . Each incident recorded in the Torah contains a multitude of deep significations and each word itself is an expression of Wisdom and the doctrine of truth.

Rabbi Simeon

———Before an egg can turn into a chicken, it must first totally cease to be an egg. Each thing must lose its original identity before it can be something else. Therefore, before a thing is transformed into something else, it must come to the level of Nothingness.

Dov Baer

———Think of yourself as nothing and totally forget yourself as you pray. Only remember that you are praying for the Divine Presence. You may then enter the Universe of Thought, a state of consciousness which is beyond time. Everything in this realm is the same . . . life and death, land and sea . . . but in order to enter this realm you must relinquish your ego and forget all your troubles.

Maggid of Mezerich.

Since the Middle Ages, the Zohar (Book of Splendor) is considered essential for understanding Jewish mystical practices. It tells the story of a 2nd Century sage called Rabbi Simeon bar Yohai and his son Eleazar, who lived in a cave for thirteen years to escape the Romans who had ransacked the city. Sustained by a carob tree and a fountain which miraculously burst forth at the mouth of the cave, the father and son sat buried in sand during the day to protect themselves from the burning sun. In this environment they studied the Torah under the guidance of the Prophet Elijah.

In the 13th year of their forced banishment, the Roman emperor Trajan died permitting the two exiles to return to their home. Filled with horror and aversion at the absence of spirituality among the Jews, Rabbi Simeon returned to the cave. At the end of a year, he heard a voice from within the cave urging him to disregard those who deviated from their faith and to only teach those who were ready to listen. It was the discourses given by Rabbi Simeon to his loyal disciples, who were transformed spiritually by his mere presence, that make up the subject matter of the Zohar. He expounded that all things were reflected in a higher world, a Cosmic existence, and that nothing, absolutely no thing or person survived independently on any plane, regardless of their station. ''All souls form but one unity with the Divine Soul,'' was the basis for all his teachings. He stated: ''All things of which this world is composed, as the soul and the body, will return to the principle and to the root from which they sprang. For God is the beginning and He is the end of all degrees of creation.''

INTERPRETATIONS FROM THE CABALLAH

Adam Kadmon — The Cosmic reflection of the Body of God.

Agla — Strengths.

Aravot — A secret place inhabited by departed souls of Saints and sages.

Ayin — No-thing.

Bahir — Book of Light.

Binah — The sphere of 'Understanding' on the Cosmic tree.

Bittul ha-yesh — The annihilation of the desiring ego.

Caballah — The name for Jewish mystical tradition.

Chaverim Meaning 'Comrades'; a group of mystics in the 16th Century Safed.

Chayay Olam Habah — Life of the Future World.

Chayot —— Highly vibrating living beings composed of pure energy.

Cheshek —— Mystic enthusiasm.

Daath — The secret sphere of 'Knowledge' on the Cosmic tree.

Devekuth — Cleaving to God.

Dillug — 'Skipping', an exercise in free association of ideas in reference to specific code words.

Dodi — 'Dear friend', The stage at which the mystic is bound to God by love rather than awe.

Elohim Hayim — ''The Living God''

En Sof —— The Infinite.

Etrog — 'citron fruit', Visualized at the core of the heart during meditation.

Gilgulim — Incarnations

Hakhanot — Hasidic preparations for ritual washing, prayer, meditation and dressing in non-woolen garments.

Halakha —	The Jewish legal tradition.
Haluk —	Garment of light surrounding God's glory visible to Merkabah mystics.
Hasagah —	Emphasis on 'Intellect' as the way to God.
Hasid —	A mystic devotee.
Hasiduth —	Devotion to God.
Hebel —	'Breath', Meditative breathing exercises using the text of Ecclesiastes.
Hebli —	Vanity.
Hekhalot —	The halls of God's palace.
Histapkut —	'Making do', The ascetic attitude of the medieval school of Isaac of Akko.
Hitbodedut —	'Meditation'.
Hitlahavut —	Hasidic enthusiasm.
Hitpaalut —	Hasidic rapture following contemplative prayer.
Hokhmah —	The sphere of 'Wisdom' on the Cosmic tree.
Ibbur —	The additional soul lent to all Sabbath observers on that day.
Kavanna —	One pointed concentration.
Kavannot —	Special symbols to induce one pointed concentration.

Kedusha —	Sanctification.
Kisupha —	Yearning for the Divine.
Lulav —	A palm branch; symbolic of the human spine in meditative visualization.
Madregot —	Levels of mystic ascent.
Mafteach ha-hokhmoth —	Keys to wisdom.
Maggid —	A preacher in ordinary life; A celestial guardian in spiritual life.
Mashav —	Contemplating.
Maskil —	Enlightened.
Matrona —	The female aspect of God.
Mechavenim —	Those who make prayers with meditation.
Merkabah —	Throne mysticism.
Midot —	Qualities
Mikhtav —	Writing
Miryat Eynayim —	What the eyes can see.
Mitzvoth —	Divine precepts.
Mishnah	'Oral Law'
Mivta —	Articulation of the letters.

Mohin Degadlut—	Expanded consciousness in Hasidic ecstasy.
Neshamah —	The spiritual portion of the soul.
Niggun —	Wordless melody to induce meditation.
Ofanim —	Wheel-shaped angelic beings.
Or Ha-Sechel —	Light of the Intellect.
Otzer Eden Ganuz —	Hidden treasure garden.
Otzer Ha-chayim —	Treasure of Life.
Pachdiel —	Guardian of the Fourth chamber.
Pachad —	Fear.
Pardes —	The 'garden' symbolizing Jewish mystical practices.
Rav —	Master and teacher.
Rav Ha-Hasid —	Master of devotion.
Rebbe —	Hasidic master.
Sefer Ha-Malbush —	Book of clothing.
Sefer Ha-Tzeruf—	Book of Permutations.
Sefer Yetzirah —	A first century manual of letter contemplation.
Shedim —	Demonic beings who confuse the mind in meditation.
Shefa —	Divine influx.

Shekhinah —	Immanent presence and female aspect of God.
Shema —	Daily recitation of God's oneness.
Shem Hameforesh —	The specific Name of God.
Shiur Komah —	Measure of the body.
Shulkhan Aruch —	Legal code.
Tahor —	Pure.
Tamim —	With God.
Tetragrammaton —	YHVH: the sacred Name of God.
Tevunah —	A stage in contemplation where subject-object separation disappears.
Tikkun —	Spiritual 'correction' exercise.
Totrosyai —	The symbolic guardian of the threshhold at the first stage of higher consciousness.
Tzaddik —	An enlightened saint.
Tzeruf —	Mental Hebrew letter permutation.
Yashar —	Sincere.
Yechidah —	Union with the Absolute.
Yichud —	Mental 'binding' exercise.
Yichudim —	Binding of the spheres.
Zohar —	"The Book of Splendor"

A YIDDISH MEMORY BANK

Compiling the memorabilia in this compendium has been a nostalgic and memorable experience. Wracking my brain, as I embarked on the mental journey back into my childhood, I strived to remember the sundry incidents and Jewish expressions that occurred a half century ago. It might have seemed an impossibility yet, as I retraced the past, digging into the environment of my childhood, the flood of memories rushed into my consciousness as if they happened only a few days ago.

The vividness of that era, in contrast to life as it is today, was never more evident than when you begin to recall the relationships between the parents and children of the first generation Americans and the impersonal attitudes and relationships of the families today.

I can remember so well. . . . . . .

THE FRIDAY NIGHT RITUAL OF MAMA 'BENCHING LICHT' WHILE THE CHILDREN STOOD AROUND WATCHING IN AWE.

MAMA MAKING THREE GLASSES OF TEA FOR THE CHILDREN BY DIPPING ONE TEA BAG FROM ONE GLASS TO ANOTHER.

GETTING A PENNY FROM PAPA, THEN GOING INTO A CANDY STORE WHERE YOU HAD A HUNDRED SELECTIONS TO CHOOSE FROM.

MAMA SINGING THE OLD JEWISH 'LIEDELE', "MY GREENEH KOOZINEH".

MAMA CURING MY EARACHE BY DIPPING A COTTON BALL INTO MY URINE AND APPLYING IT INTO THE INFECTED EAR. (THE YIDDISH EXPRESSION FOR THIS ACT WAS CALLED 'PAHSSLIN'.

BEING TAKEN TO THE SECOND AVENUE THEATRE TO WATCH MOLLY PICON IN A YIDDISH PLAY.

MAMA GIVING US A NICKEL ON SUNDAYS THEN PACKING US OFF WITH A BAG OF KAISER ROLLS AND BANANAS TO THE MOVIES WHERE WE WOULD WATCH PEARL WHITE, IN "THE PERILS OF PAULINE" FOR THREE PERFORMANCES.

THE MANY FIGHTS IN THE SCHOOL YARD AFTER BEING CALLED 'A GODDAMNED JEW'.

GOING TO THE SYNAGOGUE WITH PAPA FOR THE DAILY EVENING SERVICES AND LISTENING TO THE TEN OLD, BEARDED MEN READING THE 'CHOOMISH' BETWEEN 'MINCHA' AND 'MAHRIV'.

THE DELIGHTFUL TASTE OF A KOSHER CORNED BEEF SANDWICH AND AN EGG CREAM ON A SATURDAY NIGHT . . . ALL FOR 15¢.

PUTTING A RAW POTATO ON A STICK THEN ROASTING IT OVER AN OPEN FIRE.

MAMA MAKING DELICIOUS PASSOVER WINE IN THE CELLAR FROM GRAPES THAT HAD BEEN SQUEEZED FOUR TIMES PREVIOUSLY.

DELIVERING THE FIRST GALLON OF THIS WINE TO SOME POOR FAMILY.

TAKING TURNS WITH MY SISTERS ON COLD WINTER NIGHTS TO WARM OUR FEET IN THE KITCHEN STOVE.

MAMA MAKING AN X FOR HER SIGNATURE WHEN SHE HAD TO WRITE HER NAME.

THE NEIGHBORLY DISCUSSIONS AND ARGUMENTS OF THE WOMEN ON THE STREET AS THEY STUCK THEIR HEADS OUT OF THEIR APARTMENT WINDOWS AND YELLED ACROSS THE ALLEY.

THE FAMILY CONVERSATIONS IN YIDDISH AFTER DINNER . . . ALWAYS STRESSING HONESTY, RELIGIOUS ADHERENCE, CHARITY AND THE GREATNESS OF AMERICA (THE GOLDENEH MEDEENA).

TRIVIA

Old Yiddish cures and remedies brought over from the villages of Poland and Russia by our parents and grandparents when they came to America.

GAUGLE MAUGLE: (For the sore throat)
A sure fire remedy consisting of milk, a raw egg and a wad of butter; heated to a boiling point then swallowed in one gulp.

PAHSSLIN: (For the earache)
A cotton ball at the end of a wooden match, dipped into the urine of the ailing person, then applied to the affected ear.

TRIVIA

One of the most popular Yiddish folk songs that was brought over from Russia and Poland all the way to Ellis Island. It tugged at your heartstrings with its beautiful, plaintive melody. Although the name of the song is known as ''Oyfin Pripehchik'' (a wood burning stove) the original name is ''Dehr Alef Bais'' (The A,B,C's).

DEHR ALEF BAIS

Ofyin Pripehtchik brent ah fyeril
Un in shtoob iz hayss
Un dehr rebbe lehrnt klayneh kinderlech
Dehm Alef Bais

Zeht'zshe kinderlech, Gedenkt'zshe tyereh
Vos eer lehrnt daw
Zaugt'zshe nauch amaul, un tahkeh nauch amaul
Kumitz alef uh.

(Translation)

In the stove, a small fire is burning
And it is warm in the room.
And the rabbi teaches little children
The A,B,C's.

Look here, little children; remember dear ones,
What you are learning here.
Repeat it once again, and over and over again,
The A,B,C's.

Eli, Eli

Adagio
Traditional Yiddish Folk Song
E7 Am E7
mp E - li E - li, la-ma a - sav - ta -
espress.
Am E7 Am
nu? E - li, E - li,
E7 Dm E E7
la - ma a - sav - ta - nu? Mit Fei - er und Flam
f
F7 E7 Am Dm F7 E7
hat men uns ge - brent i - ber - al hat men uns ge- macht zu Schand, zu Schpot;

Am Dm Am E7 Am
Ob - zu-tre-ten fun uns hot doch kein-er net ge - wagt, fun
p
un - ser hei - lig - er, Toï - re fun un - ser Ge - bot.
meno mosso
rit.
Dm E7 Dm E7 Am
Mazel Tov
Allegro
Traditional Yiddish
mf
Dm
Oy, oy, oy Cho - sen Kal - le ma - zel tov, Oy, oy, oy
E7 Am A7 Dm
Cho - sen Kal - le ma - zel tov, Oy, oy, oy Cho - sen
E7 A7 Dm
Kal - le ma - zel tov, Wintch all - e heint a yom tov is heint.

JEWISH WIT AND HUMOR

JEWISH WIT AND HUMOR

An old Yiddish saying:
"Ah mensh trahcht un Gott lahcht"
(translation)
"Man thinks and God laughs"

Throughout the complexity of their amazing history, the Jews have been noted for their ability to come up with satirical and ludicrous tales that either reflected their joy or heartbreak, or portrayed their ancient yearning for understanding and justice. Their wit and sense of humor, never diminishing even under the most perverse conditions, many times directed against themselves, was one of the dominant forces that helped to sustain them through situations, that otherwise might have proven fatal. In a much deeper significance, it emphasizes their never ending quest for absolute truth.

During the period of slavery in Egypt, their only recourse, to offset the indignities practised against them, were the allegorical expressions by their Rabbis, whose subtlety and satire helped to provide the hidden strength and mental stability to survive under the dire conditions imposed by their persecutors.

One such story tells of an Egyptian taskmaster, who while watching an Israelite funeral, questioned one of the mourners. "Why is it," he asked a bearded mourner, "that your funerals are so sad and gloomy while ours are full of pomp, music and feasting?"

"I really can't answer you," acknowledged the old Jew, "perhaps that is why we would rather attend your funerals than ours." The subtle story is designed to create a smile and to make the recipient think about it, never to cause hilarity or obvious insult.

Many anecdotes came into being in the Yeshivas of Poland and Russia where the advanced students, after long study periods, would retire in the evenings to their 'bivouac' areas and tell stories to relax and amuse themselves. Typical of virile young men, their conversations would inevitably begin with sex and women, then unalterably turn to the legends, folk stories and tales about prominent members of the community. These conversations were transposed into humorous and satirical tales.

On completion of their studies and returning to their respective countries and villages, the students retold these stories to whoever would listen. The artful perception in their tales immediately gained wide acceptance and became a standard chronology of traditional Jewish humor and folklore.

Inherently, the telling of a Jewish joke, related by a Jew and satirizing a Jew, has a more significant meaning. Psychologically, it can be considered a release from tension, from the chain that, throughout history, the non-Jewish world has placed around his neck for being a Jew. It is the only way of expressing his anger and frustration in combatting the scorn and ridicule that have been heaped against him from time immemorial. He has the awareness that he is merely a plain human being, not unlike anyone else, with all the weaknesses to which mortals are prone. However, with it all, he has the courage of his convictions to be cognizant of those weaknesses and to satirize them; added to this he flays his contemporaries for their own shortcomings.

The unusual reaction of a Jew to a Jewish joke, regardless of where he may live; either in a "stet'l" in Russia, a "medina" in Casablanca, in modern Israel or in the more sophisticated environment of America, is relatively the same, considering the wide diversification of his background or life style. Each will react with the same interpretation, and the reason is, that beneath the surface, in their subconsciousness, they are molded together in the same identity with one another; in the awareness that for over 3000 years their faith, their ancestry and their lot has been interwoven in a constant cycle of pogroms, slavery and persecution.

A true Jewish joke reflects the entire panorama of the Jewish caravan through history. With its ups and downs, its constant striving for understanding and acceptance; the bottom line for every Jewish joke that has been written was the deeply rooted desire for a position of equality with their international non-Jewish neighbors. Perhaps this prelude is too serious for the humorous anecdotes that follow but it may be able to inject the motive and principle behind each punch line.

****

Finishing an oil portrait of her aged grandmother, the modern American artist, Sylvia, put the finishing touches on the painting, picked it up, then turned and showed it to the old woman sitting on the couch. ''Well, baubi, do you like it? What do you think?'' Her grandmother glanced at it for several seconds then murmured in whimsical Yiddish. ''It is nice but then I never did take a good picture.''

****

Jake Greenburg, just two weeks in America from Minsk, rushed into his apartment on Delancey Street and headed straight into the bathroom. He yelled to his wife who followed him worriedly. Jake pointed to the water in the toilet. ''How much do we pay for this water?'' he panted.

''We pay nothing for this water, why?'' she exclaimed. ''Then we're going to make a million dollars.'' he smiled exultantly. ''I just saw a sign in Macy's Department Store. They're selling toilet water for $2.00 a bottle.

****

A conversation:

''Good morning, Mr. Bernstein. How's by you?''

''Eh!''

''How is business? Are you making money?''

''Eh!''

''How's your wife? Is she well?''

''Eh!''

''Well, goodbye, Mr. Bernstein. It's always nice talking to an old friend.''

****

On Hitler's birthday, a fourth grade teacher in Berlin asked her pupils, ''If Hitler was your father and you could have any wish granted, what would you ask for?''

''I would want to be a Storm Trooper.'' one shouted.
''I'd want to be a pilot.'' yelled another.
''A General!'' called a third.
''An orphan.'' shouted Izzy Cohen.

****

Rebbi Davidson, a demanding melamed, was furious when little Abie handed in a poor paper. ''This is ridiculous, Abie, I don't see how one person could have made so many mistakes.''

''One person didn't,'' Abie muttered sheepishly. ''My father helped me.''

****

At an adult night school for immigrants in New York, the teacher asked Mr. Feinstein, newly arrived from Bialystok, where elephants were to be found.

Feinstein, confused and unaware of the answer, replied. ''How can anyone lose an elephant?''

****

At a divorce trial, the Judge asked Mrs. Goldbloom, ''Why do you want a divorce for incompatibility? Aren't your relations satisfactory?''

''My relations are fine, Judge,'' she countered. ''but his relations; you never saw such busybodies in your life.''

****

The Yeshiva baucher asked the Rabbi. ''Rabbi, why did God make man before woman?

''Because He didn't want any advice on how to make a man.'' was the curt reply.

****

Sam called at the Special Delivery window of the Post Office for a package. The clerk checked the incoming mail then held up one of the packages. ''I don't know whether this is for you or not. The name is obliterated.''

''It's not for me.'' answered Sam. ''I'm not obliterated; I'm Bernstein.''

****

Mrs. Jakovsky thought the opportunity was ripe. ''If you really loved me,'' she said to her husband. ''you'd buy me a mink.''

''O.K., I'll buy you a mink,'' her husband replied, ''but on one condition.''

''What condition?'' she asked curiously.

''That you feed him.''

****

Morris Lefkowitz sat down across the desk from the interviewer to answer questions about a driving license. Your name, please?''

''Morris Lefkowitz''

''Your birthplace?''

''Bialystok, Russia.''

''Your occupation?''

''Kosher butcher.''

''Your religion?''

''A Catholic, what else.''

****

Mr. Koogle walked into a tailor shop on Rivington Street to have his suit pressed

''That will be two fifty,'' said the tailor as he handed him the pressed garment.

''Two fifty!'' Mr. Koogle was indignant. ''In Moscow we could have this suit pressed for fifteen cents.''

''I believe you,'' answered the tailor. ''but look at all the time and money you save by not taking the trip.''

****

Moishe, a nature lover, came home one day and saw his mother in a new mink coat. ''Mama,'' he said in accusation, ''don't you know how much that poor animal suffered so you could have a fur coat?''

''Shame on you, Moishe, for calling your father an animal.''

****

A noted anti-Semite, very rich and very important, was arranging a coming out party for her daughter and decided to hire the finest entertainment. She sent for Jascha Heifetz, the violinist.''My fee is $5000.'' she was informed.

''Very well,'' she agreed. ''but I do not permit Jewish entertainers to mingle with my guests.''

''In that case,'' Heifetz replied. ''The fee is only $500.''

****

Its no disgrace to be born poor, and its no disgrace to die poor but do we have to spend our entire life in that condition?

****

The very orthodox Mendel Rosenblum went to the hospital and was put in a room with an Irishman and an Italian. The following morning, he arose early and began to roll the tefillin on his arm. Murphy the Irishman looked over at the Italian. ''Look at that Jew, Giuseppe, he's taking his own blood pressure.''

****

The head of the Communist cell in New York was preaching about the advantages of Communism. He talked on and on; for three hours he talked, until looking down at the second row he saw one of his flock asleep. ''Comrade,'' he shouted in anger, awakening the man. ''if you have to sleep why don't you go home.''

''What do you mean, telling me to go home.'' the listener retorted. ''Where do you think you are—in Russia?''

****

At the end of the nature class, the teacher announced, ''And don't forget, of all the animals in the jungle, an elephant never forgets.''

''What does he have to remember?'' shouted Jakie Abramovitz.

****

The Chairman of the Israel Bond banquet was pleading for funds. ''For the first time in history,'' he expounded, ''we are growing apples in almost every part of the country.''

Jacob Weinstein, with a little too much Israeli wine under his belt, rose to his feet. ''Just a minute, Mr. Chairman,'' he said vociferously. ''I must disagree with you. What did Adam bite into—a pickle?''

****

The patient walked into the doctors office. ''What seems to be wrong?'' asked Dr. Davidson.

''I'm really worried, Doctor,'' the patient replied. ''Lately it seems that my memory is going. I can't seem to remember anything from one day to the next. What do you suggest?''

''Well,'' the doctor quickly replied. ''the first thing you must do is to pay me in advance.''

****

ANTHOLOGY OF JEWISH CULTURE

ANTHOLOGY OF JEWISH CULTURE

This section contains an interesting compilation of traditional and religious facts pertaining to Judaic customs, beliefs, services, prayers, holidays, history and other characteristics related to Jews and Judaism.

Alphabetically compiled, this information is presented in order to enlighten the reader on the many aspects of ancient and modern Jewish cultural and religious experiences.

Aleph

All things grow with time --- except grief.

(Talmud)

ADONAI (From the Hebrew: 'My Lord God')

This title, sacred in its own identity, is only used in the synagogue while reciting solemn prayers. The word 'Hashem' is substituted during ordinary conversation.

In Hebrew, four consonants, YHVH denote the name of God. It is probably a derivative of Jehovah but this definition has been disproved. The diacritical marks, dots and dashes, that usually form the vowels, making pronunciation possible, is missing from this word creating a mystery as to how this word came into being.

The word YHVH was so sacred that only in the temple of

Jerusalem was it permitted to be mentioned, and then in a tone so low that the congregation would be unable to hear it.

ADON OLAUM

Adon Olaum is the first two words of a popular hymn chanted in the synagogue in many services. It expresses the relationship between God, the Universe and Man. It is believed to have been written in the 12th Century.

AFIKOYMEN

The Afikoymen is the middle matzo of the three matzos placed on the Passover Seder table. It is considered the dessert of the feast and is broken into pieces by the head of the household and passed around to the persons at the table to be eaten as an after-bite. It is usually hidden during the feast by the person presiding at the services and the youngster who is able to find it is rewarded with a coin as a ransom.

ALEPH

The first letter in the Hebrew and Yiddish alphabet. Placing the Aleph together with the second letter (BET), they form the word 'Alephbet' or 'alphabet'.

Its physical structure was presumed to represent the head of an ox.

ALIYAH

A Hebrew derivative meaning 'going up', signifying the honor bestowed upon a Jewish member of the synagogue to be called for a reading of the Torah.

A second usage has to do with Immigration to the land of Israel. The first Aliyot were the immigrants who arrived in Israel between 1880 and 1905; the second group arrived from 1905 to 1914; the third from 1919 to 1924.

ALTAR

The Hebrew term, 'MIZBAYACH' refers to a pile of stones used in the offering of sacrifices. During the period of the Temple in Jerusalem, the Altar symbolized the sanctity and unity of the Jewish people.

AMIDAH

The Hebrew word for 'Standing', recited at the services in which the worshipper stands. The basis of Amidah has three applications: The opening benedictions (ADORATION); the closing benedictions (THANKSGIVING); and the intermediate benedictions.

During weekday prayers and services there are 13 benedictions and on Sabbath and Holidays there is one.

AMORAH

From the Hebrew: "Interpreter".Amorah refers to the sages and scholars who interpreted the 'Mishna' from the 3rd Century in the Academies of Babylonia and Palestine until the completion of the Talmud in 500 C.E.

An ordained Amorah is called Rabbi or Rov.

AMOS

The first of the Jewish literary prophets. His prophecies are written in the 'Book of Amos' which forms an integral part of the Hebrew Bible.

ANGEL OF DEATH

From the Hebrew 'Malach Ha-mauves'.

One of God's messengers whose function is to destroy and end one's life. The name is found primarily in Jewish folklore which includes numerous legends on the subject.

ANOINTING

There are over 200 references in the Bible to 'Anointing' or the procedure of applying ointment to someone. Since the time of Abraham, 'Anointing' was widely used by the ancient Israelites and was believed to be endowed with sacred powers. All men of stature, priests and kings were anointed with either an elixir of olive oil or oil of Myrrh.

The title: the Anointed of Yahweh, the most sacred name of the Lord, implies the high omnipotent value set upon the rite of anointing and a guest was honored and welcomed by anointing his head or feet.

APOCRYPHA

From the Greek, the term applies to the 14 Jewish writings excluded from the Bible. Special historic interest is centered on the apocryphal writings of Ben-Sira and the Maccabees. The Apocrypha includes prophecies, poems, proverbs, etc.

ARAMAIC

A Semitic language adopted as a Jewish tongue in Babylonia during the 5th Century B.C. Similar to Hebrew, it spread to Egypt and then to Palestine. It flourished for two centuries and was then replaced by Arabic.

Many important Jewish documents are written in Aramaic including the 'Ketubah' (the marriage contracts); the 'Get' (the Jewish writ of Divorce); and the Kaddish (the mourner's prayer). Much of the mystical writings of the Caballah is written in Aramaic.

ARARAT

The Bible's reference to the mountain 'Mount Ararat' on which Noah's Ark rested after the flood.

ARBA KANFES

In Yiddish - (Tzitzes)

A small four cornered shawl traditionally worn under the shirts by Orthodox Jews. It has tassles on all four corners and an opening for passing it over the head. Its basic function is to remind the wearer to think constantly of the 'Almighty'.

ARBA KOSOT

Arba Kosot is the Hebrew expression for the four cups of wine used in the ceremonial at the Passover Seder. They are to remind one of the liberation from bondage in Egypt which is accompanied by four words: ''Bring out'', ''Deliver'', ''Redeem'', and ''Take''.

AHKDAUMOHS

Ahkdaumohs is a poem written by Myer ben Isaac Neharai in the 11th Century. It is accompanied by a special melody before the reading of the Torah on Shavuot. It relates to the religious devotion of the Jews, the future blessings for the faithful and the Glory of God.

AURON HAHBRISS

Hebrew for: ''The Ark of the Covenant.''Under the command of Moses, through a divine inspiration, the Ark of the Covenant was constructed by the Biblical master craftsman Betzahlel.

Carried by the Israelites during their wandering in thc wilderness, it was brought to the sanctuary at Shiloh. Later, after the construction of the Temple in Jerusalem, it was carried there by David and placed in the holy shrine by King Solomon.

AURON HAKODESH

Hebrew for ''Holy Ark''.

Auron Hakodesh refers to the beautifully designed cabinet in the center of the East wall of the synagogue in which the Torahs are kept. Covering the doors of the Ark is an artistically embroidered curtain, called the 'Pauroches' and directly over the doors, hangs the Eternal Light, the 'Nehr Talmid'.

AUSHAMNU

Hebrew for: ''We have trespassed.''

It is the beginning of a listing of sins, placed in alphabetical order and intoned during Yom Kippur. To emphasize his repentance, the worshipper praying continues to beat his breast as he recites each sin.

ASHKENAZIM

The name 'ASHKENAZ' is derived from a kingdom in ancient Armenia. It is a name applied to the Jews of Poland, Russia, Roumania, Czechoslovakia and Turkey.

There are two primary branches of Jewry; the Sephardim and the Ashkenazim. The Ashkenazim moved from France, through Germany then continued on to Eastern Europe where they came upon large groups of Jews who had originally migrated, thousands of years before, from Egypt, Palestine and Assyria.

The variance between Ashkenazic and Sephardic Jews is extensive. They greatly differ in their pronunciation of language, their style of liturgy, their trends of thought, rites, ceremonials and the type of food they eat. Yiddish, as we know it today, is purely an Ashkenazic conception. Their people are basically of a humble, pious nature; content to live simple lives and are bound, mentally, spiritually and physically, to the orthodox tradition of the Talmud and to the belief of the coming of the Messiah.

It was with this group of people that the Jews reached the highest level of their teachings. The Yiddish language, with its idioms, colloquialisms, expressions and warmth became a living reality. A beautiful example of their dreams and their nightmares is the play, ''Fiddler On The Roof.'' At the turn of the 20th Century, due to the recriminations against them, almost the entire Jewish population emigrated to America. What was left, was almost completely destroyed in the Nazi Holocaust.

AULEYNU

Auleynu is the first word of the closing prayer of the daily liturgy. From the Hebrew, it means, ''It is incumbent upon us.'' It is one of the oldest prayers known in the Bible; its basic theme being, 'The ultimate turning of all mankind to God.' It holds an important place in the liturgy of the High Holidays.

AVINO MALKAYNU

From the Hebrew, meaning: ''Our Father, Our King.''

The beginning of a prayer intoned during the Penitential Days between Rosh Hashonah and Yom Kippur: Also during the days of fasting. It symbolizes God in the vision of Divine Mercy (Father) and Divine Justice (King).

AUVOS

Also known as PIRKAY AUVOS, ''Ethics of the Fathers''. A section of the Mishna composed of selected wise sayings, rules, ethics, conduct and religious principles as stated by the Teachers of the Mishna.

There are six chapters which are read on the Sabbaths between Passover and Rosh Hashonah.

Auvos, in principle, teaches the love of Peace, about human behavior and relationships, and the importance of modesty, humility and charity.

B בּ
Baiz

Being poor is no disgrace ---- which is the only good thing that can be said about it.

(Talmud)

BAAL KOREH

From the Hebrew, "Master Reader."

The designated reader of the Torah during Sabbath and Holiday services in the synagogue.

BAAL SHEM

From the Hebrew, "Master of the Name."

A person with Divine Inspiration who possesses the power to perform miracles. These people were famous for their piety and their knowledge of Caballah, the Jewish art of mysticism.

BAAL TOKEA

The Hebrew name for the person who sounds the Shofar on the High Holy Days.

BERAKOT OR BROCHOS

The Hebrew for "Blessings."

Brochos is an ancient Jewish tradition offering blessings and thanks to God. These benedictions are recited as daily rituals when a person partakes of food, when witnessing the wonders of the universe (like thunder and lightning) and when performing certain commandments. The benedictions all begin with the words, "Blessed art thou, O Lord, our God."

BALFOUR DECLARATION

On November 2, 1917, a letter was written by the British Secretary of State for Foreign Affairs, Arthur Balfour, to Lord Rothschild. It was a brief but world shaking document that was to complicate British policy in the Middle East for their entire period of occupation. It had a similarly complicating effect on American and Russian foreign policy, and influenced greatly the geopolitics of the Arab-speaking world.

Why the letter was written, nobody knows. Some say it was in appreciation to Dr. Chaim Weizmann, the famous Jewish scientist, for his work on behalf of Britain, but this has been discounted. The letter follows:

Dear Lord Rothschild,

I have much pleasure in conveying to you, on behalf of His Majesty's Government, the following declaration of sympathy with Jewish Zionist aspirations which has been submitted to, and approved by, the Cabinet: ''His Majesty's Government views with favour the establishment in Palestine of a national home for the Jewish people, and will use their best endeavours to facilitate the achievement of this object, it being clearly understood that nothing shall be done which may prejudice the civil and religious rights of the existing non-Jewish communities in Palestine, or the rights and political status enjoyed by Jews in any other country.

I should be grateful if you would bring this declaration to the knowledge of the Zionist Federation.

Yours sincerely
Arthur Balfour.

BAR MITZVAH

Translation from the Hebrew meaning a boy, having reached the age of thirteen, has become ''A man of religious and moral duty.''

Upon the Saturday of the week of his thirteenth birthday, the boy, now having reached the status of manhood in respect to his religious duty, is brought into the synagogue where he reads a ''Haftorah'', a writing by one of the prophets and related to that Sabbath's Torah reading.

Through the ages, the Bible states that a Jewish boy, upon reaching his thirteenth year, assumes the role of adult and has a lifelong moral and religious committment to the Jewish community. A boys parents have been responsible for instilling this committment but from this point on, the responsibility belongs to the Bar Mitzvah boy.

In the synagogue, the boy is brought up to the altar where he recites certain prayers, reads the Haftorah and sometimes delivers a speech in which he speaks of some phase of Judaism and thanks his parents for his upbringing.

Once the ceremony is completed, he is, from the religious viewpoint, considered a man. He is obligated to wear phylacteries (Tfillin) every morning while he recites his prayers. At services in the synagogue, he is legally considered a member of the Minyan, one of the ten adults required before any prayers can formally begin, and he can be called to the Torah for an aliyah.

BAS MITZVAH

Meaning, ''The daughter of religious and moral duty.''

A ceremony for girls, which is meant to approximate a Bar Mitzvah.

Bas Mitzvahs are relatively newly created rites having originated within the last twenty or thirty years. In the Orthodox tradition, women and men have different roles in the synagogue. Today, at least within the Reform movement in Judaism, women and men are equal in all respects, going so far as studying in the Yeshiva and even becoming ordained as Rabbis.

BEDIKAS CHAUMETZ

On the day before Passover, as soon as night falls, the chaumetz (leavened bread) is searched for throughout the house. The search is done with one candle, a feather and a bag or box in which to collect the chaumetz.

Before starting, the following blessing is recited: ''Blessed art thou, O Lord our God, King of the Universe, who hast sanctified us with his commandments and commanded us to remove the leaven.''

With the candle lit, a search is made of every room in the house, including the basement, attic, the car and the garage. Pockets in clothing must also be checked. When the search is completed, we recite: "All manner of leaven that is in my possession which I have not removed or have no knowledge of same, shall be null and disowned as the dust of the earth."

After that, all food that has been gathered is burnt in the morning.

BAIS DIN

Hebrew for a Jewish court of Law. Bais din has descended from early biblical times and was once known as the Sanhedrin. Today it is a voluntary forum for arbitration in Jewish circles and is used to settle disputes and controversies.

BES HAMEDRESH

From the Hebrew: "House of Study." Bes Hamedresh refers to a place where worshippers congregate for prayer and study. It also applies to a school for higher learning for potential rabbis.

BREAKING THE GLASS

Breaking a small glass under his heel by the bridegroom as the climax of a wedding ceremony has several interpretations.

Some people believe it to be the vestige of some primitive form of magic where a loud noise will frighten away evil spirits who are jealous of human joy.

Others say that it is a reminder of the destruction of the Temple, a symbol of sorrow. In the midst of their happiness, the bridal couple is reminded of the sorrows of their ancestors and their responsibilities in the future.

BIBLE - JEWISH

The Bible, in its present form, preserved and intact through the ages, was written on a continuous basis, covering hundreds of years, by numerous scholars, Rabbis and biblical wise men who contributed their talents in anonymity preferring to have their contributions credited to such revered historical wise men as Solomon, Isaiah, Amos and David.

Desire for acclaim or self esteem was unknown to these masters of epic narratives, rules of law and miraculous legends, and devoting their lives to the Bible was merely their humble way of serving God.

The Bible is basically composed of three individual parts which were created at vastly different times. The earliest portion, written approximately in 600 B.C.E., was the Five Books of Moses, known as the 'Torah.' During 200 B.C.E., the ''Prophets'' was completed which involved historical analyses of Samuel and Kings, the Judges, Joshua, Isaiah, Ezekiel and Jeremiah.

The third section, called the ''Holy Writings'', took the longest to complete due to the impasse between the scholars as to what to glorify and what to eliminate. The most controversial material were the Apocrypha, which was finally eliminated from the Jewish version and the Song of Songs, which a majority of the scholars claimed was too worldly and secular a story. When the ''Holy Writings'' was finally concluded, an agreement was reached to keep the Proverbs, Psalms, Job, the Scrolls, Ruth, Lamentation, Esther and Ecclesiastes. They also agreed on Ezra, Dan, Nehemiah and the Book of Chronicles. When the complete text of 24 Books was finally assembled to everyone's satisfaction, the year was 90 A.D.

Most of the Bible was written in Hebrew, with isolated parts being penned in Aramaic.

B'NAI B'RITH

From the Hebrew, meaning: ''Sons of the Covenant.''

An American Jewish organization, founded in 1843 by a group of German Jews in New York City. Since that time it has grown into an international organization of over 400,000 people.

Originally created as an organization to provide health and sick benefits for its members, it gradually spread out to other involvements such as the creation of orphanages for homeless children, hospitals and old age homes.

In time, as the necessity arose, the B'nai B'rith branched out into other services such as the creation of Americanization classes for Jewish immigrants and the formation of the Anti-Defamation League to fight anti-Semitism.

In 1924, it established the Hillel Foundation which maintains social, cultural and religious programs on college campuses for Jewish students.

BREAD OF AFFLICTION

The first passage in the Haggadah at the beginning of the Passover Seder is 'Haulachman anyau', which means that Matzoh is the 'Bread of Affliction' that was eaten by our ancestors when they left Egypt to enter the wilderness. It expresses the hope and prayer for the redemption of the Jewish people and their return to Eretz Yisroel as free men.

BRISS

Hebrew for 'Circumcision.' The English translation: 'Covenant, in relation to the circumcision rite'.

The circumcision of a male child on the eighth day of his life symbolizes the covenant between God and Israel, that His people live a life of virtue and spiritual steadfastness in obeying and transmitting God's law.

It is a corporeal seal of the covenant to be carried for the rest of his life.

The circumcision, a quick, clean cut with a sterilized knife, is usually performed by a specially trained expert (not a Rabbi) who is called a 'Moyl'. In many instances, moylim (pl.) are called upon to perform circumcisions by doctors and other non-Jews who find them masters at their trade.

The knife that he uses is a double edged blade, razor sharp, to assure a good, clean cut the first time.

At the ceremony, the baby boy is held by his godfather, (the Sandek) as the other witnesses recite the prayer; 'Blessed be he that cometh'. During the circumcision, the baby is held on the Sandek's knees while prayers are said. At the conclusion, the Moyl recites the prayer: 'May the boy grow in mind and body - to a love for the Torah - to the marriage canopy, and to a good and healthy life.' A blessing is then offered over wine, and a small cotton ball, dipped into wine, is placed on the baby's lips to cause him to fall asleep and not cry.

Today, circumcision is not an exclusive privelege of Jews. Its hygienic advantages are so universally recognized and has become so medically approved that circumcising a newborn non-Jewish baby in the hospital is commonplace.

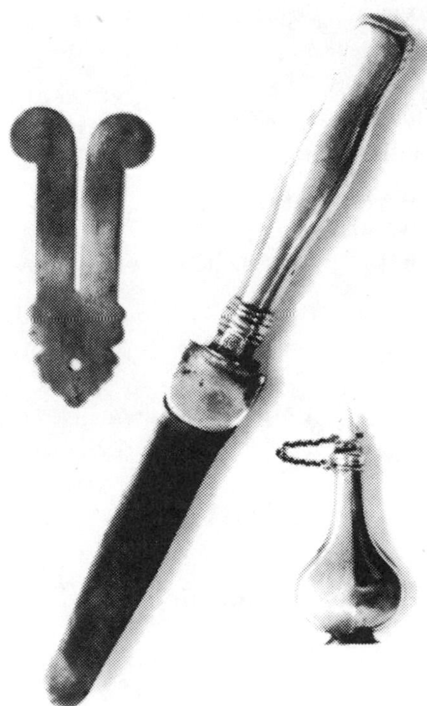

A silver circumcision set dated 1862 from Austria. Set includes a double-edged knife, clamp and powder container.

BRAUCHEH

From the Hebrew, ''Benediction''.

Brauchehs are religious ceremonial demands on pious Jews and are usually recited in silence.

Tradition calls for brauchehs to be said on many occasions where thanks is given to the Lord. Examples are as follows:

1. The first act on arising in the morning.
2. Before and after every meal.
3. Eating or drinking at any time (there are special brauchehs for each food and drink).
4. On washing one's hands.
5. Upon a safe return from a journey.
6. Recovering from an illness.
7. The arrival of a new season.

8. On the new moon.
9. On the wearing of a new garment.
10. When smelling a fragrant odor.
11. On seeing a natural phenomenon.
12. On seeing a beautiful living thing.
13. On receiving calamitous news.
14. On seeing a wise man.
15. The last thing before going to bed.

Kauf

Cherish a good heart when thou findest it in anyone.

CABALLAH

From the Hebrew word for ''tradition'', it applies to Jewish mystical philosophy and practices. It traces its origin to its ancient ancestry in Babylonia. Caballah is a philosophy dealing primarily in mysticism. Its basic involvements are the creation of the Universe, the nature of God, the final destiny of mankind, the nature of Evil and the true meaning of the written law.

It teaches that God did not create the Universe directly, inasmuch as He is above all that exists. The world itself, with all its various forms of life are merely emanations from God, not reflecting from one thing to another or from the more Holy to the less Holy.

The Cabbalistic creed declares that there are ten Spheres emanating from all existence in the following order and importance; each one flowing out of the one before it: *Crown, Wisdom, Intelligence, Greatness, Strength, Beauty, Firmness, Splendor, Foundation and Kingdom*. The Tenth Sphere, *'Kingdom'*, brought about the physical world. These Ten Spheres rule the world in this order, and thus God's rule is explained.

The soul is the foundation of Man's being. All souls were created simultaneously, at the same time, during Creation, and if the soul remains pure on contact with the physical body it becomes, after death, a part of the existence ruled by the Ten Spheres.

Evil, in itself, does not exist but is solely the negation of good. It can be overcome through repentance, prayer, self analysis and strict adherence to the Law. Many Caballists, ignoring pain and suffering, inflicted physical self punishment in atonement for committing evil or for a redemption of their soul.

CALENDAR - JEWISH

In practically all religions the calendar was originally conceived by the changes in natural phenomena; the transitions of the seasons; winter to summer, the growth and death of all vegetation, the rising and setting of the sun and the quarterly changes of the moon. Since all of these phenomena were inexplicable to the ancient mind, most of these being relegated to the supernatural, it is understandable that the use of these constant changes would lend themselves to annual observances.

In modern times, we use the days of the month to designate our annual holidays; New Years Day on the 1st of January, Thanksgiving on the last Thursday of November; Labor Day on the first Monday in September, etc. In view of our system of measuring holidays, we should not be surprised at the variances of marking holidays in the Bible and that, at different times, other types of calendars may have been used.

The most ancient calendar used by the Jews was the solar calendar, where the designation of time was reckoned entirely by the sun. In this era, the year was divided into seasons and not months. Since all vegetation comes to life in the Spring, it was decided that this phenomenon should usher in the New Year and as such, the Festival of Matzoh, originally an eight day observance, culminated in the date of the New Year.

While this primitive calendar was still in use, the solar year of 365 days was divided into seven periods of 50 days, with a seven day 'Matzoh' period and an eight day harvest festival both added to the 350 days. The eight day harvest period was called the Pentecost or "Shabuoth", because it came 50 days after the Matzoh.

However, the rabbis eventually concluded that a radical adjustment in the calendar had to be made and a change from the solar to a lunar-solar method of establishing time was inaugurated. The 'Matzoh' fell on a particular day of the month instead of a seasonal equinox. The New Year (Rosh Hashonah), fell on the first day of the seventh month in the new lunar-sonar calendar.

It was at that time, that the rabbis substituted names instead of numbers to designate the months. Beginning in the Spring, Number I became Nisan, Number II became Iyar, Number III became Sivan, etc.

Today, Jews regard 'Matzoh' and 'Pesach' as one and the same, both commemorating the release from slavery of the Israelites from Egypt. Succoth, preceding the New Year in the solar calendar, now follows it by two weeks in the lunar-sonar calendar. The significance of this change is interesting. There is a definite transition from a vague method of establishing dates for holidays to a more precise one. It eliminated all pagan elements for manners of worship and it brought about broader and more intellectual methods of religious reformation.

THE JEWISH CALENDAR (including Holidays)

TISHRE	(September and October) 30 days
	Rosh Hashonah (New Year) 1st and 2nd days
	Yom Kippur (Day of Atonement) 10th day
	Sukkot (Tabernacles) 15th to 21st days
	Shemini Atzeres 22nd day
	Simchas Torah 23rd day
CHESHVAN	(October and November) 29 days
KISLEV	(November and December) 29 days
	Chanukah 8 days (25th to the 1st)
TEVES	December and January 29days
SHEVAT	January and February 30 days
ADAR	February and March 29 days
	Purim (14th day)
NISAN	March and April 30 days
	Pesach 8 days (15th-22nd)
IYAR	April and May
	Lag B'Omer (18th day)
SIVAN	May and June 30 days
	Shavues (6th and 7th days)

TAMMUZ	June and July 29 days
AV	July and August 30 days
	Tishah B'ov (9th day)
ELUL	August and September 29 days

Note: A leap year in the Jewish calendar consists of two months of Adar; Adar Rishon (the first Adar), and Adar Shaynee (the second Adar).

CANDLE LIGHTING

A great deal of importance is attached to the lighting of candles in the Jewish religion. The lighting of candles in the Jewish home for ushering in the Sabbath and various other holidays is ordained in the Mishna and is one of the most solemn duties of the Jewish woman.

Tradition states that light symbolizes the Torah and the soul. Major events in personal lives are commemorated by lighting candles; these being during marriage services, Yaurtzeit (annual commemoration of a dead relative), and placing candles beside the dead.

CHALLAH

A white twisted bread, usually called an egg bread in English; eaten on the Sabbath and other festivals. It was originally the piece of dough thrown into the fire as a gift to the Priests during the time of the Temple.

CHUMESH

From the Hebrew: ''Fifth''. Chumesh is a term applied to the entire Five Books of Moses.

CHUPPEH

From the Hebrew: ''Covering.'' The Chuppeh is the wedding canopy used in either indoor or outdoor weddings. It is part of the traditional rites and symbols of Jewish weddings.

Its symbolism lends an air of royalty to the event, for the bride and groom are considered to be king and queen, respectively, for that day.

The Chuppeh is usally composed of a large square sheet of silk or satin held aloft at the corners by four wooden poles. Usually, it is embroidered with a large Star of David and some biblical quotation. In many orthodox weddings, a large 'Tallis' has been known to be used for a Chuppeh.

COCHIN JEWS - INDIA

A sect of approximately 1500 Indian Jews established in the early 16th Century on the Malabar coast in the South of India.

Divided by a strict caste system, the White Jews, who originally emigrated from Turkey and Syria, held the upper hand in matters of wealth, position and status. The dark-skinned Jews, ranging in color from off white to dark brown are the most populous and live very pious lives.

The liturgy of the Cochin Jews is Sephardic. They are extremely Orthodox and speak Hebrew. Typical of the Sephardim, the men have long payessen (side locks of hair), wear Yarmulkehs, and are attired in simply a loincloth. As much as possible, Kashres is observed. With the establishment of the Jewish state, ninety percent of these Jews left for Israel leaving only a small sect of about 200 people.

CHOMETZ

From the Hebrew: "Leavened."

Chometz is the name for all food prohibited from being eaten on Passover.

CHAZZIN

From the Hebrew, "A sage." The Chazzin (Cantor) is a trained singer of passages in the liturgy and one who assists the Rabbi in the performance of the services.

As liturgy in the synagogue was bred in a history of suffering and deprivation, the accompanying music incorporates all the pathos and lamentation that is synonymous with their background. The chazzin, on behalf of the congregation, bewails their despair and compassion while he emphasizes their devotion to God. His voice reaches out to the heavens with his singing; sometimes soft, sometimes sweet, and often in a low, falsetto wailing tone.

The chazzin is not a Rabbi. He can be any member of the congregation.

CHALLEF

The knife used by the Shoychet in slaughtering chickens and other prescribed animals. The method used must be as quick and painless as possible. The fowl, when killed, are plucked dry over an open gas fire.

CHASIDIM From the Hebrew, "Pious Ones"

One of the most fantastic and radical innovation that ever happened to the Jewish religion occured in the 18th Century in East Europe when the Chasidic movement was founded by a simple, peasant Jew, named Israel ben Eliezer. Wandering about in the open countryside, he preached a plain, simple gospel which immediately drew the attention of the communal Jews because it advocated a casual, laymans tongue and derogated the strong threats and punishments by the Rabbis, and the mysticism of the Talmud.

Castigating the doomsday threats of the Ultra-Orthodox Rabbis and the mystical wise men, Israel ben Eliezer, now called the Baal Shem Tov, placed emphasis on the merits of simple prayer and happy worship. The only synagogue needed is in the heart, he declared, with a happy, spontaneous outpouring of ones prayers.

The Chasidim, the followers of Baal Shem Tov, converted their worship into one of religious rapture; clapping their hands, singing and dancing while praising the Lord. Particularly, the poor discovered the warm, personal, happy relationship with their maker, who, heretofore had been dire, somber and threatening. They created happy folk songs and parables in a language that all understood.

Needless to say, Baal Shem Tov was denounced by the High Rabbis who claimed that he was an ignorant degenerate. However the movement spread throughout Eastern Europe with a tremendous flourish.

CHANUKAH From the Hebrew, "Dedication." 'The Feast of Lights'

Chanukah is the most joyous of Jewish Holidays, lasting eight days and usually falling in December.

Chanukah does not find its origin in the Bible but commemorates the great victory of the Maccabees over the Syrians in 167 B.C. It was a struggle for religious freedom and it rescued Judaism from complete annihilation. The story can be found in Maccabees I and II.

Briefly, it tells of the uprising which was led by the High Priest Mattathias and his son, Judah, the Maccabee against Antiochus IV, the tyrant, who decreed that all Jews must be converted, by force if necessary, to Greek polytheism. He ordered the Jews to build shrines and altars to these idols and put a stop to the circumcision of male infants. He built huge statues of Zeus in the Temple and used Jewish Holy Places for orgies. When this occured, thousands of Jews fled the city, hiding in caves.

The situation seemed hopeless until the Maccabees, completely untrained and ill equipped, formed bands of guerillas to fight the tyrant. They won a great victory at Emmaus.

Returning to Jerusalem, they found the Temple burned and desecrated and set about to restore it. On the 25th day of Kislev, in 165 B.C., Judah, the Maccabee, rededicated Zion's Temple by lighting the candles of a huge Menorah. The celebration lasted eight days.

Chanukah is unique in that it is the only Jewish holiday related to an event of war. It is celebrated with gifts and parties. Chanukah 'Gelt' has its origin with this Holiday.

D ד
Daled

Don't ask the doctor how the patient is --- ask the patient.

DAVNEN

From the Yiddish: 'To Pray.'

The act of praying. Jewish prayers are founded on a threefold structure: that of petition, adoration and thanksgiving. There are prayers for any occasion that may unfold in anyone's life including joyous occasions or tragic events.

DAYAN

From the Hebrew: ''A judge'' (also a sage). A Dayan is a wise man, a teacher of the Torah and trained to preside over the Jewish people in a Jewish court of Law. In any Jewish controversy, the Dayan's judgement is accepted at a Din Toyrah (a verdict of the Torah).

In countries where Jewish communities lived in ghettoes without privilege of official judicial decisions, sanction by the heads of state was given to the Dayanim to render verdicts and opinions in cases involving the Jews.

DEBORAH

For her great wisdom and accomplishments on behalf of the Israelites, Deborah was known as the 'Mother of Israel'. She was a judge and a Prophetess and under her inspiration, the Armies of Israel defeated the Canaanites in a fierce and decisive battle.

DEAD SEA SCROLLS

The Dead Sea Scrolls represent an entire library of historical facts: they are called the Library of Qumran, since they originated in the Qumran region of Palestine, near the Dead Sea. They were discovered by accident in a cave by a Bedouin boy in 1947 and were considered perhaps the most sensational discovery of the 20th Century. The Dead Sea Scrolls contain the following historical writings:

1. An oration by Moses to the people of Israel.
2. The Thanksgiving Psalms.
3. A commentary of Habakkuk, Micah, Nahum and Psalm 37.
4. Two copies of the Book of Isaiah.
5. The Manual of Discipline, with a list of regulations for the existing society who went into the desert to live a life of isolation.
6. An apocalyptical book which tells of the War of Sons of Light and the Sons of Darkness, and tale of victory of Good over Evil.

DEUTERONOMY

From the Greek: 'Dvorim' The Fifth book of the Torah. (The Five Books of Moses)

Deuteronomy tells of the happenings and experiences of the Jews while in the wilderness. Moses tells the story of the Jews during their 40 years in exile and reveals the Ten Commandments. He stresses upon the Israelites the need for adhering to the Ten Commandments, reveals Godly blessings for the faithful and threatens punishment for those who disbelieve. It concludes with the Song of Moses, including the details of his death. A remarkable feature of this book is that it is written in the first person, with Moses relating the experiences, while the others are all in the third person.

DIASPORA

From the Greek; meaning: 'Scattering'.

Diaspora refers to the dispersion of the Jews outside of Zion. Throughout history, Jews have lived outside of their biblical homeland. After the Roman conquest of Judea, Jews scattered to Europe; settling in Rome, then France, Spain, Germany and England. Due to religious persecution, they sought and found refuge in Russia and Poland where they lived until the latter part of the 19th Century when persecutions took place once again in Russia under the Czar. At that time, millions made the journey to the United States. Of the 13 million Jews in the world today, only 3 3/4 million now live in Israel.

DIETARY LAWS

The Jewish dietary laws, or 'Kashres', are founded on ancient Biblical laws and ordinances. They establish the differences between 'Kosher' food which is allowable and 'Trepheh' food which is forbidden. Since their inception in early biblical days, these laws have been in effect and have had a profound effect on Jewish life wherein an entire people courageously fought and resisted persecution wherever the observance of Dietary Laws was forbidden.

The following rules specify the exact nature of the Kashres:

1. Only cloven-footed animals which chew their cud: (e.g. cattle, sheep, goats and deer) are permitted.
2. Fish with fins and scales only.
3. All fowl except birds of prey.
4. Locusts and reptiles are forbidden.
5. Blood from animals is forbidden. Meat must be salted before cooking.
6. Animals must be slaughtered by a Shochet (ritual slaughterer) according to tradition.

7. Milk and dairy products cannot be eaten at the same time. One must wait 6 hours after a meat (Flayshig) dinner before partaking of dairy (Milchig) food.

Dietary laws are still observed today by a great number of Jewish families.

DIN TORAH

A Hebrew term applied to a hearing held before a Rabbi according to the principles of Jewish Law.

DYBBUK

From the term, 'Evil Spirit', in Hebrew.

A famous demon in Jewish folk lore, made famous by his association with King Solomon. It can be described as the nearest thing to a vampire, a witch, a ghoul; a formless spirit that enters a person's body for the purpose of inciting evil; also described as the devil.

To rid a person of the Dybbuk, a minyan of ten men is called and the Tzaddik (righteous man) will read a passage from a psalm aloud, ordering the Dybbuk to leave the body of the possessed, (The latter ritual being a form of exorcism). If the prayer has no effect, the Tzaddik immediatley calls for an individual with blameless character to blow the Shofar. This usually accomplishes the task at hand.

Aiyen

Every man does his own thing.

ECCLESIASTES A Greek derivative

It is the Book Kohelet, named after the son of David, in the last section of the Hebrew Bible called Ketuvim (Writings). It was written during the time of the Second Temple.

The book, highly controversial, gives off a pessimistic outlook of life, stating the phrase, "Vanity of vanities, all is Vanity.", implying that there is nothing in life that is worthwhile. All material possessions, the spiritual world, the joys and disappointments, and even wisdom has no value because there is never anything new in the universe. When man increases knowledge, he only builds more sorrow, that man is no better than a beast.

"Writings" implies that man should not become impatient because there are worlds beyond his comprehension and in the end, God will not forsake him. Therefore, it is imperative to fear and trust in God for this is the sole obligation of Man. "Writings" offers many quotations of practical wisdom in relation to mans behavior and his relationship with his fellow man.

AYN KELOHENU

The opening words of a hymn in the prayer book sung at the conclusion of Morning Services on Sabbath and Holidays. It means "There is none like our God."

EHCHOD MEE YODAYAH

From the Hebrew, meaning: "Who knows one?"

A plaintive chant in the Haggadah basically for children. Its words consist of 13 questions beginning with: "Who knows one?, "Who knows two?" "Who knows three?", etc. The answers are: "One is God", "Two are the Tablets of the Covenant.", "Three are the Patriarchs.", etc.

The song originated in France during the 16th Century.

ELIJAH

One of the most beloved and important prophets in Jewish history. Elijah was acclaimed as the protector of the downtrodden, the sick and poor, performing all sorts of miracles while being disguised in many different forms. He is mentioned in prayers during the Seder ceremony and Circumcision rites. The Bible states that Elijah never died but was carried directly to heaven on a chariot of fire during a gigantic whirlwind.

EYL MAULAY RACHAMIM

The opening words of the prayer for the departed, meaning "God, who is full of compassion." and is recited by Ashkenazic

Jews at funerals, on the Sabbath of the week of Yaurtzeit, and also during Yizkor in the synagogue.

ERETZ YISROEL

In Hebrew: ''The Land of Israel.''

The Bible states that Eretz Yisroel is the 'Promised Land' ceded by God to Abraham and his descendants, the land where the sacred city of Jerusalem was built and the land where all of the Jews buried in other lands will come to life again; the land, where at the end of Time, thc Messiah will appear.

It has been the dream of Jews, throughout the world, since time immemorial, to return to their Promised Land and be free to worship in religious freedom, free from prejudice and persecution, to be able to study and work and live in a manner in which their conscience dictates. Since 1948, when the State of Israel was founded, this dream has become a reality.

ESROG

A citron fruit, like a lemon, grown especially in Israel, that must be free of imperfection and used in conjunction with the Lulav (a Palm branch tied with Myrtle and Willow) during the Suhkes Holiday, (the Festival of the Tabernacles).

As the basic theme of Suhkes is Thanksgiving, the worshippers march around in a circle bearing the Esrog and Lulav.

EREV

Hebrew for 'Evening'. Erev designates the evening before the Sabbath or a Holiday, e.g. Erev Shabbas, Erev Yontiff, Erev Pesach, Erev Yom Kippur, etc.

EVIL EYE

One of the many superstitions in Jewish folklore, particularly fear of being jinxed, is brought about by creating jealousy and envy in another person. Hence, in many cases, the Jewish idiom, 'Kayn ayn ahora' is uttered after every sentence in which self praise or the glowing words of a parent as she speaks of her child in a lauditory manner.

'Kayn ayn ahora', which means ''May no evil overtake him'', is the magic phrase that shuts out the dark and evil forces that lie in wait to reverse any happy or fortunate experience or situation. e.g., ''May God bless him, my son Abie is the smartest boy in the class. Kayn ayn ahora.''

EXODUS

From the Book of Exodus, it is the saga relating to the departure of the Israelites from Egypt. Exodus, which also marks the birth of the Jewish State, is considered the most important event in Jewish history, which is referred to over and over again in the Bible and in the prayers of the synagogue. Passover, the Holiday celebrating the event, is one of the happiest for all Jews.

Fay

For Instance, --- is not proof.

FALASHAS—ETHIOPIAN JEWS

The Ethiopian word for ''Emigrants''. A sect of black Jews in Ethiopia claiming to be direct descendants of the Ten Tribes dispersed from Palestine. The Falashas speak neither Yiddish nor Hebrew and believe only in the Old Testament. They have no Rabbis and follow the teaching of Jewish monks who declare that Moses' teachings are the only basis for their religion and beliefs.

Fasting is a major part of their doctrine, abstaining from eating on Mondays, Thursday, on the day of the new moon and on Passover. Strangely, they believe in evil beings, follow soothsayers, rain doctors and those who can bring the dead back to life.

FALSE MESSIAHS

Throughout the long and bitter experiences of the Jews, so called 'holy' men, claiming to be the Messiah, have emerged from the pages of history, genuinely convinced that they had indisputable dispensation from the Lord to lead the people of Israel into salvation. Their mental states ranged from the genius to the mad, from the brazen to the ridiculous, from the sincere to the avaricious.

The disintegration of empires --- e.g. the Persian, the Byzantine, the Roman, was always instrumental in raising the Messianic hopes of the Jews and created unbelievable situations wherein some inventive individual, either dedicated or ulterior motivated, would appear with the 'answer' to the Jewish problem. Each in his own way created a furor. Many succeeded to the point where even a king or an emperor (at one time even the Pope) was convinced of their supernatural powers. But in the end, they all disappeared in the same way, either by being beheaded or burnt at the stake.

There were many false Messiahs in the pages of Jewish history: Judas of Galilee, Theudas, Benjamin the Egyptian, Menachem, a man who called himself Moses, Abu Issa al-Isfahani of Persia, Severus, Yudghan, Eldad Ha Dani, to name a few. But by far, the most celebrated and most spectacular was Shabbatai Zvi from Smyrna. His was an unbelievable tale but we shall touch on it only briefly. The tradition of ancient Jewish folklore holds that when the degradation and misery of Israel would reach its highest point and all hope for salvation be lost, the Messiah would appear to lead them out of their despair. This was the situation in the Ukraine when half of the Jewish population, over 300,000 people, were decimated by a pogrom of the Cossacks.

This was the state of mind of the remnants of the Jews when Shabbatai Zvi appeared on the scene. He was a young man, in his early twenties, who believed he was the "chosen one" to lead them out of their misery. He traveled from country to country, sent by fanatic followers who claimed that he was the "Anointed One", the true "Messiah."

After creating mass hysteria among the people throughout the Middle East, from Egypt to Turkey, he was traveling through Constantinople one day where his influence had already spread to the Turkish population. With the upheaval he caused, he was suddenly brought before the Sultan who gave him the choice of turning to the

Islam faith or losing his head. Shabbatai Zvi suddenly became Mehemet Effendi, thereby ending his charade. He died several years later without fanfare, in obscurity, as a Muslim.

FLAYSHIG

From the German: ''Flesh or Meat''

All meats, poultry or other foods prepared with animal fat, which cannot be eaten at the same time with dairy foods (Milchig).

Orthodox Jews wait at least six hours before eating milk, cheese or other dairy foods after having eaten meat products.

FOUR QUESTIONS

In Yiddish: ''Fier Kashes''

The four questions are usually asked at the Passover Seder by the youngest person there. Its purpose is to activate the children's interest and to teach the child about the Exodus from Egypt and God's love for His people.

The four questions start with ''Mah Nishtahnau'', (''Why is this night different?'' and when the child finishes asking the questions, the answers are provided in subsequent passages in the Hagaddah.

G ג
Gimmel

Give everyman the benefit of the doubt.

Gabbeh

From the Hebrew: ''Collector''

An officer of the synagogue. The Gabbeh is sometimes the Vice-President and Treasurer of the Congregation and is often times responsible for collecting charitable contributions.

GABRIEL

Gabriel is one of two angels mentioned in the Bible. The second is Michael.

GALITZIANER

A Galitzianer is a Jew from Galicia, which was formerly a part of Poland but was ceded to Austria in 1772.

In the early 1900's, the Galitzianer comprised almost 10% of the population and Jewish Galicia was a center for the study of the Talmud. There were many prominent Rabbis, scholars and numerous important Yeshivas.

Since the early days, a severe rivalry existed between the Galitzianer and the Litvaks (Jews from Lithuania) who regarded each other with contempt. Any form of relationship was frowned upon and a marriage between a Litvak and a Galitzianer was unthinkable.

GAONIM

From the Hebrew: ''Excellence or Eminence''

The Gaonim were a colony of Saboraim Jews (from the Aramaic, meaning - 'Explanation') who devoted their lives to the completion of the Babylonian Talmud. From 580 c.e. to the year 1058, almost 500 years, many of the Jews accepted the Gaonim's version of Jewish wisdom and literature, and to this day, their work is still considered outstanding. Due to their efforts, the Talmud became the accepted law book of the Jews, the Responsa literature was developed to its highest degree, liturgical poetry was created and the Caballah was brought into popular form.

Probably their most important contribution to Jewish life was their Responsa literature. Written in Hebrew, Aramaic, and Arabic, it involved every phase of human life, theology, history, philosophy, economics and social behavior.

In matters of legal jurisdiction, social relationships and human behavior, where laymen or scholars could not reach agreement, the problem was always submitted to the Gaonim, whose verdicts were returned after serious and lengthy debate, with references to the Talmud, and then rendered in a lengthy explanation after clarifying all possible consequences.

During their zenith, the Gaonim were the heads of the Talmudic academies throughout Babylonia. The term ''gaon'' (sing.) is today used to describe a person who possesses superior intellect and learning.

GAN EDEN "The Garden of Eden"

Usually referred to as the 'Paradise' in Heaven, it being reserved for the souls of the good and righteous. Jewish history maintains that this story has an allegorical meaning while others claim that it is a realistic place, located in a specific area somewhere in the Euphrates valley.

GEHENNA

From the Hebrew: "Hell"

Taken from the "Valley of Gehenem"

According to the Bible, the Valley of Gehenem, which was situated South of Jerusalem, was the scene where children were sacrified to the idols. Since that time a curse lay over the valley and it has become synonomous with Hell.

The Talmud describes Gehenna as a black hole, consumed by an everlasting fire and sulphurous fumes. It is considered the final resting place of the wicked.

GENESIS

From the Hebrew: "Brahshis" (In the beginning)

Genesis is the first of the Five Books of Moses and begins with the Creation of the Universe. It contains a detailed account of the lives of Abraham, Isaac and Jacob and ends with the death of Joseph in Egypt.

GEMATRIA

from the Greek: "GEOMETRICS"

This refers to the use of letters as numerals. In ancient days, the letters in the Hebrew alphabet also had numerical values assigned to them. Each letter and for that matter, each word, could be converted to its numerical equivalent. These numerical values were calculated in order to arrive at a solution to the meanings of the mysterious passages in the Torah. The results were often startling, and where the Holy Scripture was impossible to decipher, the numerical revelation became the uncontested solution.

GESHEM

Hebrew for ''Prayer for Rain''

Geshem is one of the oldest prayers that is recited on the eighth day of Sukkot at Shemini Atzeret. It is incorporated in the Amidah through the winter months until the first day of Passover.

GEULLEH

From the Hebrew: ''Redemption'' Geulleh is a prayer in the daily liturgy applying to the religious concept that God is the redeemer of all mankind.

GET

Hebrew for ''Divorce''.

According to Jewish Law, when differences between husband and wife are irreconcilable, and living together becomes intolerable, Judaism encourages that they divorce. Rabbinical laws have analyzed divorce from every possible angle and cause, and have made it, from a religious viewpoint, easy to obtain. The process involved is quite complex and only very few trained Rabbis can undertake the proceedings. The emphasis, however, is on reconciliation, for when young children are involved, it is they who suffer the most.

However, in Jewish law, it is deemed a greater evil if children are raised in an environment of disrespect and contempt then having them face the separation of their parents.

A divorced person is encouraged to remarry, for those without mates will look to sin.

The Talmud states that a divorce can be considered if a wife burns the supper, this apparently signifying that her mind was on things other than her husband.

GOLEM

Golem is a product of Jewish folklore applying to a figure made out of wood or clay and given animation by the magical use of a diving name. The Talmud describes Golem as an 'embryo' or 'human being without a soul'.

This belief in Golems was widely accepted during the persecutions in the Middle Ages when almost any legend was believed that gave one relief from the pogroms. The most famous Golem was the one created in the 16th Century by one of the great Rabbis of Prague, Judah Low, for the purpose of exposing a plot against the Jews in a blood accusation. When a Golem was created, it was usually believed to be under the spell and complete mastery of its creator.

Hay

He who seeks more than he needs hinders himself from enjoying what he has.

HADASSAH

"The Womens Zionist Organization of America"

Originally organized by a group of women in the United States in 1912 to raise the standard of health and hygiene in Palestine, the Hadassah has grown into an organization of 1200 chapters with an enrollment of over 300,000 members.

Today, in Israel, Hadassah's hospitals and public welfare committments are making tremendous contributions to scientific and medical research. The Hadassah Medical School is now a part of the Hebrew University.

HAFTOREH'

From the Hebrew, meaning: "Conclusion"

The Haftoreh is a specific reading assigned to each Sabbath. Since ancient times, the reading of the Haftoreh, after the Torah reading, has been observed in the synagogue.

On his Bar Mitzvah, the Jewish boy studies and learns his Haftoreh, reciting it in front of the congregation as he is being confirmed.

HORA

The favorite folk dance of Israel which came into its own on the acquisition of statehood for the Promised Land.

It probably originated in Roumania.

HAGANAH

From the Hebrew: ''Self Defense''

The Haganah was the Jewish Peoples Army in Palestine during the days of the British Mandate. It was originally established as a fighting force to protect the Jewish colonies from the attacks by hostile Arabs. When Britain opposed the Jewish self defense units, the Haganah went underground and continued their defense of the settlements against the Arabs. In World War II, many members of the Haganah joined the British Army against Germany and undertook many daring rescue missions to save Jews from Hitler.

After the war, when British occupation forces restricted Jewish immigration to Palestine, the Haganah started guerilla warfare fighting both the British and the Arabs.

In 1948, when Israel gained statehood, the Haganah became part of the Palmach, the Jewish National Army.

HATIKVAH

From the Hebrew, meaning: ''The Hope''

Hatikvah is the name of the Israeli National Anthem. Written by the poet Naphtali Herz Imber and set to music by a Palestine colonist, Samuel Cohen, it has a plaintive Sephardic melody and became the song of the Zionist movement in 1898.

HAGGADAH

From the Hebrew, meaning: ''Tale''

The Haggadah is a compendium of Jewish metaphorical conceptions which include vast amounts of material from the Talmud and the Book of Exodus. It contains folklore, history, theology, ethics, mysticism, religious facts, proverbs, prayers, hymns, superstitions and even amusing songs for small children. The Haggadah embraces all the ethical, poetical, historic, and scientific discourse found in classic Judaism.

It thrives on fascinating stories and the strange behaviors of rabbis, saints, martyrs, and scholars. Everything is explained in detail, even the answer to the Four Questions, asked by the child at the Passover Seder.

The Haggadah is the second book of Jewish literature and Tradition, the first being the Halacha, which is devoted exclusively to the Law.

HALACHA

From the Hebrew, meaning: "Law"

The Halacha is the first book of the Talmud; (the Haggadah being the second). It is the accumulation of statutes and regulations originating as far back as the statutory Torah of Moses (the Ten Commandments) and spelling out in detail the Oral Law; then following that with codes, decisions, rulings and digests of recorded law. Through the ages, sages and Rabbis have clarified these statutes, adapting them to changing times and conditions.

HAVDOLEH

From the Hebrew, "Separation"

Havdoleh is a simple ceremony usually conducted by the head of the family at the end of the Sabbath. When the man of the house returns home from the synagogue, the members of the family gather around while he lights a braided candle, fills a goblet of wine and recites the prayer, "Blessed art Thou, O Lord our God, King of the Universe, who distinguishes between holy and profane, light and darkness, between the Sabbath and the six days of labor and between Israel and other nations."

A scented box is then opened and members of the family sniff the contents to bring back the spirit saddened by the end of the Sabbath.

HOSHANE RABBEH

Hoshane Rabbe is the seventh day of Suhkes at which time seven processions are made in the synagogue. It applies to the willows used by the worshippers whose discarded leaves symbolize their petition to God to cast off their sins. It is a solemn service for, by tradition, Hoshane Rabbeh is considered the day when man's blessings for the coming year are decreed in Heaven.

HASKALAH

From the Hebrew, meaning: "Enlightenment"

In the middle of the 19th Century, in Germany, a movement was begun to modernize the Jews and Judaism to relieve the persecution against them due to their difference in language, culture, dress and mannerisms. The movement quickly spread to Austria, Poland and Russia.

The Maskilim, as the proponents of the Haskalah were called, claimed that if the Jews adopted the manners and the culture of their Gentile neighbors, they would be treated as equals and would become emancipated. As a result, modern Jewish schools were established in all the major German cities and a major Jewish newspaper was started to eliminate the ghetto side of Jewish life.

This movement was greatly opposed by the Orthodox Jews who saw in it a dire threat to Judaism. In time, the large majority of Jews in Eastern Europe began to realize that this was a gigantic hoax to Germanize and Russify their people, for it did nothing to abate the persecution and pogroms. Finally, the Haskalah movement was shattered and the Jewish leaders came to a final realization that their only hope lay in the Zionist movement.

I י
Yud

If I am not for myself, who will be for me?
And when I am only for myself, what am I?
And if not now, when?

INQUISITION

The order of the Catholic Church in Spain during the 13th Century to seek out and punish heretics. The Inquisition turned against the Jews who returned to Judaism after having been forced to convert to Christianity. These converted Jews (the Marranos) underwent the most fanatic type of torture by Thomas de Torquemada, the General Inquisitor of Spain in 1483. Over 400,000 persons were tried and persecuted by the Inquisition, many of them burned alive at the stake. Its evil continued unabated until the beginning of the 19th Century.

ISAAC

Son of Abraham and Sarah, he was the second of the Biblical Patriarchs. In the Bible it tells that God, in order to test Abraham's faith, commanded him to sacrifice his son Isaac. As Abraham was ready to comply, an angel told him to sacrifice a ram instead. Isaac died at the age of 180 and was buried with his ancestors in a cave at Machpelah.

ILLUI

The Hebrew word for an exceptionally gifted young person applied particularly to those given to a student of the Talmud with great intellect.

ISAIAH

One of the greatest Hebrew Prophets. He is credited with having written the first 39 Chapters of the ''Book of Isaiah. His emphasis is on the holiness of God and the need for having faith in Him. Isaiah projected the vision into the future, ''at the end of time'', when peace will be established on earth; (the wolf shall dwell with the lamb); a son of David will rule with wisdom and justice, and all nations will stream to Jerusalem from whence will come the word of the Lord.

His words of comfort to the people have rung through the ages, and the concept of people, as the suffering servant of God gave them strength to endure the evils of persecution.

IRGUN TZEVAI LEUMI

The name of the secret Jewish, ''National Military Organization''; commonly known as the ''Irgun''. Founded in 1936 in Palestine, its primary objective was to fight against Arab terrorists and to establish an independent Jewish State in Palestine.

The Irgun led the most vigorous and unorthodox campaign against the British authorities for their anti-Jewish policy.

Today, in the Knesset, the Irgun is represented by the Herut Party.

J ש
Shin

Judge not thy fellow man until thou reachest his place.

JEHOVAH The Almighty --- GOD

The name Jehovah appeared in English for the first time in the middle of the 16th Century and it is assumed that it was derived from the unutterable Hebrew connotation for the Almighty; the four letters, 'YHVH'; in which they added the vowels to form a pronouncable word.

The letters YHVH is the most sacred name for God; only permitted to be spoken in the ancient Temple in Jerusalem by the High Priest.

Other synagogues use different synonyms to substitute for use of the four letters such as Adoshem, Eloha, Elohim, Shaddai and Jehovah. The actual meaning of YHVH in the Old Testament is 'the essence of his being'' and is never used during ordinary discourse or conversation.

JUDAISM

Judaism is the religious faith of the Jews, who, without formal affiliation, accepts the teachings of Judaism, in all its complexities, as their own.

Judaism can literally be called a 'civilization' whose people are the Jews; linked together by a common heritage, a common language of prayer, a vast compendium of literature, folklore and above all, a common destiny. Judaism is basically a way of life.

JEREMIAH

Jeremiah was one of the major Hebrew prophets who was most outspoken in his condemnation against the worship of idols and social injustice. He was adamant in the fact that every individual was responsible for his own conduct, stressing religious adherence. Predicting that the Temple would be destroyed because of the transgressions of the Jews, he invoked the wrath of the King of Babylon and was forced to flee for his life, hiding out in a cave.

He lived to see the fall of Jerusalem and the destruction of the Temple by the Babylonians. He then fled to Egypt and his written prophesies became the guiding spirit of the dispersed Jews. It is said that he wrote the Book of Lamentations which tells of the despair and hopelessness of the Jews upon the desecration of Jerusalem which was once the prosperous and joyous capitol of Judah.

JERUSALEM

Jerusalem is one of civilizations oldest cities. David conquered it from the Jebusites and it became the capitol of the United Kingdom of Israel. During the reign of King Solomon, it became the spiritual center of the Jews as they erected the Holy Temple.

Jerusalem was successively conquered by the Babylonians in 587 b.c.e.; the Romans in 70 c.e.; the Moslems in 637; the Crusaders in 1099; the Moslems in 1187 and the British in 1918.

Today, Jerusalem is the capitol of Israel and is once again a symbol of the nations glorious past.

JOB

Job is one of the greatest books in the Wisdom Literature of the Bible, contained in the Book of Writings (Kesuvim). Its basic theme is delving into devine justice by questioning the reason behind, "Why do the righteous suffer?"

The Book of Job, a long sequence of 42 chapters, is basically a series of dialogues between Job and his friends.

In the prologue, there is a discourse between Job and Satan wherein Satan questions Job's sincerity in his obedience to God. To prove this point, God permits Satan to test Job's faithfulness at which time, Satan proceeds to bring forth all types of misfortune. Job's wealth is taken away, his children die and he is afflicted with a deadly disease.

In the subsequent dialogue between Job and his friends, Job pours out his soul in protest against God's unjustifiable punishment while insisting upon his innocence. His friends, however, insist that Job is guilty for God's punishment, though not understood, is nevertheless always deserved.

Later, as God appears to Job in a violent storm, he is made to realize that man is insignificant in the face of God's omnipotence and it is futile to try and understand God's actions.

Kauf

Know whence thou camest;
know whither thou art going;
and know before whom thou art about
to give account and reckoning.

KADDISH

From the Hebrew: "Sanctification"

Kaddish is the name of a prayer written in Aramaic, used for many centuries as a mourner's prayer. Kaddish is recited by a mourner at the graveside and during the three daily prayers in the synagogue for the first eleven months following the death of close relatives.

KAYN AYN AHORA

From the Yiddish: "Without the evil eye"

This is a superstitious phrase created to ward off a jinx or demon when someone is given to excessive praise or boasting.

In ancient times, the Jews were constantly in fear lest they offend their God by boasting of success or praising a loved one in front of others. They felt that by creating envy or jealousy in another person, it would bring about an unspoken reaction that would immediately jinx them and revert the situation into one of disaster. This was particularly true when parents boasted of or praised their children. Automatically, the tag word in their sentence would be, 'Kayn ayn ahora'. e.g. "My boy Abie, God bless him, is so good. He was just made valedictorian of his class, kayn ayn ahora."

KADASHIM

Kadashim is the Fifth of the Six Orders of the Mishnah, dealing with the details of sacrifices, Temple regulations, and the duties of its priests. This Order (Sedorim) is in turn subdivided into eleven other tractates.

KARAITES

The Karaites were Jewish priests under Roman rule who opposed the Talmud, or any other interpretation of the one, true law, the Torah. Forming an anti-rabbinical movement in 760 A.D., known as Karaism, they demanded that only the Torah was the law for Israel, and that other verbal or written laws, such as the Talmud and the Oral Laws, were blasphemous.

They were countered by the Pharisees and the Talmudists, who bitterly opposed them. It is now almost extinct. Aman Ben-David (740-800 A.D.) was an important Karaite leader.

KAPOREH

Kaporeh is an ancient Jewish sacrificial rite which Maimonides condemned as idolatrous. It entails swinging a chicken over one's head three times while reciting a prayer to atone for sins committed during the past year.

Older Jews, who have migrated from Europe, still refer to the old axiom, "Shlogn Kaporis", which means "To become a scape-goat."

KASHRES

From the Hebrew: "Fitness"

Kashres is fitness or cleanliness as applied to food, sacred objects and persons meeting the religious requirements of traditional Jewry. The basic laws of Kashres were originally laid down in the Bible and later refined in the Talmud. Most Jewish communities set up boards

The Ketubah (marriage contract). This parchment dates back to 1758 from Monticelli, Italy. It is colorfully decorated with birds, flowers, a crown and coat of arms.

for the supervision of the slaughtering and handling of meat in accordance with Jewish dietary laws.

KRIEH

From the Hebrew: ''Tearing of Garment''

Krieh is the ancient custom of a mourner tearing his garment as a token of his grief on the death of a loved one.

KETUBAH

Hebrew for: ''Marriage Certificate''

The Ketubah is a document used as evidence of a marriage to protect the woman's rights. It contains an obligation on the part of the husband to pay his wife a certain amount of money in the event of a divorce.

The Ketubah is traditionally written in Aramaic and is signed by witnesses.

KHAZARS

The Khazars were a Mongolian sect of Jews who flourished from the 8th to the 10th Centuries on land between the Don and Volga rivers. Originally, Bulan, the pagan King of the Khazars, desiring to embrace the 'true religion', after summoning representatives of the Christian, Moslem and Jewish faiths to expound their views on the validity of their respective religions, became convinced of the truth of the Jewish faith.

Their devotion to Judaism lasted for two centuries until their defeat by the Russians. The remnants of their people either converted back to Christianity or inconspicuously merged with their Jewish brethren.

KIDDISH

From the Hebrew: "Sanctification"

Most often, the Kiddish is the prayer recited before the Friday night dinner, over a glass of wine. Its purpose is to sanctify the Sabbath. The head of the family recites two brauches (blessings) thanking the Lord for having created wine and for having created the Sabbath as a memorial of the Creation. All members of the family share in the Kiddish wine.

KITTEL

German for "Smock".

A Kittel is a white, loosely woven garment worn by the head of the house during the Seder and other religious functions. It is also worn by Orthodox Jews in the synagogue during Yom Kippur. Old, pious Jews are buried in their Kittlen (pl.) as a mark of their piety.

KNESSET

Hebrew for: "Parliament"

The Knesset is the Israeli Parliament whose members are chosen by all citizens over 18, regardless of sex, race or religion. It consists of 120 members, representing all parties, using a system of proportional representation. The Knesset has the sole power to enact laws and is approved for the sole power of approving a government before it can take office. Elections are held every four years in Israel.

KOL NIDRE

From the Aramaic: ''All Vows''

Kol Nidre is a prayer sung at the start of the evening service on Yom Kippur, cancelling all negative vows made during the year under brutality, persecution or duress.

The chant was regarded with disgust by the learned men who claimed that once a vow is made it can never be annulled.

KOSHER (also see Dietary Laws)

The word 'Kosher' means ''Fit'' and has been used to help condition Jews to Holiness by its restrictive rules and regulations. For over 20 Centuries, Rabbis have laid out an elaborate system of regulations pertaining to food. Each particular detail is prescribed with such minute care that a great deal of study must be done to master the Kashruth's complexities.

A few of the rules are:

It is permissible to eat the meat of animals which have a split hoof and chew their cud. It is not permissible to eat rodents, beasts of prey, reptiles, swine, horses, and pachyderms. All food grown in the ground is permitted. Of forms of sea life, only those with scales and fins can be eaten. Most, but not all, fowl and birds are permissible. There is also a ban on eating the flesh of an animal that dies of old age or disease or one that meets a violent death.

The slaughtering of an animal must be accomplished in the quickest and least painful way possible. The shochet (ritual slaughterer) must kill an animal with a single stroke of his knife. The severing of the carotid artery, in the neck, is the most humane way to kill. The blood pours out, the blood supply to the brain is cut off, and the animal's consciousness vanishes. The shochet is permitted to do his work under the careful eye of inspectors, who watch every move. Many modern Jewish leaders hold that strict observance of the Kosher laws (Kashrut) is outmoded, while others claim that Kashrut helps remind the Jews of their identity and heritage.

L ל
Lamed

Let thy house be a meeting place for the wise; sit amidst the dust at their feet; and drink their words with thirst.

LAMENTATIONS

The third of the Five Scrolls of Ketuvim (Writings) in the Bible. Written by the Prophet Jeremiah, there are five chapters of poetic elegies describing the fall of Jerusalem. Jeremiah was an eye witness to the destruction of the first Temple in 586 B.C.E.

The Book of Lamentations is recited in the synagogue on Tisha B'ov in commemoration of the destruction.

LEVITICUS

The third of the Five Books of Moses, called Vayikra in Hebrew.

The name is derived primarily because it deals with the functions of Priesthood, which was the tribe of Levi.

Its great significance and value lies in the 27 Chapters explaining the vital laws of the Bible such as the Law of Sacrifice, consecration of Priests, the Law of Purity, the Ceremony of Yom Kippur, Sexual morality as well as Dietary Laws and Laws of Festival Regulations.

LULAV Hebrew for 'Palm Branch'

The Lulav is used, together with the Etrog (Citron) during Succoth. As the blessing is said, while the Lulav is held in the right hand the Esrog in the left, the Lulav is waved in 6 directions; Up, down,

North, South, East and West symbolizing Gods presence in the Universe.

(see Succoth and Esrog)

LUAH Hebrew for 'Calendar'

See Calendar for complete analysis.

LADINO From the Spanish: "Several Languages." Also called 'Judesmo'

Ladino is the multi-mixed language spoken by Sephardic Jews in Spain, Turkey, Portugal, Morocco, Tunisia and by Spanish Jews of South and Central America

Its base is Spanish and has a mixture of Arabic, Turkish and Greek phrases. This, plus a profuse injection of Hebrew words and Talmudic idioms is the structure of Ladino.

Ladino dates back to the Middle Ages and the first known book of this language was found in Turkey in the early 16th Century.

LAG BA-OMER From Hebrew, meaning: "The 33rd Day of Omer"

Lag Ba-Omer is a Jewish festival observing several historical events: the cessation of a plague which threatened the students of Rabbi Akiva, the Hadrianic persecution of the Jews against teaching the Talmud and Torah, and the anniversary of the death of Rabbi Simeon ben Yohai, who authored the most sacred book of the Caballah, the ZOHAR.

Lag Ba-Omer is a favorite childrens holiday marked by bonfires and picnics in the fields.

LAMED-VOVNIKS

According to Jewish folklore, the Lamed-Vovniks are "thirty six righteous men" who live in every generation and by whose saintliness and devotion to God, the world is able to continue existing. They are supposed to be living humbly and undetected among their neighbors and if by chance their identity is revealed, he immediately loses his saintly usefulness. There are hundreds of stories about these people in the Hasidic folklore.

LE CHAYIM Hebrew, meaning: "To Life"

Le Chayim is a popular Jewish phrase used most commonly in offering a toast over a glass of wine or liquor.

LITURGY From the Greek: "Public Worship"

Liturgy is the set procedures for religious services or prayers.

Jewish liturgy dates back to the Holy Temple in Jerusalem when prayers were offered during the ritual of sacrifice. As time passed, Jewish liturgy assumed the standard procedure of three daily services: the morning prayers (Shachres); the afternoon prayers (Minchah); and the evening prayers (Myriff). On Sabbaths and Holidays, a fourth prayer is offered, (Musaf).

There are two distinct major versions of Jewish liturgy; the Askhenazic ritual (used by East Europeans) and the Sephardic version (used by the Spanish and the Portuguese).

Mem

Man is only wise during the time that he searches for wisdom;
when he imagines he has completely attained it, he is a fool.

MENORAH

A special candlestick holding nine candles, (eight plus one for the Shammus). It is used during the Chanukah festivities and either candles or oil burners with wicks is commonly used.

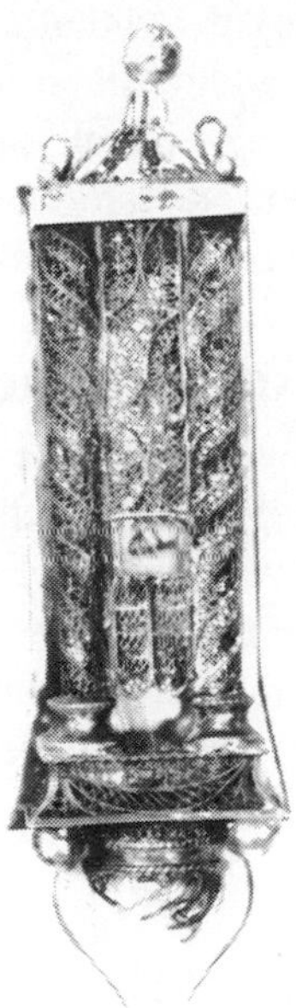

A hand-wrought 18th Century silver mezuzzah from Russia.

MEHITZAH-Partition

In old Jewish law there must be a partition between men and women worshippers. In ancient Orthodox synagogues, a special balcony was built for female worshippers where they prayed without taking an active role in the proceedings. Conservative and reformed Jewry eliminated this custom by having special pews designated where entire families sat and prayed together.

MAHZOR

The Mahzor is a special prayer book based on the Siddur (the daily Prayer Book). It contains additional prayers which are sung as hymns, and is used on holidays e.g. Pesach, Suhkes, etc.

MEZUZAH

A Mezuzah is a small metal case, about three inches in length, which is placed on the doorpost of a Jewish home. It is usally placed at an angle, about five feet from the floor, to the right of the entrance. In Orthodox homes, they are found on every door in the house.

Inside the case is a tiny parchment on which is inscribed fifteen verses from the Book of Deuteronomy. The first sentence is the watchword of Israel. "Hear O Israel, the Lord our God, is One."

The Mezuzah is a constant reminder of Gods presence. To the visitor, the Mezuzah denotes that the house is Jewish.

MAGGID-Hebrew for "Preacher"

A Maggid was usually a traveling preacher who would go from town to town (stet'l to stet'l) to preach his sermon, known as the Derashah. Their sermons were of a religious and moral nature and their ability to sway people emotionally was well known. They were gifted speakers, able to give much comfort and raise hopes for a better future. The Maggids achieved great fame in the Jewish communities of Poland and Russia and it has been only recently that their popularity has waned.

MINYAN

A Minyan is a quorum of ten men (any male over thirteen years of age) required before the services can be held in the Synagogue. The figure 'TEN' has always held a particular significance for the ancient Jews. When Abraham asked God to save the righteous in Sodom and God replied that He would spare them if Ten righteous men could be found in that den of iniquity.

Other instances where the number Ten held particular meaning were:

The Ten Commandments

Ten Days of Penitence.

God's presence is represented upon any ten men who gather in his name.

The Ten plagues on the Egyptians.

Ten is the unit of clan structure established by Moses.

Ten generations are recorded between Adam and Noah; and between Noah and Abraham.

Other rituals requiring Ten men are:

Marriage, Kaddish, Shivah.

Ner Tamid—Hebrew for "eternal light" is usually constructed of silver or bronze. The Ner Tamid hangs in every synagogue in front of the holy ard and contains an ever-burning light. It symbolizes the immanence of God and undeviating reverence for the Torah.

MESSIAH or "Mesheeach"

A steadfast belief, a hope that had kept them believing since the days of Isaiah, was in the coming of the Messiah, a descendant of the House of David, who would redeem all of mankind and establish God's Kingdom here on earth.

The Messiah, according to legend, would appear as a human being with rare talents consisting of wisdom, integrity and leadership. He would come to stimulate a social upheaval that would usher in a future of perfect peace and equality.

However, before he would appear, a generation of preparedness would be forthcoming where Man would hear his footsteps and turn their hearts to God.

In modern times, only the most orthodox still believe in the coming of the Messiah. Today, the majority of Jews believe that mankind as a whole, only by their own deeds and actions, can bring about a Kingdom of Heaven. When mankind has reached the pinnacle of human rights, justice and kindliness; only then will there be a coming of the Messiah.

MOGEN DAVID (SHIELD OF DAVID)

The Mogen David is a six pointed star consisting of two triangles pointing in opposite directions.

In medieval days, a mystic declared that the six pointed star represented the royal shield of the House of David. Although it was a cabbalistic statement, it gradually was accepted as authentic and took on a special significance to Judaism.

The Mogen David has become a distinct Jewish symbol and is found as decorations in Jewish architecture. With the growth of Zionism, it has taken on national stature wherein the national Flag of Israel is a white banner with the Mogen David emblazoned thereon.

MARRANOS From the Spanish: "Pigs"

"Marranos" was the derogatory name given to converted Jews by the Spanish and Portuguese Catholics who, at heart, remained Jewish.

The tales of torture performed on the Jewish population to force conversion defies the imagination. Implemented by Torquemada, the Chief Inquisitor for King Ferdinand and Queen Isabella, the methods of torture superceded those of Hitler. Conversion was forced in the name of Christ by use of torture racks, branding irons, skin pealing, limb separation and many other fiendish means.

Many Marranos who formerly had risen to positions of great influence found themselves purged of all worldly possessions and their lives in ruin. In the latter part of the 15th Century, literally hundreds of thousands Jews were sacrificed by so called pious Christian fanatics, who finally succombed to the final solution, that of expelling every Jew from Spain.

Since that time, Spain has never recovered from that disaster. The Marrano Jews finally found a haven in Holland, Sweden, England, Italy, Turkey and South America.

MILCHIK From the German: "Milky"

Any food that contains a dairy product.

In Jewish dietary laws, all dairy food cannot be eaten with meat products or within the necessary time for the meat to be digested. It is stated that dairy foods, consumed with meat, absorbs the acid and blood residue of the meat causing it to curd and sour in the stomach.

MIDRASH From the Hebrew: "Interpretation"

In the 5th Century B.C., in the time of the Second Temple, sages and scholars, convinced that the Bible lent itself to many complex interpretations, initiated intricate Midrashic meanings and interpretations to the Bible.

After the Jewish dispersion in the 4th Century, these scholars rewrote the Biblical texts and compiled a mass of over one hundred books involving clarified interpretations, parables, proverbs, allegories and other illustrative stories.

MEGILLAH

The Megillah is the descriptive narrative describing the Book of Esther and the Purim Holiday. The Megillah, in itself, is a group of beautiful and intricately illustrated scrolls where famous Jewish artists were able to express some of their finest talents. Many of these scrolls, some from the Middle Ages, have been preserved in the original metal cases which hold them. The cases were made of silver filigree, exquisitely designed, representing artistry of the greatest craftmanship.

MISHNAH From the Hebrew: "To repeat one's learning"

The first of the two basic divisions of the Talmud (the second being the Gemara). It is the coded heart of the Oral Law which analyzes and interprets that which was not written down. The Mishnah is divided into six parts, called (Sedarim) and then redivided into sixty three tractates. Each tractate is divided into chapters (Perakim) which are then divided into paragraphs.

The six parts of the Mishnah are: 1. Seeds, 2. Festivals, 3. Women, 4. Damages, 5. Sacred Things, 6. Purifications.

The famous Rabbi Akiba initiated the work of collecting and assorting the vast amount of Oral Laws and Traditions and this work was continued at his death by Rabbi Judah, the head of the Sanhedrin; the Highest Court in the land. It was finally finished in 200 A.D. and was accepted as authentic, to this day.

MITZVAH From the Hebrew: "Commandment"

A Mitzvah is a good deed performed out of the goodness of ones heart as an obligation and must be performed with a joyous feeling of Godliness, regardless of the burden it may incur.

It is a Godly command instilling the joy of fulfilling a holy and pious act and must not have a mental or physical ulterior motive in the act of giving.

The Talmud states that the only reward for a Mitzvah is another Mitzvah. Another interpretation states that the Mitzvahs of the Jews can be classified as "Sacred Sociology."

MIKVAH From the Hebrew: "A pool"

Orthodox Jewish law and tradition requires that a woman upon entering into wedlock and after bearing a child must take a ritual bath called a Mikvah.

A husband and wife cannot come in close physical contact let alone, make any attempt to cohabit during her menstrual period. On the seventh day after her menstruation she is required to take a bath of running water. There are rules and regulations governing this ritual. In Europe and in the Jewish areas of the United States, religious women still observe this ancient custom.

It is the emphasis that Judaism places on hygiene and cleanliness that keeps a family healthier and psychologically cleaner in spirit that has inspired such a custom.

MOHEL From the Hebrew: "A Circumciser"

A Mohel is a man, (not a doctor) whose profession is to circumcise male infants on the eighth day after their birth. He holds no special reverence in the Jewish hierarchy but is regarded as a technician and in many cases, is called in by physicians to perform this type of work.

Jewish Law requires a series of stringent rules for the licensing of a Mohel. He must have expert surgical skill and must be a religious Jew.

(See Briss)

MYRIFF

The daily evening services in the synagogue which begins after the setting of the sun. Myriff follows the afternoon service (Minchah) and if there is a pause between the two services, while they wait for the sunset, the congregation passes the time reading the Chumash and the Talmud.

MOSES

Moses, according to many historians, was the greatest historical figure of all time. He was the son of Amran and Jochebed, Levites, and lived during the time when Pharoah decreed that all newly born Jewish male children were to be killed.

Left in a basket on the Nile, he was found in the bulrushes by Pharoah's daughter and was raised in the king's court.

The biography of Moses is completely bound up with the early history of the Jews and is found throughout the Torah. He was known as Moisheh Rabbenu, (Moses our Teacher) and in Jewish history, his name looms largest for his divine interpretations, his ethics and his concern for his fellow man.

MOAB

Moab was an ancient country of the Middle East, located in the area of what is now Jordan. Involved in many wars with their neighbors, they disappeared as a nation on the rise of the Babylonian empire.

MASADA

The famous historical fortress on the West shore of the Dead Sea where the Zealots (Jewish patriots) made their last heroic stand in the war against Rome, (66-72 c.e.)

The Masada, to this day, is a symbol of Jewish dedication and heroism and fires the imagination of the Zionist youth.

MAROHR

The Hebrew term applying to the bitter herbs eaten during the ceremonial at the Passover Seder to remind one of the suffering and slavery of the Jews in Egypt before Moses led them to freedom into the wilderness.

MANNA From the Hebrew: 'Mah Hoo' (What is it?)

Manna was the magic food sent from Heaven which sustained the Jews in the wilderness during their forty years of wandering.

The manna fell from heaven during the night upon the dew and Moses instructed the Jews to gather (one omer) about four quarts, and twice that much on the Sabbath.

The manna was baked and tasted like wafers cooked in honey.

The popular phrase, 'like manna from heaven' is derived from this biblical event.

MAFTEHR

Maftehr is the Hebrew word applied to the verses in the Bible which concludes the reading of the Law on Sabbaths and Holidays. The person who is called to the Torah to pronounce the benedictions over the Maftehr also reads the selection of the Haftorah.

Nuun

Nine wise men do not a minyan make but ten cobblers do.

NAHUM

One of the Twelve Minor Prophets. His prophecies foretold the destruction of Nineveh and the downfall of the Assyrian Empire. His time and place of birth are unknown.

NAZERITE—From the Hebrew: "Nazir"

Applying to a person who consecrated himself by not drinking wine or liquor, not cutting his hair and by not touching a dead body. His life was dedicated to the sacred and priestly form of life. Sampson was a Nazerite by angelic direction.

NEDAN

Nedan is the dowry offered by the parents of a bride to her future husband. It was also a gift from the bridegroom to the father of the bride.

NAPHTALI

One of Jacobs twelve sons and head of the Israeli tribe of that name. The Naphtali tribe lived on a strip of land in Northern Palestine and were known for their courage and ferocity in battle. In the Song of Deborah, their deeds were proclaimed for their bravery.

NEGEV

A large stretch of desert in the Southern part of Israel extending all the way to the Gulf of Aqaba. This desert, which in ancient days, was an inhabited and productive area has been barren for centuries.

The Negev is now a vital part of Israel where massive colonization projects are being initiated. A water pipeline from the Yarkon river has been extended throughout the desert which has been a great help for the new developments to flourish.

The Port of Eilat, at the base of the Negev, is tremendously strategic both militarily and economically.

NEILAH From the Hebrew: "Conclusion"

This term is applied to the closing services on Yom Kippur. Regarded as the most solemn service in the Temple, the Neilah symbolizes the closing of the gates of Heaven on the day of Atonement, when the fate of MAN is sealed. The Neilah service is concluded by the blowing of the Shofar which signifies the end of the fasting period.

NUMBERS

The Fourth of the Five Books of Moses, (Pentateuch), known in Hebrew as Bemidbar (In the desert Wilderness). It is called 'Numbers' because it opens with a census of the people when they arrived in the wilderness; and later, the Book of records a second census taken after the Israelites entered the Promised Land.

Bemidbar deals with the many experiences of the Israelites in the desert, such as the Sinai legislation, the role of the Levites, and the important happenings on the way to MOAB; such as the sending of spies to the land of Canaan, the rebellion of Korah, the wars in the desert, the story of Balak and the conquest of East Jordan.

Aleph

Only shlimazels believe in mazel.

OLAM HA-ZEH—OLAM HA-BA

From the Hebrew, meaning ---- "THIS WORLD -- AND THE WORLD THAT IS TO COME"

Olam Ha-Ba -- refers to both the life of the soul after death and to the Messianic Age of Bliss (the Millenium). These two ideas began in the teachings of the Prophets and were developed in the Jewish Classics from then on. Olam Ha-Zeh is merely a preparation for Olam Ha-ba, and the suffering of an individual in 'this world' will be compensated for in the 'world to come.'

ORAL LAW (THE MISHNAH)

The Oral Law is the body of Jewish Laws not contained in the "Written Laws" (the Torah). The Oral Law (Torah Shebe-al Peh), was believed to be devinely inspired and was carried on from generation to generation, without being written down. This media has been going on through the ages.

The Oral Law was sustained by the Pharisees and has been kept sacred throughout history.

ORTHODOX JEWS

The first time Jews were referred to as Orthodox was by Furtado when Napoleon convened the Sanhedrin in Paris. In broader terms, it applies to the old and historic religion of the Jewish people.

Today, with the advent of Reformed Judaism, 'Orthodox' Jewry are the adherents of strict traditional Judaism and for that reason, had to be reconstructed to conform with modern and changing times.

According to Orthodox Judaism, the Torah is considered a way of life to be expressed by practices, ceremonies and in conformity with the Mitzvos (commandment of the Law).

OMER

A Hebrew term having two meanings; "a dry measure of grain" (which is a tenth of an ephah) and "Sheaf", applied to the sheaf on the First Fruits which the Jews were commanded to offer in the sanctuary on the Second day of Passover. The counting of the days of the Omer, between Passover and Shavuos, is still a part of the Jewish ritual.

OBADIAH

Obadiah was one of the Twelve Minor Prophets whose book of prophesies contains Twenty One verses. He forecasted vengeance on the enemies of Judah and predicted their return from Babylonian captivity. He lived approximately during 586 B.C., after the destruction of the First Temple.

Pay

Pray for the welfare of the government, since but for the fear thereof, men would swallow each other alive.

PUSHKEH Yiddish

A small can or box in the home where charitable contributions are dropped in a regular procedure during the week. Every Jewish home kept one of these boxes in which to keep money for their favorite charity. The money was usually placed there before lighting the candles on the Sabbath.

PIDYEN HA-BEN

From the Hebrew, meaning, 'Redemption of the Son'. It is stated that the Bible requires the redemption of the first born son 30 days after his birth. In tradition, the father of the boy offers coins to a Kohen (a member of a Priestly family) for the redemption of his son. If either the mother or the father is a Kohen or a Levite (Levi), no Pidyen Ha-Ben ceremony is necessary.

PALMACH

Originally known as the Haganah Shock Companies, the Palmach were groups of Jews formed from the British Army and included members of the Haganah and Etzel for the purpose of seizing the Mufti in Baghdad from where he was helping the Axis powers.

In 1941, the Palmach and Haganah undertook intelligence operations missions to Syria and Lebanon, sometimes under the direction of the British authorities. When the British invaded Syria and

Lebanon in July of 1941, a Haganah platoon acted as scouts and saboteurs in behalf of the British forces.

Later, the idea became firmly entrenched in the British minds that the entire Zionist leadership was now given to terrorism after a Palmach operation liberated 200 interned illegal immigrants, creating a half-day general strike with violent demonstrations and fostered the proclamation of ''The Jewish Resistance Movement'' by Kol Yisroel.

On the night of the 31st of October, Palmach troops sank three naval craft and wrecked railway lines in 50 different locations. The attacks were accomplished with great skill and little loss of life.

When Israel achieved statehood, the Palmach succeeded in incorporating members of all other military fringe groups to join with them establishing the Israeli National Armed Forces.

PENTATEUCH

The Pentateuch is the Torah, which consists of the Five Books of Moses: Genesis, Exodus, Leviticus, Numbers, and Deuteronomy.

PURIM

Purim is a festive holiday, falling in February or March, recalling the victory of Queen Esther and Mordecai over their arch-enemy, Haman.

It is a happy time, calling for masquerade parties, singing and dancing, and symbolizes the release of pent up anxieties for Jews who had suffered from persecution and slavery.

During Purim, the congregation gathers in the synagogue and listens to the dramatic story of Purim. Whenever Haman's name is mentioned, the children raise a din with their 'gragehrs' to express their indignation.

With all its joy, Purim is a day of spiritual meditation and comfort, reminding Jews that all tyrants eventually disappear into the unknown.

PASSOVER - (PESACH)

From the Hebrew: ''To Pass over''

Pesach or Passover is perhaps the most outstanding festival in Jewish life. Meaning the ''Festival of Freedom'', Pesach lasts eight days of which the first two days and the last two days are full holidays.

Pesach falls in the spring of the year, usually during April, and is basically a home ceremonial. Prior to the holiday, the house is scoured from top to bottom to remove any sign of leavened bread or any other food containing leavening agents. For the duration of Pesach, only Matzos and other unleavened products are eaten. The highlight of Passover is the Seder where the family observes an elaborate ritual. The table is decorated with Passover china and silverware and wine cups are placed before each participant.

In the ceremony, the father recites the story of Exodus and the youngest child asks his father "The Four questions" (FIER KASHIS); Why is this night different from all other nights?: 1. Why do we eat unleavened bread, 2. Why do we eat bitter herbs, 3. Why do we dip food in salt water, 4. Why do we lean at the table?

The father answers from the book, the Haggadah, in which he tells of slavery in Egypt, Moses courageous leadership, and finally the miracle of redemption.

Passover has become the symbol of the Jews most cherished ideals; freedom from persecution and slavery. From generation to generation, each Jew must regard himself as having been personally delivered from the hands of the Egyptians.

PHARISEES

The Pharisees were members of a political-religious party in ancient Israel during the time of Christ. Representing the middle and lower class of people, in contrast to the Sadducees, who represented the upper classes, the Pharisees believed in the worship of God in a simple way, through love and equality.

Opposing the Pharisees, the Sadducees, were reactionary, insisting on strict observance of the law.

Later, the preaching of the Pharisees were adopted by Christianity and compose an important link between Judaism and Christianity.

PIRKE ABOTH—From the Hebrew: "Sayings of the Fathers"

Pirke Aboth is a small tractate in the Nezikin order written in the Mishna of the Talmud. It was written by famous scholars and teachers who flourished during a 500 year period up to the 2nd

Century c.e. when the Mishna was assembled. Pirke Aboth contains proverbs, epigrams, maxims and pithy sayings and became highly popular and widely read among the Jews, gradually being incorporated into the daily prayer book, the Siddur.

The wisdom of Pirke Aboth not only found favor among the Jews but the Gentiles as well, with many of its proverbs being adopted with ready acceptance.

The Talmud declares: "He who wants to become truly pious and virtuous, let him study and practice the teachings of Pirke Aboth." (Babba Kamma 30a)

PIYYUTIM

The Piyyutim are poetic compositions written by Hebrew poets in Spain during the Middle Ages. They were added to the liturgy on special occasions such as holidays and festivals to serve as interpolations in the services. The most famous poets who have written Piyyutim are Kalir, Ibn Gabriel, Judah Ha-Levi and Moses ibn Ezra.

Raysh

Rivalry of scholars advances wisdom.

ROSH HASHONAH

Hebrew for 'new Year'

It is the first of the two most sacred holidays in the Jewish religion; the other being Yom Kippur.

Rosh Hashonah is the start of the Ten Days of Penitence, when all persons are judged before God. It is during these ten days that God examines the acts of men which involves their deeds and their motives. This is also the period of the year when Jews sit in self judgement of their deeds and permit their conscience to decide whether they have lived up to their resolutions and behaviour.

The most important symbol of Rosh Hashonah is the blowing of the Shofar (Rams Horn) which is sounded during worship on each of the Ten Days. It calls upon the congregation to repent their misdeeds, to return to God with humility so that the coming year may be marked by proper observance of God's commandments and by ethical conduct toward their fellow man.

RABBI

A Rabbi is a teacher --- a man who has the knowledge and can transmit the heritage of Judaism to the members of his congregation. His position rests not upon his title but upon his learning and knowledge. A Rabbi cannot be assumed to be a priest or prophet. He has no special Godly priveledges and is in no way an intermediary between God and Man. The influence and respect of a Rabbi is determined solely by his ability to maintain the respect and cohesiveness of his congregation as an interpretor of Jewish law and tradition.

The title of Rabbi was first used 1900 years ago. Modern rabbis are graduates of recognized seminaries or Yeshivas where they complete specialized courses in religious studies. Among the Orthodox, a man is not a rabbi until he obtains ''smicheh'' (ordination).

REVISIONISTS

A fringe Zionist party founded in 1925 by Vladimir Jabotinsky. Unhappy with the mild aspirations and the slow progress of the main body of Zionists, they demanded more drastic revisions, even the use of military force to establish a Jewish State in Israel. Their main opposition was the Histadrut, the Labor Party, and in 1935, they withdrew from the World Zionist Organization and established their own organization, the New Zionist Organization.

The Revisionists had many followers in the Diasphora and in Palestine itself. From them, emerged the Irgun, an illegal military force to fight the British, who were obstructing their progress with their entire army. Today, the Revisionists are represented by the Herut Party in the Israeli Knesset.

RUTH

In the Book of Writings (Ketuvim), the third section of the Bible, it tells of the Moabite woman who converted to Judaism and married a Jew. After her husbands death, together with her mother-in-law, Naomi, she left Moab and traveled to Bethlehem where she married a wealthy farmer, named Boaz. King David was one of their descendants.

ROSH CHADESH

From the Hebrew, meaning: ''Beginning of a Month''

Rosh Chadesh is the name of the half-holiday denoting the appearance of the New Moon; which is the beginning of a new month in the Hebrew calendar.

In olden days, Rosh Chadesh was considered an important time of the year for based on the lunar system, the New Moon was used by the Jewish High Court (Sanhedrin) as a means of setting the calendar.

On the Sabbath preceding a New Moon, a special prayer is offered in the synagogue for a good month ahead.

REVELATION

A basic belief of Orthodox Judaism is that God, through a revelation of Himself or his Teachings, will contact certain individuals, either one man or a group. Since Adam, God has revealed Himself to Prophets and other chosen men to emphasize His will and authority.

The greatest revelation was at Mt. Sinai where the Israelites, through Moses, received His Law. Since these Laws were given to the Jews by God, Himself, they are therefore unchangeable and fundamental for the duration of Time and Man.

RESPONSA—In Hebrew; "Sheelot U-Teshuvot", meaning 'questions and answers'

The Responsa is a branch of rabbinical literature comprised of rulings and opinions on matters of Jewish law. The Geonim, whose authority was unquestionably accepted by all Jews, issued written opinions on all legal questions submitted to them by the Jewish population. Covering over 1200 years of Jewish development, the Responsa provides invaluable information about the religious, social, moral and political life of the Jews during the time.

S ס
Samech

Soldiers fight and kings are the heroes.

SANHEDRIN From the Greek 'Synedrion' meaning "Assembly"

The Sanhedrin can be compared in stature to the Supreme Court; it represented the highest court of authority in the ancient Jewish nation. It was composed of seventy aged wise men and included a Patriarch called the Nasi. Their decisions were final regarding matters of theology, ethics and political matters. Being of learned and knowledgeable backgrounds, they interpreted the scriptures and combined religious and civil authority to make it binding. Their authority lasted until 70 A.D. when Titus destroyed the Great Temple.

Driven to Tiberias, they founded orders of rabbinical scholarship and learning which later established the Bet Din, the modern version of the Jewish Court of Law. History states that Moses was the first Nasi, who declared to his followers, "Gather unto me seventy elders of Israel.", but its true origin is vague.

When in session, the Sanhedrin met in the Hall of Hewn Stones in the Temple. They sat in a semi-circle making it easier to discuss the problem at hand while open discussion prevailed. Standing before the court were disciples of the judges who were learned men and were present for consultation. If an accused person was being tried for a discrepancy of the law, he was required to wear mourning clothes. In the matter of the Torah and Mosaic Law, the Sanhedrin exercised supreme authority.

SEPHARDIM

From the Hebrew, the word 'Spanish', 'Portuguese' and 'North African Jews'. It is derived from the Hebrew word 'Sepharad' meaning Spain, and was mentioned in the Bible as the land in which the Jews found refuge when they were driven from the Holy Land in the middle ages.

Sephardic Judaism flourished in Spain for a period of over 800 years, reaching its cultural heights in the 15th Century, during which time they excelled in their knowledge of medicine, astronomy, mathematics, music and the sciences.

Until their expulsion from Spain at the end of the 15th Century, their scholars and financiers had attained the highest positions in the land including the honor of being advisers to the king and queen. Many of them were found among the aristocracy and their mode of living plus their lavish synagogues reached the ultimate in magnificence.

Driven from Spain during the Inquisition, they settled throughout Europe crossing the Mediterranean Sea to Greece, Turkey, Palestine, England, France and Holland. Many came to the United States in what proved to be the first Jewish colony in America.

The Sephardic language is called Ladino which is a mixture of Spanish, Turkish, Arabic and Hebrew. Their words and sentences are an amalgamation of Spanish and Hebrew roots which form the prefixes of verbs and adverbs, creating a hodge-podge of idiomatic slang, completely alien to the Yiddish spoken by the Ashkenazim in Eastern Europe.

Today, the Sephardim comprise 7% of the worlds Jewry. The chasm, separating them from the main body of Jews, can be attributed to differences in language, their trends of thought, their customs and their style of liturgy in the synagogues.

SUCCOTH

Succoth is known as the Festival of the Tabernacles, beginning five days after Yom Kippur and continuing for nine days. Its origin was in ancient Palestine to celebrate the harvesting of the crops and the approach of the rainy season.

A small lean-to hut (Succah) is built out of wooden boards with branches and leaves serving as a roof; with open spaces in the roof so that those inside can see the sky. It is symbolic of the temporary dwellings lived in by the Israelites during their 40 years in the wilderness.

On the walls of the Succah are hung various types of fruit of the season, and a plain wooden table and benches are placed inside. During the week of Succoth the family eats their food in the Succah.

SABRA

Sabra is the name of a prickly cactus plant which is sturdy, endurable, and able to withstand hardship and yet it is good tasting. By extension, it applies to all native born Israelis.

STERN GANG

A group named after its founder, Abraham Stern, that fought the British during the prelude to the birth of Israel.

Abraham Stern, a strange and dedicated young man who had shown remarkable ability as a student by Judas Magnes, was a brilliant poet and his philosophy, which he imposed on his followers, was a dedication to Zionism and primitive, orthodox Judaism. He was driven by an almost maniacal single mindedness.

Stern's theory was that anyone against the National Homeland of Israel was an enemy; the end justified the most violent means, compromise of any sort was treachery, and there was no distinction between the Nazis and the British occupation forces because both were against a future Jewish homeland.

His faithful followers named him 'Yair', after a Roman hero against oppression. He was imprisoned in 1939 and released in 1940. His mind was cluttered with hate and he even hated the Jews who disagreed with him, more than he hated the enemy.

In January 1942, the Stern Gang murdered two officials of the Histadrut. Shortly thereafter, in February of 1942, after the capture of twenty of his men, Stern was killed in a police raid.

SHOFAR

A ram's horn that is sounded on the High Holidays and on special significant occasions. The Shofar, or rams horn, symbolizes the ram who appeared as a substitute for the sacrifice of Isaac. In Jewish history, the rams horn was sounded to alert the Jews to danger, as a call to arms, as a sign of Peace, to usher in the new moon, and as a routine sound of assurance.

There are several variations in the blowing of the Shofar, these having been developed by Rabbis and sages. Broken notes denote weeping, followed by long, steady notes; then by a staccato of broken notes for sobbing and wailing.

SIMCHATH TORAH

From the Hebrew; "The Day of Rejoicing in the Law"

The festival of Simchath Torah falls at the close of Succoth and is dedicated to the glorification of the Torah. It is a happy occasion, with feasting and dancing to mark the end and the new beginning of the weekly readings of the Torah. On this day, the last chapter of Deuteronomy is read and immediately after, the Book of Genesis is begun, denoting the continuous cycle of worship with the symbolic reference that the Torah has no beginning and no end.

Despite its solemn liturgy, Simchath Torah is the happiest day of the year. The honor of being called to read the last verses of the Torah is bestowed on a distinguished member of the synagogue, who is referred to as "The Bridgroom of the Torah."

SADDUCEES

The Sadducees were a group of fundamentalists whose views were similar to the later-appearing Karaites. They accepted only the Torah as the true law for Israel and rejected any other interpretation of its teachings, such as offered by the Talmudists.

SHALOM

Hebrew for; "Peace"

Shalom, for many years, has been the word used to indicate a greeting and a departure. Peace has always been of such importance in Jewish tradition that in ancient teachings, Shalom was considered to be one of the names of the Almighty.

''Shalom Alaychem'' means, ''Peace be with you.''

SHAMMAS

A Shammas is the sexton of the synagogue (shul).

His duties are generally those of a caretaker. In addition, he serves as an assistant to the Chazzan, as a general secretary, etc. He attends all daily services and is typically the first to arrive and last to leave the synagogue.

SHAVUOT

The Hebrew for: ''Feast of Weeks''

Shavuot, also known as the Pentecost, is celebrated on the 6th and 7th days of Sivan (May-June), commemorating the completion of seven weeks of counting the Omer (sheafs of barley) which begins on the 2nd day of Passover, when a sheaf of barley (Omer) was offered as a sacrifice.

Wheat is harvested after barley, and fifty days after, on Shavuot, two loaves of bread, made from wheat, were offered as first fruits of the harvest.

Deeper meaning also centers around Shevuot. It denotes the time that God gave the Ten Commandments on Mt. Sinai, thus the name, ''Zeman Mattan Toratenu'', (the Season of the Giving of our Torah.)

Usually, Jewish homes and synagogues are decorated with plants and flowers to portray its botanical significance.

SHEITEL

The ancient Yiddish word for wig, worn by orthodox, Jewish, married women as a token of their modesty.

Traditional Jewish law states that it is sinful for a married woman to be seen by other men or to attend the services without a hair covering. Extremely pious women would cut their hair off on their wedding day and wear a kerchief as a covering.

This custom, although adhered to in rare instances, is not followed at the present time except by Chasidic women.

SEDER From the Hebrew, meaning; "Order"

The Seder is the family ceremony in Jewish homes on the first two nights of Passover. It is a reminder of the Passover meal during the time of the Holy Temple. It is a happy ceremony, commemorating the deliverance from Egypt of the Jewish people and with it, the hopes and prayer for the redemption of the people to their homeland.

The high points of the Seder are the recitation of the Kiddush by the head of the family, the reading of the Haggadah, which entails the situation of the Jews in Egypt during the time of Moses, the asking of the Four Questions by the youngest member present, the eating of the matzos and the bitter herbs; then the Passover meal with all the Pesachdiki dishes, the drinking of the four cups of wine, reciting of the Hallel, (Psalms of Peace), and the singing of songs by the entire family.

SHEMA

The Shema is the oldest and most important of Hebrew prayers. It is considered to be, in sense, Israel's complete affirmation of its faith: ''Hear, O Israel, the Lord our God, the Lord is One.''

When Shema is intoned, it is accompanied by the reciting of three other selections from the Pentateuch.

SIDDUR

From the Hebrew; meaning, ''Order''

The Siddur is the prayer book used in the synagogue for daily liturgy. It is distinguished from the 'Mahzehr' which is used during the High Holidays and Festivals.

The Siddur contains the three daily services: Shachres (morning service), Mincheh (afternoon service), and Myriff (evening service). It also contains prayers for the Sabbath services.

Aside from the prayers, the Siddur also contains blessings for special occasions; Psalms, the Song of Songs, Zmires (Sabbath hymns) etc.

The oldest prayers in the Siddur are the Shema, which was recited in the Second Temple, and the Amidah or the Shimoneh Esray.

The basic prayers in the Siddur are recorded in the Mishneh and the Gemara.

SHIVAH

The Hebrew word for ''Seven''

It refers to the first seven days of mourning which begins immediatley after the burial of a close relative. ''Sitting Shivah'' means the mourners stay at home, do not wear shoes, and do not sit on chairs, but on a low stool or on the floor.

For the seven days, daily services are said in the home, including the Kaddish. The following kin are considered close relatives: Spouse, father, mother, son, daughter, brother and sister.

SHIMONAH ESREH

Shimonah Esreh is the principal prayer of the three daily prayers in the synagogue. It is a series of blessings, called the 'Amidah' (standing) and is recited while the worshippers are on their feet.It is usually recited in a low tone of voice, while facing the East. At its conclusion the Chazzan repeats the prayers aloud.

Shimonah Esreh has three basic divisions: The three benedictions of Adoration (Avot, Gevurot, Kedusha Ha-Shem); the thirteen Petitions (personal prayers); and the concluding three which are for Thanksgiving (Avodah, Hodaah, Shalom), or the Priestly benediction.

SHALISHUDIS

From the Hebrew ''Shalosh Seudot'' Meaning, 'Three Meals'

This term is applied to the meal that is eaten on Saturday after the Minchah service. The Talmud states that all Jews should honor the Sabbath with Shalishudis; three festive meals, one on Friday evening and two on Saturday.

SHADCHIN

A Yiddish term for a marriage broker which profession flourished during the Middle Ages. Later, in the stet'ls and ghettos of Russia and Poland, it became very common and was considered to be a 'mitzvah' to bring the proper man and woman together which could culminate in the perfect marriage.

SHEKEL From the Hebrew, "To Weigh".

The Shekel was the accepted measure of money during the biblical days of Abraham. A shekel was worth eight grams of silver and the Bible states that Abraham bought a burial place for himself and his family for 400 shekels.

In reality, the shekel was a weight, rather than a coin, until the 1st Century. At that time, the government issued a shekel as a coin and stamped it with the imprint of three pomegranates.

In February of 1980, the modern government of Israel replaced the Israeli pound with the shekel, evaluating 10 pounds to the shekel. The same impression of three pomegranates appear on the modern version as on the biblical coin.

Tess

The best horse needs a whip;
the wisest man needs advice and the best woman needs a man.

TALLIS In Hebrew, meaning: "Cloak"

A Tallis is a white, silk or wool prayer shawl worn by Jews in abeyance with ancient biblical law. The Tallis is worn at all morning services (never at night because in ancient times, services in the evening were held indoors and an outer shawl was not worn). Many Jews wear the Tallis folded over the shoulder for comfort but the more pious and holy wear it unfolded, covering their head and shoulders, symbolically feeling that they are taking refuge in the shadow of God's wings. A Tallis is usually given to a boy on his Bar Mitzvah which denotes his manhood and the priveledge of wearing it.

The pious Jew wears his Tallis to the grave for it is considered part of his burial robe.

TEFILLIN or "Phylacteries"

Tefillin consist of two small black cubic boxes, approximately 1½ inches wide, to which black leather straps, about ½ inch wide, are attached. Inside the boxes are four separate pieces of parchment on which are inscribed verses from the Book of Exodus and Deuteronomy, proclaiming God's unity, His providential care and Israel's deliverance from slavery.

Nineteenth century Tefillin cases from Warsaw, Poland for both the hand and head phylacteries.

The two boxes are worn in a specific manner while reciting special prayers. One box is placed on the left arm and the other fastened to the forehead. In a prescribed manner, the worshipper wraps the Tefillin on his person to remove any mental intrusions and to help him concentrate on his praying.

Symbolically, its purpose is to act as a reminder of Mans closeness to God and of his committment of heart and body to God's will. The phylacteries on his left arm, near the heart, represents his emotional ties to his faith; the box on his forehead, near the brain, denotes his intellectual acceptance of God's will.

TORAH

The Torah is the most sacred and revered object of Jewish life and ritual. It is a hand written scroll which contains the Five Books of Moses which is housed in the Holy Ark of the Synagogue. Upon the Torah, is written the complete Bible from Genesis to Deuteronomy.

An early 19th Century Torah breastplate from Vienna, Austria.

The scroll is made of parchment, wrapped around two wooden poles or rollers and covered with an embroidered cloth. Two silver ornaments rest on the poles and across the face of the scroll hangs a silver breastplate which adorns the covering.

The text of the Torah, hand written in Hebrew, has been unchanged through hundreds of generations and must be meticulous and literally letter perfect. It there are two written errors, the scroll may not be used in worship.

In Jewish folklore, the Torah precedes the time of Creation. It was at God's side when the Universe came into being and is considered the breath of MAN.

Throughout history, Jews have been persecuted and have died to save the Torah from desecration. Forced to flee from tyranny and persecution, they carried the Torah with them, leaving all their worldly possessions behind.

TU BISHVAT "Arbor Day"

Tu Bishvat usually falls in February and denotes the planting of trees in ancient Israel. In Israel today, young children participate in a ceremonial planting of trees, for reforestation is an important necessity for the reproduction of the land.

Tu Bishvat has become increasingly important as a gala and festive holiday.

TAANIS BECHORUM

"The Fast of the Firstborn Sons"

When the Almighty slew the first born sons of Egypt, he spared the first born sons of the Children of Israel. Therefore, all first born Jewish males must fast on the day before Passover in gratitude to the Almighty.

In modern times however, the fast day has been broken by a Seudas Mitzvah, a festive meal in celebration of a mitzvah, such as the "Siyum" meal held at the conclusion of a study of a Book of the Talmud which takes place in the synagogue.

TESHUVAH—From the Hebrew: (Repentance -- Return)

Teshuvah means that anyone having sinned will be forgiven if he returns to God, which includes turning away from sinful ways and returning to righteousness.

Both in the Bible and rabbinic literature, it is stated that the 'gates of prayer' may be shut but the 'gates of repentance' are always open.

There is a definite distinction between sinning against God and sinning against a fellow man. A wrong against God may be forgiven if the sinner confesses and vows not to do it again. However, a sin against man is not forgiven until the sinner first apologizes and makes amends to the person he has wronged. Jewish tradition regards repentance as one of the most important functions of piety.

TABERNACLE

The Tabernacle refers to the portable sanctuary carried by the Israelites in the wilderness, constructed by Betzalel, at the direction of Moses. It was a tent like structure, containing an outer court where offerings were burnt on the altar, and an inner sanctuary leading to the Holy of Holies, "the Ark of the Covenant", accessible only to the High Priest on Yom Kippur.

After the conquest of Canaan, it was mentioned for the last time as being located in Shiloh during the time of Eli, the High Priest.

TZADDIK

A Tzaddik is an extremely righteous and religious man. Among the Chasidim, a Tzaddik is one who is considered their leader and adviser.

TISHAH BOV Hebrew for "The Ninth Day of the Month of Av."

Tishah Bov is observed by Jews as a day of mourning to commemorate the destruction of the First and Second Temples. As time passed, other disasters, such as the expulsion of Jews from Spain, occurred on that day. During services, the worshippers sit on the floor or on low stools as expression of their sorrow.

TANNAIM (Tane, sing.)

The Tannaim was a group of about 225 Jewish sages and scholars in Palestine during the 200 years after Hillel's death. They were the authorities of the Oral Law, with their opinions recorded in the Mishna of the Talmud. The most famous of the Tannaim was Rabbi Akiba.

U י
Yood

Unless you know what will happen today, don't worry about tomorrow.

UNLEAVENED BREAD - MATZOS

Matzos is a thin, finely perforated, crisp sheet of bread, baked without yeast or other leavening agents and formed in square sheets for easy breaking. It is eaten by Jews on Passover.

Matzos commemorates the bread eaten by the Jews in the 13th Century as they fled from the Egyptians during their flight through the wilderness when they couldn't wait for the dough to rise. Matzos is also used as part of the festivities at the Seder and is intimately involved in the proceedings.

URIM AND TUMMIN

The Urim and Tummin were two objects that decorated the breast plate of the High Priest. The Bible states that they possessed the mystic power of an oracle which could answer questions put to them, expressing the will of God. This was particularly true during times of stress, danger or crises.

The breastplate, containing the Urim and Tummin, has been adopted by Yale University as their seal.

Vov

Verily, no crown carries such royalty with it as doth humility.

VIDDUI From the Hebrew: "Confession of Sin"

Viddui refers particularly to the prayers Ashamnu and Al Het, which are recited on Yom Kippur. Some orthodox Jews recite the Viddui every night before retiring.

Vov

When a father helps a son, both smile; when a son helps a father, both cry.

WAILING WALL

The remains of King Solomon's Temple in Jerusalem which was destroyed in 70 A.D. It is considered the most sacred place in the world by Jews everywhere. For the first time in 2000 years, the wall has been in Jewish hands since 1967.

The facade of uneven stones rises to 75 feet. The lower portion has been polished to an alabaster sheen by the caresses of thousands of hands, lips and foreheads of humble and grateful Jews.

In the crevices between the stones are many thousands of scraps of paper--prayers to God, prayers for Peace.

A pure silver alms box, dated 1744 from Russia.

WRITTEN LAW

The Written Law is the Torah or the Five Books of Moses, that God revealed to Moses on Mount Sinai. It is the first division of the Bible, or the "Pentateuch".

There are two other divisions of the Bible which have strong authority.

In the second division, the fast days during the year were instituted by the Prophets; called NEVIIM. In the third division, Mordecai and Esther instituted the Festival of Purim, called KETUVIM.

WANDERING JEW

A well known legend in European literature involving a Jewish shoemaker named Ahasuerus who was cursed to wander eternally as punishment for taunting Jesus of Nazareth while on his way to the crucifixion.

The story of the Wandering Jew became a popular folk tale for writers and artists, and a best seller based on this legend was written by Eugene Sue, called "The Wandering Jew."

Yud

You are wrong if you persist long enough that you are right.

YARMULKEH

From the Polish, 'Skullcap'

In the early days of the Temple, Jewish men were instructed to cover their heads as a designation of their respect to God, whose radiance emanated above them. Although Reform Jews are deviating from this ancient tradition, Orthodox and Conservative Jews counter that baring ones head is a non-Jewish demonstration, counter productive to Jewish custom and religion.

In other activities, apart from wearing the Yarmulkeh in the synagogue, Jews have taken to wearing the yarmulkeh in public gatherings and other protest marches as a source of identification that they are Jewish.

YESHIVAH

From the Hebrew, (to sit).

A house of study where students sit for hours on end studying the Talmud. Their concentration is basically on the spiritual and eternal concepts of the Torah, analyzing and disecting the Mishna and Gemara to perpetuate themselves as Jews. The old Orthodox Jews feared that secular and worldly knowledge would gradually diminish the Jewish influence in their youth if they were permitted to allow their minds to become interested in non-Jewish subjects. However, in Poland, during the latter part of the 19th Century, Yeshivah students were permitted to study such secular subjects as science, fiction and philosophy.

The first American Yeshivah was founded in 1886 in New York City. Later, merging with other schools of that kind, it gradually became the Yeshiva University which contains a medical school as well as a seminary.

YORTZEIT

Yortzeit is the Yiddish term for the anniversary of the death of parents and other close relatives. It is observed yearly on the day of the relative's death by reciting Kaddish in the synagogue and the lighting of Yortzeit Licht.

YIZKOR

Yizkor is the Memorial Service for the dead recited in the Synagogue on the Eight day of Passover, the Second day of Shavuouth, on Yom Kippur and on Shemini Atzeres. It is also called Hazkarat Neshamot (remembering the souls.)

YOM TOV—Hebrew for, "Good day" Pronounced "Yuntiff"

"Good Yuntiff is used as a greeting and salutation on major Jewish Holidays and festivals.

YETZER HA-RA YETZER-TOV

According to Jewish tradition, a person is born with two different impulses or inclinations: the inclination to do wrong (YETZER HA-

RA) and the impulse to do right (YETZER TOV). MAN has the freedom of choice to choose between the two opposite impulses.

The Torah teaches that it is the obligation of every man to seek the knowledge and character for developing the YETZER TOV.

However, the substance of Yetzer Ha-Ra, the impulse and inclination for evil, was very much in evidence. The human factor could not be denied or ignored so the Rabbis reiterated that, without the YETZER Ha-RA, there would be no ambition, no passion, no marriage and no civilization. They stated that YETZER HA-RA was not all bad. It is the manner in which a person responds and reacts that determines its ethical value.

YOM HA-DIN

Yom Ha-Din is known in Hebrew as Judgement Day and refers to Rosh Hashonah (Jewish New Years) as the day when each persons fate for the coming year is determined by God. By tradition, the entire period of the High Holy Days is centered around the idea that one's fate is determined during this time. The common phrase, "The Day of Judgement" is also used for the 'end of time' when the Messiah will appear.

YAD

A Yad is a silver ornament in the shape of a hand with the forefinger extended. As it is considered irreverent to touch the Torah with ones bare hand, the Yad is used to point to the passage to be read. Through the centuries, many of these Yadim were considered to be works of art.

YOM KIPPUR

Yom Kippur, the Day of Atonement, is considered the holiest and most solemn day in the Jewish religion. It falls on the 10th day of Tishre (Sept-Oct) and marks the culmination of the Ten Penitential Days which begin on Rosh Hashonah.

Food, drink and work are forbidden and the day is spent in the synagogue in prayers for forgiveness of sins and reconciliation with both God and Man.

The services commence with the traditional prayer of Kol Nidre and are concluded with the sounding of one blast of the Shofar.

YISHUV Hebrew for: "Settlement".

The word "Yishuv" applied originally to a Jewish community in what was former Palestine. Today, a yishuv is applied to a settlement in Israel which is similar to a Kibbutz, but considerably larger in size and more complex in its operations.

Z ז

Zieyen

ZOHAR (The Book of Splendor)
"All souls form but one Unity with the Divine Soul"
(Rabbi Simeon bar Yohai)

ZION

The Biblical land of the Jews---Israel; Jerusalem.

The age old concept of the reunification of the Jews in their own, traditional land.

Through the ages, wherever they lived in the world, Jews would turn in the direction of Zion and pray that--"Next year in Jerusalem."

The first modern Zionist was Chaim Weizmann, the great and distinguished scientist, who later became the first President of Israel.

ZOHAR

The most important book in the teaching of Caballah is the "Book of Splendor", or in Hebrew "Sefer ha Zohar."

Sefer ha Zohar is a complex digest of Jewish superstitions,

folklore, and mysticism designed to diagnose and reveal the mysterious meanings of the Bible. It contains an olio of symbols, dreams, nightmares, cryptology and various other forms of unusual events. It deciphers exorcism, deals in the metaphysical and delves into mathematics, astrology and numerology as it assigns numerical equations to each letter of a word to find a solution as to the meaning or intent of that which is written. This Book of Splendor, in addition to its unique writings, contains magnificent historical tales, beautiful proverbs and heart rending prayers.

The Chasidic movement, steeped in religious tradition, were completely immersed in the study of Zohar.

ZERAIM—From the Hebrew, meaning 'Seeds'

It is the name of the first division of the Mishnah in the Talmud. It has eleven tractates, most of which deal with the rules and regulations of charity and agriculture.

ZEMIROT Hebrew for 'Hymns'.

These hymns are chanted during meals on the Sabbath.

Many of these hymns are anonymous while a great number of them were written by Jewish poets during the years of the Crusades.

ZECHARIAH

Zechariah, the Eleventh of the Twelve Minor Prophets, advocated the rebuilding of the Second Temple. He lived during the time following the return of the Jewish people from Babylonian captivity.

ZEALOTS—In Hebrew, "Kannaim"

The Kannaim were devoted Jewish patriots who zealously defended the honor of God and Israel. They were members of an extremist party who were active for about a century before the destruction of the Second Temple by the Romans in 70 a.d.

They often resorted to violence, including the means of assassination. As they usually carried a dagger, called the (Sica), the Romans called them "Sicarii."

TEACHINGS FROM THE TALMUD

TEACHINGS FROM THE TALMUD

THE TALMUDIC AGE

Locations of the great Talmudic academies of learning throughout the Middle East. (200 b.c.e. to 500 c.e.) Palestine Talmud (500 c.e.) Babylonian Talmud

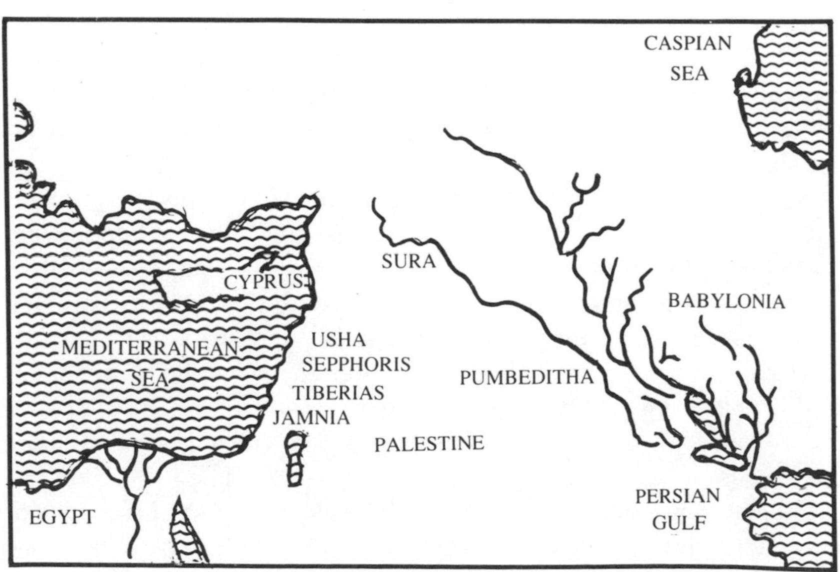

The Talmud

The Talmud, one of the most extraordinary writing achievements undertaken in the history of mankind, is a massive repository of Jewish law and Ritual consisting of sixty three books which are divided into two divisions, the Mishna and the Gemara.

The Talmud is a monumental conglomeration of Jewish religious experience and wisdom throughout their long history and contains a mass of debates, monologues, dialogues, conversations, discussions, conclusions, suppositions and commentaries by their sages, scholars, teachers and rabbis who, for thousands of years, interpreted the Torah for the teaching of law, liturgy and tradition. It is the source for divine inspiration, insight and ethical behavior that will instruct mankind until the end of time.

The Mishna, the first division of the Talmud, is called ''The Teaching''. It is the foundation of Jewish law. Originally compiled and recorded by Rabbi Judah, the Prince of Palestine at the end of the second century, a.d., it was universally accepted and became the heartbeat of the Talmud.

The Gemara; which means ''Completion'', records the many debates on Jewish law in the academies of Babylon and Palestine during the 3rd, 4th and 5th Centuries. This, together with the Mishna, is the text of the Talmud.

However, the composition of the Talmud contains many other elements beside the specifics of the Mishna and Gemara. Interwoven with the opinions of the scholars, are literally thousands of proverbs, parables, anecdotes, epigrams and humorous sketches that display an intimate and glowing aspect of Jewish life prior to and after the destruction of their land. It is truly a treasury of wisdom, much of which has been carried over to this day.

Inasmuch as the two divisions of the Talmud were written hundreds of years apart, conditions dictated that they be written in different languages. The Mishna, the basis of the Oral Law, which was not written but handed down from generation to generation, was composed in Hebrew, while the Gemara, the Second Division of the Talmud; the vast accumulation of commentaries from the Mishna, was written in Aramaic. The compiled material in the Gemara took over three centuries before it was finally approved and completed.

For over two hundred years, the two rival schools of thought in Jerusalem, the Hillel and the Shammai, fought bitter debates on the religious and judicial doctrines in the Talmud. The majority of these debates and discussions were won by the Hillelites whose presentations were always forebearing and filled with humility and compassion.

It was the power of the Talmud, studiously read, studied and meticulously observed that retained the cohesiveness and held together a people dispersed and driven all over the world. In Europe, the Middle East, North Africa and numerous other places in the world, the Talmud made them one family, held together by a common bond of laws, morals, ethics and obligations to a most loved and revered Almighty God.

Parables

There was once a king who was told that humility lengthens man's life. Deciding to live humbly, the king dressed himself in rags, lived in a small hut, and forbade his courtiers to bow before him. A wise man, having noticed that the king was proud of his accomplishments, remarked: "This is not the right way, O King. Dress like a king, behave like a king, let people serve you like a king. Yet be humble in your heart. This is what humility means.

(*Baal Shem*)

A man died and left a will which no one understood. His three sons asked the help of Rabbi Banaa. He read: "Give my oldest son a barrel of dust, my second son a barrel of bones and my youngest son a barrel of threads." The Rabbi asked: "Did your father leave land, cattle and cloth?" "Yes," was the answer. "Then," said the Rabbi, "the oldest receives the land, the second son the cattle, and the third, the cloth."

(*Babba Batra 143*)

The great king Alexander asked for admission at the Gate of Paradise. "Only the righteous may enter here." was the reply.
He then pleaded for a gift, and a piece of human skull with one eye open was thrown to him. Alexander wished to weigh it on his scales and placed on the balance gold and silver, but the skull was heavier. More gold was added, but to no avail. Acting upon the advice of the

Sages, he placed some earth on the eye and at once the gold became heavier. "This teaches," they said. "that a human eye is not satisfied with all the gold that exists until it is covered with the earth of the grave."

(*Tamid 31*)

Doctrines

WOMAN

(With respect to the formation of a woman from Adams rib)

God considered from which part of man to create woman. He said:

I will not create her from the head that she should not hold up her head too proudly; nor from the eye that she should not be too curious; nor from the ear that she should not be an eavesdropper; nor from the mouth that she should be too talkative; nor from the heart that she should not be too jealous; nor from the hand that she should not be too acquisitive; nor from the foot that she should not be a gadabout; but from a part of the body which is hidden that she should be modest.

(Gen. R. xviii, 2)

MARRIAGE

To marry and rear a family was a religious command; indeed the first of all commands addressed by God to Man.

(Gen. i. 28)

Male and female created He them and blessed them and called their name Man.

(Gen. v. 2.)

The conviction was general that not only are marriages made in heaven but forty days before the birth of a child, his or her husband or wife is determined in heaven. In Deuteronomy it states: A man should first build a house, then plant a vineyard and after that marry. So important is it to take a wife that one may sell a Scroll of the Torah for the purpose of marriage.

DIVORCE

Under the law of the Talmud if husband and wife wished to separate there was no difficulty in dissolving the marriage. ''If one has a bad wife, it is a religious duty to divorce her.'

(ibid)

The Patriarchal system of the Bible was continued under the Rabbis according to which the husband exercised absolute authority. This accounts for the ruling which is never disputed in the Talmud, ''A woman can be divorced with or without her consent but a man can only be divorced with his consent.

(Jeb xiv. 1.)

That such a procedure necessarily placed disabilities upon the woman was recognized and certain safeguards were devised. One was the fact that it entailed the payment of the Kethubah, or marriage settlement, to which the wife was entitled under certain conditions described very meticulously in the Talmud.

CHILDREN

It is written that a childless person is accounted as dead since he failed to carry out his principal duty which devolved upon him, and his name will perish with him.

(Gen. R. lxxi. 6)

Children are builders; they not only build the future of the family but likewise of the community.

(Ber. 64a)

A fathers love is for his children, and the childrens love is for their children.

(Sot. 49a)

If one refrains from punishing a child, he will become utterly depraved but one should not chastise a child who is grown up. The proper course to adopt with children and women is to push away with the left hand and draw them near with the right hand.

(Semachoth II. 6)

A person should never tell a child that he will give him something and not keep his promise, because he thereby teaches the child to tell lies.

(Suk. 46b)

Be careful of what parents speak in front of a child for children have a tendency to repeat what they hear said at home. "The talk of the child in the street is that of his father and mother."

(ibid 56b)

EDUCATION

The main responsibility of parents was to train their children to become members of the community and, in time, to take their place as Jews. The idea was to implant them as secure links in the chain of continuity so that the religious heritage which had been bequeathed by their parents would follow unbroken. The primary requisite was the instilling into their children a knowledge of the Torah. Gods command; "Thou shalt teach them diligently unto thy children." This was included in the prayers offered every day.

The Talmud has many quotations which dwell on the education of children: "He who rears his children in the Torah is among those who enjoy the fruit in this world while the capital remains for him in the World to Come." "Whoever has a son labouring in the Torah is as though he never dies".

(Gen. R xlix 4)

One reason for the high value set upon education was the love of learning for its own sake. "If you have acquired knowledge, what do you lack? If you lack knowledge, what have you acquired?"

(Lev. R. i. 6)

"The world only exists through the breath of school children," "We may not suspend the instruction of children even for the rebuilding of the Temple" "A city in which there are no school children will suffer destruction."

(Shab. 119b)

"If one learns as a child it is like ink written on clean paper; if one learns as an old man, it is like ink written on blotted paper."

A teacher is accorded the greatest dignity and in certain matters takes precedent even over a parent, 'because the teacher brings the child into the life of the world to come whereas the parent only brings the child into this world."

(B.M. II. 11)

FILIAL PIETY

The duty of a child to honour one's parents is one of the most important obligations in the Talmud. It is one of the precepts by which a man enjoys the fruits in this world and the capital remains for him in the World to Come. (Peah I. i) 'The Bible places the honouring of parents on an equality with the honouring of God; it is said, "Honour thy father and they mother" and also "Honour the Lord with thy substance." A lesson is drawn that the duty to parents is even stricter than that which is due to God. If you are destitute and unable to fulfill a commandment of God, you can be relieved of the obligation. However, with the honoring of parents, whether you have the means or not, you must fulfil the commandment; even if it means begging from door to door.

Under most circumstances, a child must honour his father first. "Leave the honouring of your mother and honour your father, because both you and your mother have the duty of honouring him"

(Kid. 31a)

Respect for parents must be continued after they are dead. When dead, if a child has the occasion to quote him, he should not say, "Thus said my father," but "Thus said my father, my teacher, may I be an atonement for his decease."

SOCIAL LIFE

Man is a unit in the body of humanity, and that fact creates many duties for him with respect to his relationship with his fellow men. His life is not his own to do with as he pleases. His conduct affects his neighbours as their conduct affects him. "If I am not for myself, who will be for me? And being for myself, what am I? (Aboth l. 14) If an individual, however exalted his status, were to understand that the work he performs in is in service of the community, harmful class pride would be avoided. It is stated: "I am a creature of God and my neighbour is also His creature; my work is in the city and his in the field; I rise early to my work and he rises early to his. As he cannot excel in my work, so I cannot excel in his work. But perhaps you say, I do great things and he small things. It matters not whether one does much or little if only he directs his heart to Heaven."

(Ber. 17a)

Although the spirit of independence is a virtue, it must not be carried to the extent of believing that the individual can dissociate himself from his fellow men. Since life has grown more complex, man's requirements are so many that he must realize how much of his comfort he owes to the toil of others. The consciousness of the extent to which the wealthy are beholden to the men whose humble occupation contributes to their well being should have the effect of obliterating the sharp dividing lines between all classes. "If the body is taken away, of what use is the head." ,(Gen. R.C. 9) which emphasizes the truth that all classes are interdependent. Cooperation and mutual assistance are essential factors in life, as the following proverb tells. "If you will lift the load I will lift it too; but if you will not lift it too, I can not."

(B.K. 92b)

Mankind is comprised of many types of people, some praiseworthy and others the reverse. There are four different types among men. He who says, What is mine is mine and what is yours is yours; is a neutral character: He who says, What is mine is yours and what is yours is mine, is a boor: He who says, What is mine is yours and what is yours is yours, is a saint: He who says, what is yours is mine and what is mine is mine, is a wicked man."

(Aboth v. 13)

HUMILITY

'Humility is the greatest of all virtues' as it is stated by the Lord, one Rabbi declared. 'The spirit of the Lord God is upon me because the Lord hath anointed me to preach good tidings unto the meek. It is not stated "to the saints" but "to the meek", hence learn that humility is the supreme virtue. "Whoever runs after greatness, greatness flees from him; and whoever flees from greatness, greatness runs after him" (ibid)

"A name made great is a name destroyed" "Reflect upon three things and you will not come within the power of sin: know whence you came, and whither you are going and before Whom you will in the future have to give account and reckoning. Whence you came—from a putrefying drop; whither you are going—to a place of dust, worms and maggots; and before Whom you will in the future have to give account and reckoning before the Supreme King of kings.'' ''Be exceedingly lowly of spirit, since the hope of man is but the worm.''

In the Bible it states; ''Humility must accompany knowledge for meekness is one of the forty eight qualifications requisite in a student of the Torah.'' Hillel once said, ''My abasement is my exaltation and my exaltation is my abasement.

CHARITY

Morality and the quality of compassion, which play such an important part in the tenets of the Talmud, place extreme emphasis on the desire to be as considerate and charitable as possible to another human being whenever in need of assistance. Charity, as devised in the Talmud, falls into two separate schools of thought. The first is almsgiving which signifies the giving of monetary assistance to the poor and needy; and the second is the bestowing of loving acts.

Almsgiving, which is called ''Tzedakah'', also has the significance of ''Righteousness.'' The giving of alms has several implicit connotations attached to the act. In giving alms one is merely acting in a righteous manner for it is written that all mans possessions are but a loan from the Creator and by his charity he merely assures a more equitable distribution of Gods gifts to mankind. The Talmud also states that even the professional beggar who is maintained by charity must himself practice charity. No one is exempt.

An act of charity not only helps the needy but confers spiritual benefit on the donor. Most importantly, charity must be practised in secret. The true charity is when a person gives alms without knowing who receives it and the person receiving alms does not know who has donated it (B.B. 13b) For it is then that the receiver has not been put to shame.

The second aspect of charity is the bestowal of benevolent and loving acts (Gemiluth Chasadim). It is one of the three pillars upon which the social order of the world rests. In three respects is Benevolence greater then almsgiving:

Almsgiving is performed with money whereas Benevolence with money and personal service.

Almsgiving is solely for the poor; Benevolence can be offered to the rich and poor.

Almsgiving can only be given to the living; Benevolence can be displayed to the living or the dead.

Benevolence comprises all the kindly acts which alleviate the misery of the afflicted and binds together human relationships.

HONESTY

Much importance is attached in the Talmud to integrity in business dealings for it distinguishes the virtue of a moral life. It is written that "when a person is brought before the tribunal (after death) the first question put to him is, Have you been honest in your transactions?" ((Shab. 31A). The disastrous consequence of dishonesty was that 'Jerusalem was destroyed because honest men ceased therein'

(Shab. 119b).

Strict laws are laid down in the Talmud for the regulation of the business world: 'The shopkeeper must wipe his measures twice a week, his weights once a week and his scales after every weighing.'

(B.B. v. 10).

Even practices which are now regarded as lawful are denounced in the Talmud: Storing up the produce to increase the price; practicing usury, giving short measure and unsettling the market.

Not only actual fraud, but every form of deception, is forbidden. It is forbidden even to deceive a Gentile. With the righteous a "yea" is "yea" and their "nay" is "Nay." The Holy One, blessed be He, is intolerant of a person who says one thing with mouth and another in his heart.

(Pes. 113b).

FORGIVENESS

It should be the desire of all citizens to see that quarrels are quickly ended when harmony is disturbed between two individuals who have created enemity between one another. To achieve this result, two conditions are essential. The first is that the party who is in the wrong must admit his fault and beg the pardon of the person he offended. The Talmud is very firm on this point; however, there is a limit to the number of times attempts at reconciliation are made; according to one view, not more than three times.

Secondly, it is the duty of the aggrieved party to accept the apology when made to him and he should not nurse his grievance. It is written: "A man should always be as flexible as a reed and not hard like a cedar"

(Taan. 20b).

A wise recommendation, which would tend to lessen quarrels and quickly heal them when they did happen is: 'If you have done someone a little wrong, let it be in your eyes great; if you have done him much good, let it be in your eyes little; if he has done you a little good, let it be in your eyes great; if he has done you a great wrong, let it be in your eyes little'

(ARN xli).

To refuse to repair a breach and reject an overture when it is made is an attitude which is censured.

PEACE & JUSTICE

There are three things that preserve the peace and happiness of a community according to the Talmud. They are: Truth, Judgement, Peace. "It is the experience of the world that if a man takes a bundle of reeds he is unable to break them while they are tied together; but if they are taken singly, even a child can break them (Tanchuma Nitzabim I)

To avoid quarrelling is the ultimate in saintliness. A proverb declares: Happy is he who hears an insult and ignores it; a hundred evils pass him by.

There are four kinds of temper: he whom it is easy to provoke and easy to pacify, his loss disappears in his gain; he whom it is hard to provoke and hard to pacify, his gain disappears in his loss; he who it is hard to provoke and easy to pacify is a saint; he whom it is easy to provoke and hard to pacify is a wicked man. (Aboth v. 14)

The Talmud indicates that it is essential to maintain Peace for—'The sword comes into the world for the delay of justice, and for the perversion of justice,' Truth and justice are the prerequisite to Peace and its surest safeguard.

GOD

In the Bible, the existence of God is regarded as an axiomatic truth. No proofs are offered to convince the Jew that there had to be a God. The existence of God follows inevitably from the existence of the Universe.

When Pharaoh asked Moses, "Who is your God that I should hearken unto His voice?", he replied. "The Universe is filled with the might and power of God. He existed ere the world was created, and He will continue in being when the world comes to an end. He formed you and infused into you the breath of life. He stretched forth the heavens and laid the foundations of the earth. His voice hews out flames of fire, rends mountains asunder and shatters rocks, His bow is fire and His arrows flames. His spear is a torch, His shield the clouds and His sword the lightning. He fashioned mountains and hills and covered them with grass. He makes the rains and dew to descend and causes the herbage to sprout. He also forms the embryo in the mother's womb and enables it to issue forth as a living being.'' (Exod. R. v. 14)

Not only is God the Creator of the Universe, but the cosmic order is ever dependent upon His will. Creation is not an act in the past which continues automatically. The processes of Nature represent the unceasing functioning of the Divine creative power. Every hour He makes provision for all who come into the world according to their need. In His Grace He satisfies all creatures, not the good and righteous alone, but also the wicked and idolaters. (Mech. to xviii. 12;)

The sum of the matter, when everything has been heard, is this: Revere God and observe His commandments, for this is the whole (duty) of man; for God brings every work into judgement concerning even the hidden thing, whether it is good or whether it is evil. (12:13-14)

ETERNITY

Time has no meaning in relationship to God. In his capacity as Creator of the Universe He must necessarily have been the first, and He will also be the last in time, continuing in existence when all else has passed away. With man his works outlive him; but the Holy One, blessed be He, outlives His works (Meg 14a)

A parable relates: 'A human king once entered a city and all the inhabitants came out to applaud him. Their acclamation pleased him so much that he said to them: 'Tomorrow, I will provide you with a water-conduit, I will erect various kinds of baths for you', He went away to sleep, but never rose again. Where is he or his promises? But with the Holy One, blessed be He, it is otherwise, because He is a God who lives and reigns for ever' (Lev. R. xxvi. i) Shall we, then forsake Him who lives for ever and worship dead objects?

(Lev. R. vi6)

MERCY

In Talmudic literature, an eternal conflict is represented as being waged between God's justice and mercy. There is scarcely a passage which refers to His capacity as Judge which does not also allude to His attribute of compassion.

The divine appellation Elohim, translated 'God', was understood to denote His aspect of Judgement and JHVH, translated 'Lord', His aspect of mercy; and the combination of the two names in the verse is explained as follows; 'It may be likened to a king who had empty vessels. The king said, ''If I put hot water into them they will crack; if I put icy cold water into them, they will contract.'' What did the king do? He mixed the hot and cold and poured the mixture into the vessels, and they endured. Similiarly, said the Holy One, ''If I create the world only with the attribute of mercy, sins will multiple beyond all bounds; if I create it only with the attribute of justice, how can the world last? Behold, I will create it with both attributes, would that it might endure!''

(Gen. R. xxii. 15)

If compassion was the deciding cause of Creation, its victory over stern justice is the reason for the world's continuance in the face of wickedness. (Aboth v. 2.) When Abraham addressed his plea to God, 'Shall not the Judge of all the earth do justly?' the meaning of his words was: 'If You desire thc world to continue there cannot be strict justice; if You insist on strict justice, the world cannot endure'

(Gen. R. xxxix. 6)

In the same strain it is declared: 'During three hours of each day He sits and judges the whole world. When He sees that the world is deserving of being destroyed because of evil, He arises from the throne of justice and sits upon the throne of mercy.'

(A.Z. 3b)

FATHERHOOD

Throughout the teachings of the Talmudic sages, the relationship which exists between the Creator and His creatures is conceived under the image of Father and children. God is constantly addressed as, 'Father Who is in heaven' and it was considered a mark of exceptional grace on His part that this intimate relationship exists and was revealed to man.

In addressing the people of Israel, God is accredited with these words: 'All the miracles and mighty acts which I performed for you were not with the object that you should give Me a reward, but that you should honour Me like dutiful children and call Me your Father.'

(Exod. R. xxxii. 5)

There is the parable: 'A man walking by the way, having with him his child whom he allowed to proceed in front. Brigands came to kidnap the child, so the father took him from in front and placed him behind. A wolf appeared in the rear, so he took the child from behind and again placed him in front. Afterwards, brigands came in front and wolves behind, so he took the child up and carried him in his arms. The child began to be troubled by the glare of the sun, and the father spread his own garment over him. The child hungered and the father fed him; he thirsted and the father gave him to drink. So did God act toward Israel when he was delivered from Egypt.

(Mech. ad loc.; 30a)

HOLINESS

'Holiness' implies apartness from everything that defiles as well as actual perfection. Both the divine holiness and its meaning for human beings are emphasized in this passage: 'The Holy One, blessed be He, says to man, "Behold, I am pure, My abode is pure, My ministers are pure, and the soul I give you is pure. If you return it to Me in the same state of purity that I give it to you, well and good; if not, I will destroy it before you.'

(Lev. R. xviii. 1)

The term 'holiness' has a special connotation when applied to God. It has a level of perfection which is beyond the attainment of any human being. 'He is holy with all kinds of holiness, i.e. He is the perfection of holiness. It is possible to imagine that man can be as holy as God; for this reason Scripture adds, "for I am holy—my holiness is higher than any degree of holiness you can reach."

(Lev. R. xxiv. 9)

In most matters Jewish law draws a distinction between a wrong done wilfully or inadvertently, but no such allowance is made in connection with in the profanation of the Name. 'Whosoever profanes the Name of Heaven in secret will suffer the penalty for it in public; and this, whether the heavenly Name be profaned unintentionally or in wilfulness.' (Aboth iv. 5)

HEAVEN

The Hebrew term for Heaven, 'Shamayim,' was explained as the combination of 'sham' and 'mayim', (the place where there is water) or 'esh' and 'mayim', (fire and water), and from these two Heaven was made. (Chag. 12a)

The Bible contains seven different designations for heaven; therefore there must be seven heavens. They are named, respectively: Vilon, Rakia, Shechakim, Zebul, Maon, Machon and Araboth. Vilon performs no other function that that it retires in the morning and issues forth in the evening, and renews the work of Creation daily; Rakia is that in which the sun, moon, stars and planets are fixed; Shechakim is that in which the millstones are located which grind manna for the righteous; Zebul is that where the celestial Jerusalem is and the Temple in which the altar is erected; Maon is that in which are bands of ministering angels, who utter a song in the night but are silent during the day for the sake of the honor of Israel; Machon is that in which are the treasuries of snow and the treasuries of hail, the loft containing harmful dews, the lofts of the round drops (which injure plants), the chamber of the whirlwind and storm, and the cavern of noxious smoke, the doors of which are made of fire; Araboth is that in which are righteousness, judgment and charity, the storehouses of life, of peace and of blessing, the souls of the righteous, the spirits and souls which are still to be created, and the dew which the Holy One, blessed be He, will hereafter revive the dead.

LIGHT

The question is raised whether the creation of light preceded the creation of the world. Since the sun was not created until the fourth day, whence did light have its origin?

There are two answers: One Rabbi affirmed; 'The Holy One, blessed be He, enwrapped Himself in light like a garment and the brilliance of His splendour shone forth from one end of the Universe to the other.' (Gen. R. iii 4); The second Rabbi maintained that light emanated from the site of the Temple which was the center of the earth's creation (ibid). Both utterances express the same thought; that only through the medium of spiritual light which radiates from God could chaos be reduced to order.

DARKNESS

It is stated that darkness was not thought of as the absence of light but a created substance. According to legend, the elders of the South were asked, 'Which was created first—light or darkness? The majority decided in favor of darkness (Tamid 32a). Darkness issues to the world from the North. (Num. R. ii. 10)

WATER

There was a conflict of opinion between the two principle schools of thought during the first century on many questions, including the subject of whether heaven or earth was created first and whether water was to be included among the original elements.

These three things; heaven, earth and water are the three primal elements in the creation of the Universe; and He waited three days and each brought forth three species. Earth was created on the first day; waited three days and produced trees, herbage and the Garden of Eden; Heaven was created on the second day, waited three days and produced the sun, moon and the planets; Water was created on the third day, waited three days and produced the birds, fish and leviathan.

Another extreme view was that water was the ultimate origin of the elements from which the others were formed. It is written; 'The spirit of God moved upon the face of the waters' (Gen. i. 2.) He then turned it into ice, then cast forth the ice like crumbs. He then turned it into earth.

(Job. xxxvii 6)

MAN

The human being, created in the image of God, lies at the root of all Rabbinic teaching concerning man. In this context, Man is pre-eminent above all other creatures and represents the culminating point in the work of the creation. "For in the image of God made He man"

(Gen. ix. 6)

This fact gives the human being his supreme importance in the economy of the Universe. 'One man is equal to the whole of Creation' (ARN xxxi) An affront to man is an affront to God. 'Thou shalt love thy neighbour as thyself' is an important basic principle of the Torah.

(Lev. xix. 18)

The purpose of mans creation was to afford him an opportunity to glorify the Maker of the Universe. Life must therefore be interpreted and conducted in that light. To spend one's existence in toiling for material possessions is senseless, since wealth has only a transitory value. This point is illustrated by the following parable: It may be likened to a fox which found a vineyard fenced around on all sides; but there was just one small hole to crawl through. He wished to enter the vineyard but was unable to do so. What did he do? He fasted three days, until he became very thin, and then went through the aperture. He feasted there and, of course, grew fat again. When he wanted to go out, he was unable to pass through the hole. So, he fasted another three days until he had grown thin and went out. When he was outside, he turned back and, gazing upon it, cried, "O vineyard! What use have you been to me and what use are your fruits? All that is inside is beautiful and praiseworthy, but what benefit has one from you? As one enters so he comes out."

Such, too, is the world. When a person enters it his hands are clenched as though to say, "Everything is mine; I will inherit it all." When he departs from the world, his hands are open, as though to say, "I have acquired nothing from the world."

(Eccles. R.V. 14)

The thought that 'man is here today and gone tomorrow' is often mentioned to urge man to action and not to waste the fleeting years.

PRE-NATAL CHILD

To what is a child like in its mothers womb? The views of the Rabbis on the pre-natal stage and that of birth are contained in this extract? 'To a book which is folded up and laid aside.' Its hands are upon its two temples; the two arm-joints upon the two knees; the two heels upon the buttocks, and the head is set between the knees. The mouth is closed and the navel open. It is nourished from what the mother eats and from what she drinks, but it does not perform evacuation lest it kill the mother.

When it emerges into the air of the world, what was closed, opens and what was open, closes; for were it not so, the child could not survive even a single hour.

ANATOMY

The anatomy of the human being is explained as follows; 'There are two hundred and forty eight bones in the human body: thirty in the sole of the foot, six in each toe; ten in the ankle; two in the foreleg; five in the knee joint; one in the thigh; three in the hip-joint; eleven ribs; thirty in the palm of the hand, six in each finger; two in the forearm; two in the elbow; one in the arm and four in the shoulder. There are one hundred and one on each side. In addition, there are eighteen vertebrae in the spinal column; nine in the head; eight in the neck; six in the thorax and five in the genitals'

(Ohaloth I. 8)

The fantastic construction of the body excited the wonder of the Rabbis and called forth exclamations of praise. 'If a bladder is pricked by only a needle all the air in it comes out; but man is made with numerous orifices, and yet the breath in him does not come out. The face which the Holy One, blessed be He, created in the human being is in measure equal to the space between ones outstretched fingers, yet it contains several sources of water which do not intermingle. The water of the eyes is salty, of the ears greasy, of the nose evil-smelling, and of the mouth sweet. Why is the water of the eyes salty? Because when a person weeps for the dead constantly he becomes blind; but since tears are salty, he stops weeping. Why is the water of the ears greasy? Because when a person hears bad news, were he to seize it with his ears, it would entwine his heart and he would die; but because the water is greasy, he lets the news into one ear and out the other. Why is the water of the nose evil-smelling? Because when a person inhales a bad odour, were it not that the water of the nose was evil-smelling and preserved him, he would die on the spot. And why is the water of the mouth sweet? At times when man eats something which is repugnant and spews it out, were it not that his spittle was sweet, his soul would not return to him'

DEATH

According to scriptures, death was held to be the consequence of sin and a sinless person would necessarily be immortal. Death is the strongest thing which God made in the Universe, and as such cannot be overcome. 'Ten strong things have been created in the world: a mountain is strong but iron can break it; iron is strong but fire can melt it; fire is strong but water can extinguish it; water is strong but clouds can bear it; wind is strong but the body can carry it (breath); the body is strong but terror can break it; terror is strong but wine can drive it out; wine is strong but sleep can counteract it: Death, however, is stronger than them all.'

(B.B. 10 a)

The Rabbis sought to minimize the dread with which the end of life was normally contemplated. Many saying come from the Bible which emphasized that death is a normal process: 'There is a time to be born and a time to die' (Eccles. iii.2) 'From the moment of birth there is always the possibility of death. (Shab. 153a), The time of death is determined by God, and none dare anticipate his decree. Suicide was regarded with the utmost abhorrance and denounced as a sin.

Proverbs

Alls well that ends well.

****

Give every man the benefit of the doubt.

****

No man sins for another.

****

An ignorant man cannot be a pious man.

****

Don't look at the flask but what it contains.

****

Do not threaten a child. Either punish him or forgive him.

****

An old maid who marries becomes a young wife.

****

All brides and grooms have glass eyes. (Love is blind)

****

One man chops wood; the other does all the grunting.

****

A man's worst enemies can't wish on him that what he can do to himself.

****

Your health comes first, you can always hang yourself later.

****

To a wedding walk; to a divorce run.

****

Man comes into the world with an OY, and leaves with a GEVALT.

****

A man is not honest just because he has never had the chance to steal.

****

Gentiles are not used to Jewish problems

****

Not only did he break the commandment; he also stole the Bible.

****

Being poor is no disgrace—which is the only good thing that can be said about it.

****

We are born into the world with clenched fists and leave with outstretched fingers for we take nothing with us.

****

A full purse is not half as good as an empty purse is bad.

****

The best horse needs a whip; the wisest man needs advice and the best woman—a man.

****

A man who pursues KOVID; from him glory runs away.

****

All things grow with time; except grief.

****

Don't ask the doctor how the patient is, ask the patient.

****

It's not money that makes everything good, it's just that no money makes everything bad.

****

Ten lands are more easily known than one man.

****

Every man does his own thing.

****

Nine wise men don't make a minyan but ten cobblers do.

****

One mitzvah leads to another.

****

The reward for a mitzvah is another mitzvah.

****

'For instance', is not proof.

****

You are wrong if you persist long enough that you are right.

****

A slap is forgotten but a harsh word remains.

****

Many complain of their looks but none complain of their brains.

****

By three things a man gives himself away; by his tumbler, his tipping and his temper.

****

Only shlimazels believe in mazel.

****

A table is not blessed if it fed no scholars.

****

When a father helps a son, both smile; when a son helps a father, both cry.

****

A father can support ten children but ten children cannot support one father.

****

Don't worry about tomorrow; who knows what will happen today.

****

Past troubles are a pleasure to relate.

****

Withhold not good from him for whom it is due.

****

Silence is a fence around wisdom.

****

Alas for the bread that a baker calls bad.

****

The best preacher is the heart; the best teacher is time; the best book is the world, and the best friend is God.

****

Tell no secrets, for the walls have ears.

****

He who takes from a thief, smells of theft.

****

Rivalry of scholars advances wisdom.

****

Teach thy tongue to say, I do not know.

****

Truth is heavy; therefore, few care to carry it.

****

The soldier fights and the king is the hero.

****

No crown carries such royalty with it as doth humility.

****

The highest sacrifice is a broken heart.

****

The finest thing man can do is to forgive a wrong.

****

There is no skill to be compared to that which avoids temptation.

****

Against all evils, silence is the best safeguard.

****

To drink a deadly poison is better than to worry.

****

None is so poor as the man who is fearful of becoming poor.

****

The eye of a needle is not too narrow for two friends, but the entire world is not wide enough for two enemies.

****

He who seeks more than he needs hinders himself from enjoying what he has.

****

Man is only wise during the time that he searches for wisdom; when he imagines he has attained it, he is a fool.

Sayings of the Fathers

(PIRKE ABOTH) Ethics and Morals

Let thy house be a meeting place for the wise; sit amidst the dust of their feet; and drink their words with thirst. (1:4)

If I am not for myself who will be for me? And when I am only for myself what am I? And if not now, when? (1:14)

He who makes great his name (self-praise) loses it; he who adds not (knowledge) destroys it; he who does not learn deserves to die. (1:13)

Make a teacher for yourself, obtain a friend, and judge every man in the scale of merit. (1:6)

Love peace and pursue peace. Love mankind and bring people nigh to the Torah. (1:12)

Let thy house be open wide; let the poor be as members of your household; and engage not in much conversing with the women (gossip) (1:15)

Specify a time for the Torah. Say little and do much. Receive every man cheerfully. (1:15)

Be cautious with ruling power: it befriends a man for its own benefit. (2:3)

Keep far from an evil neighbor, associate not with the wicked. Expect retribution (even if late in coming) (1:7)

An evil eye, evil thinking, and hatred of people drive a man out of this world. (2:16)

Separate not thyself from society. Trust not thyself until the day of thy death. Judge not thy fellow man until thou reachest his place. The diffident cannot learn. The angry cannot teach. Not everyone who does much business is wise. In the place where there are no men (good men) try to be a man. (2:5)

Let the honor of thy fellow man be as dear to you as thine own. Do not get angry on any light pretense. (2:15)

Let the property of thy fellow man be as dear to thee as thine own.

(2:19)

He with whom the spirit of men is pleased, the spirit of God is also pleased. (3:13)

More flesh, more worms. More wealth more anxiety.
More maid servants, more promiscuity.
More men servants, more robbery.
More Torah, more life.
More counsel, more understanding. (2:8)

All my days I have grown up among the wise, and I have not found anything better than silence. Study is not the chief thing, but action. (1:17)

Reflect upon three things, and thou wilt not come to commit transgression: Know whence thou camest; know whither thou art going; and know before whom thou art about to give account and reckoning. (3:1)

Pray for the welfare of the government, since but for the fear, thereof, men would swallow each other alive. (3:2)

Pacify not thy fellow in the hour of his anger. (4:23)

There are three crowns: the crown of Torah, the crown of priesthood, and the crown of kingdom; but the crown of a good name excells them all. (4:17)

Merriment and levity accustom a man to lewdness. (3:17)

Who is wise? He who learns from every man.

Who is mighty? He who subdues his passions.

Who is rich? He who rejoices in his portion.

Who is honored? He who honors others. (4:1)

Love which depends upon something else is no more when the thing is no more. (5:19)

Folklore & Legends

When one refers to Jewish folklore and legends, it is not the modern historian, who employs analytical research, that finds the answers to questions of supernatural belief. More precisely, intense research cannot penetrate beyond obvious or peripheral acts. It is a mistake to view the findings of these modern scholars as a valid answer to the supernatural events in the Bible for ancient biblical sages and authors were not historical analysts and as such, the import of preciseness and detail did not carry the same weight or importance in their estimation.

Being a part of that environment, living among their peers and witnessing the tremendous influence of the supernatural, these ancient writers encompassed all of the myths, legends and beliefs that were so prevalent at that time, for to avoid them, would create a void, an illogical absence of biblical truth and validity.

The basic rhetoric question, looming large in this variance, is whether the statements in the Bible are factual or legendary. The Bible states, without equivocation, that in the act of revelation, God acts on His own judgement and that man is the passive recipient of those acts. The word ''revelation', itself, has been subjected to many interpretations. With the advance of time, it has been said that 'man takes the initiative while God is passive'. Others claim that 'revelation is progressive' and with these beliefs and progressive explanations we arrive at the fact that these unfolding conclusions give man a constantly revealing knowledge of God and the Universe. The differences in opinion is that modern historians tend to analyze and dissect the word 'revelation', while the ancient scholars were constant in their belief that a 'revelation' is exactly what it means, a 'revelation'. It is simply a matter of faith and one can either believe or disbelieve.

Demonology

The belief in evil spirits was so strong among the Israelites, both educated and uneducated, that it is included in the Talmud. There are many legal decisions prescribed for events that include the existence of demons. Illustrated here is an evolutionary hypothesis of a demon: ''After seven years the male hyena becomes a bat; the bat after seven years becomes a vampire; the vampire after seven years becomes a nettle; the nettle after seven years becomes a thorn; the thorn after seven years becomes a demon.'' (B.K. 16a)

Characteristics: In three respects demons resemble the ministering angels and in three are they like human beings. Like the administering angels, they have wings, they fly from one end of the world to the other and they know the future. Like humans, they eat and drink, propagate and die. They have the power of altering their appearance and can see but are invisible. (ARN XXXVII)

Although they are normally invisible, yet there are means of detecting their presence and even of seeing them. ''Who wishes to perceive their footprints should take sifted ashes and sprinkle them around his bed. In the morning, he will see something resembling the footprints of a cock.'' (Ber 6a).

The most reliable safeguard against demons was in Divine protection. Were it not for the word of the Holy One, blessed be He, which protects the human being, the harmful spirits would slay him. The Divine protection against these demons is secured by obedience to His commandments. If a man performs a religious precept, one angel is assigned to him; if he performs two precepts, two angels are assigned to him; if he performs all the precepts, many angels are assigned to him; and it is said; "For He shall give His angels charge over thee, to keep thee in all the ways." (Ps XCI 11)

The Evil Eye

In ancient days, the utter fear of the Evil Eye was universal. It is very evident in the folk-lore written in the Talmud. In the application of the Evil Eye, there are two distinct senses involved. The first trait is ENVY; and the second is GREED.

Envy and Greed create harmful feelings towards the person who excites these passions in others and give rise to a wish for a calamity to overwhelm him. This is usually concentrated and communicated by a glance of hatred; hence the phrase, 'the Evil Eye.'

That the evil glance of the eye can have harmful effects is asserted in the Talmud, particularly when attributed to the Rabbis. One tale refers to Rabbi Judah: "He saw two men throwing pieces of bread at one another, and shouted. "One might think that from this there is plenty to eat in the world." He stared at them and brought about a famine. There are many such anecdotes about the Rabbis in the Talmud and it is not surprising that the masses had a firm belief in the harm that might befall him from the Evil Eye. One statement declared; "Ninety-nine die from the Evil Eye as against one from natural causes" (B.M. 107b); Because of its widespread dread, the Rabbis had to make allowances for it in their legislation. "It is permitted to utter a charm against the Evil Eye, or a serpent or scorpion, and avert the Evil Eye on the Sabbath." (Tosifta Shab. VII 23)/

The chief protection against the Evil Eye was to avoid arousing envy and jealousy in another person. Do not brag about your good fortune or your possessions else you arouse the envy of your neighbor and he will look upon thee with the Evil Eye. Hence the expression: "Kayn ayn ahora", from the Yiddish, meaning, "May no evil overtake him.", which was quoted after every statement of self importance to offset any token of jealousy and to display humility and thankfulness.

Magic and Superstition

There was a bitter debate waged in the Talmud between the rational doctrines advocated by the Rabbis and the debased superstitions which pervaded the world of the Jews. The Bible vehemently denounced every form of magic and all attempts to pierce the veil that concealed the future. There was a constant battle by the Rabbis to offset the tide of sorcery that was so prevalent but in the end they failed and magic prevailed. To offset the practice of divination, the Talmud presented this illustration. "At the time when King Solomon wanted to build the Temple in Jerusalem, he wrote to Pharaoh. 'Send me workmen for hire, as I desire to build a temple.' The Egyptian King gathered all his astrologers and told them. "Foresee and select all the men who are destined to die this year and I will send them to Solomon." When the workmen came to King Solomon, he foresaw, by means of the Holy Spirit, that they would die in the course of a year; so he provided them with shrouds and sent them back with a letter. "Since you have no shrouds to bury your corpses, I am forwarding you a supply." (Pesikta 34a). The context here is strongly emphasized, between the Egyptian King who consulted astrology and the Hebrew King who derived his knowledge from the Holy Spirit.

The time of birth was considered to have an influence upon the fate of the individual. "One born on a Sunday will be wholly good or wholly bad, because on that day, light and darkness were created. One born on a Monday will be bad tempered because on that day the waters were divided. One born on Tuesday will be rich and lustful, because on that day the herbage was created. One born on Wednesday will be wise because on that day the luminaries were suspended in the firmament. One born on Thursday will be benevolent because on that day the fish and birds were created. One born on Friday will be active and zealous to perform the precepts. And one born on the Sabbath will die on the Sabbath because on his account, the Holy Day was profaned.

The Talmud continually refers to sorcery as a practice of the heathens to alert the Jews against its usage. They declared that Egypt was the foundation of evil. "Ten measures of sorcery descended to the world; Egypt took nine and the rest of the world one." (Kid 49b). But despite all their efforts to suppress them, a belief in magic and sorcery inundated the lives of the Jews and gained the upper hand over all classes. Many of these supernatural tales were attributed to the Rabbis of whom many extraordinary tales were told. The following story describes the difference in thinking between two Rabbis. One Rabbi said to R. Chiyya, "I saw an Arab take a sword and dissect his camel. He then made a clatter with a timbrel and it stood up.'' R. Chiyya said in reply. ''Was there after it any blood or dung? If not, it was merely an illusion.'' (ibid 67b)

R. Jochanan declared that nobody should be appointed to a seat on the Great Sanhedrin (Supreme Court) unless, among other qualifications, he had a knowledge of sorcery (ibid 17a). The commentator Rashi explains that this knowledge was necessary to put sorcerers to death who relied on their magical skill to escape the penalty inflicted upon them by the Court, and also to expose them when they tried to deceive the judge with their tricks.

As all other ancient people, the Jews interpreted an eclipse of the sun as a manifestation of divine anger. The Rabbis taught that the eclipse of the sun is a bad omen for the entire world. To what is matter like? To a human king who made a banquet for his servants and placed a lamp before them. When he became angry with them, he ordered a slave to remove the lamp and leave them in darkness. So it is with the Lord when He becomes angry with the world.

The eclipse of the moon is a bad omen for the enemies of Israel, because Israel fixes the calendar by the moon and the Gentiles by the sun. If the eclipse occurs in the East it is a bad omen for those who dwell in the East; if it occurs in the West, it is a bad omen for those who dwell in the West; if it occurs in the center of the heaven it is a bad omen for the whole world. ''On account of four things are the planets eclipsed: forgers of documents, perjurers, those who rear small animals in the land of Israel and those who cut down trees.'' (Suk. 29a)

Dreams

Dramatic importance was attached to dreams in the the Bible and it was accepted by all the Jews that visions which came to them while they were asleep would have a deep significance. To them, it was a medium by which God communicated with His people. The Talmud makes the following statement. ''Although I have hidden My face from Israel, I will communicate with him through dreams'' (Chag. 5b) Dreams were declared to be a'sixtieth part of prophecy.' (Ber. 57b)

Scriptural texts were used as a means to interpret dreams. ''Who dreams of a well will see peace as it is said, ''Isaac's servants dug in the valley and found there a well of living water (a symbol of peace). (Gen xxvi. 19)

Various objects seen in a dream had various connotations, depending on the interpretation. There are three types of dreams which indicate peace—a river, a bird, and a pot. Seeing an animal in a dream has its peculiar significance. Who dreams of an ass may hope for salvation; who dreams of a cat, a beautiful song will be composed in his honor; who dreams of a white horse, whether standing still or galloping, it is a good omen; who dreams of an elephant, will have mircales performed for him.

Other objects of dreams have the following interpretations: Who dreams of wheat will have peace; who dreams of barley, his sins will all depart; who dreams of a well laden vine, his wife will not miscarry; who dreams of pomegrantes, his business will bear fruit.

There are a list of miscellaneous dreams: Who dreams of a goat, for him the coming year will be blessed; who dreams of a citron will be honored before his Maker; who dreams of a goose, may hope for wisdom; of cocks, may hope for sons; of hens, he may hope for a beautiful rearing of his children; who dreams of eggs, his request is in suspense; if the eggs are broken then his request will be granted. To dream of any animal is a good omen with the exception of the elephant, monkey and the long-tailed ape. To dream of any kind of fruit is a good omen with the exception of unripe dates. To dream of any color is a good omen with the exception of blue.

Angelology

The Universe, as envisaged in the Talmud, is comprised of two separate classes of beings. They are the 'ELYONIM' (those above), which consists of the angels; and the 'TACHTONIM' (those below) which is the human race. Often mentioned in the Bible is the celestial court with God as the King and a host of angels as His faithful and devoted servants.

The primary motive of Rabbinic angelology was the glorification of God. As in a kings court on earth, the more magnificent the surroundings of the monarch, the more admiration extended to him. So it was for the true glorification of the Almighty. God being the King of Kings, the Sovereign of the entire universe, it was so bethought fitting and proper for Him to have an enormous amount of ministers and angels to carry out His bequests.

The angels, being worthy to stand in proximity to the Throne of Glory, necessarily were more perfect creatures than man. Nevertheless, they too were created and could never attain the perfection of God. The creation of the angels is to be found in a conversation between the Emperor Hadrian and R. Joshua b. Chananyah, the former asking: "Do you maintain that a band of ministering angels do not offer praise to God more than once and He daily creates a fresh band who sing before Him and then perish?" "That is so." "Where do they go?" "To the place where they were created." "Whence are they created?" "From the river of fire." "What is the nature of the river of fire?" "It is like the Jordan, which does not cease its flow day or night." "Whence does it originate?" "From the perspiration of Chayyos which they exude while carrying the Throne of the Holy One, blessed be He." (Gen. R. LXXVIII. 1)

As it is known, angels are delegated special duties, and one of them is appointed to function in connection with prayer. It was written: "After all the places of worship have completed their services, the angel who is appointed over prayers gathers up all the devotions which had been offered in all the places of worship, forms them into crowns and sets them upon the Head of the Holy One, blessed be He." (Exod. R. XXI. 4)

At the head of all the angels are four archangels, corresponding to the four divisions of the army of Israel as described in Numbers ii. "As the Holy One, blessed be He, created four winds (directions) and four banners (the Israeli army), so also did He make four angels to surround his Throne . . . Michael, Gabriel, Uriel and Raphael. Michael is on its right, corresponding to the tribe of Reuben; Uriel on its left, corresponding to the tribe of Dan; Gabriel in front, corresponding to the tribe of Judah as well as Moses; and Raphael in the rear, corresponding to the tribe of Ephraim, in the West." (Num. R. II 10). Michael and Gabriel are the most prominent of all the angels. They were the two groomsmen at Adam's marriage at which God Himself officiated. (Gen. R. VIII. 13). They also assisted at the burial of Moses (Deut. 10). Each nation has its guardian angel; Michael being the guardian angel of Israel. He acts as the counsel for Israel's defense when the wicked angel Samael brings charges against them before God (ibid. XVIII. 5). He brought news to Sarah that she would give birth to a son and he was the instructor of Moses. In the history of Israel, he often proved himself a reliable protector. When

Haman plotted to destroy the Jews in Persia, Michael defended them in heaven. (Esth. R. VII 12).

In addition to the administering angels, there is a host of evil angels designated by the Satan, with their chief who is called Samael. Satan is the personification of wickedness and evil, among them being the Angel of Death. Satan performs three functions. He seduces men, he accuses them before God, and he inflicts the punishment of death (B.B. 16a). It is related that when Israel left Egypt, the evil angel, Samael, stood before God to accuse them. He said, "Sovereign of the Universe, up to now they have been worshippers of idols, and now wouldst Thou divide the sea for them?"

(Exod. R. XXI. 7)

The principal antidote to the allurements of Satan and the danger of the Angel of Death is the Torah. It was said: When Israel stood by Mount Sinai and proposed the statement, "All that the Lord hath spoken will we do and hear", the Holy One, blessed be He, summoned the Angel of Death and said to him, "Although I have appointed you a world ruler over human beings, you have no concern with this people because they are My children."

(Lev. R. XVIII. 3)

JUDAIC LITERATURE

JUDAIC LITERATURE

Judaic culture, throughout the long history of the Jews, preserved and protected its precious heritage through the 'written' word, painstakingly and methodically recorded by its scholars and sages, many of whom dedicated their lives to scholarship so that the Jewish monotheistic civilization could remain intact; regardless of the fact that they were driven like outcasts from country to country and dispersed among nations, as the unwanted.

Their history is unparalleled among the peoples of the world; microscopic in numbers, negligible in power, scorned by nations yet uncontested in valor, boldness and achievement.

Israel's most artistic achievement, the 'written' word, encompasses thousands of poems, psalms, proverbs, rules of life, studies of religion, folklore, mysticism, ethical writings, etc. This is the literature of the Jewish caravan. Handed down from generation to generation, through the centuries, protected with an almost fanatical reverence by its heirs, this priceless and sacred body of literature will remain, until the end of time, the heart and soul of the Jewish people.

The Jewish caravan through history has been traveling throughout the world for thousands of years. A myriad of events encompasses their lives, traversing the entire gamut of human emotions and experiences. With all their trials and tribulations, never once have they deviated from the basic belief that motivated their purpose of living, and this consciousness was the neverending, underlying source of strength that enabled them to survive. Recorded by their historians; preserved and sustained by a succession of miracles, this peerless display of literary genius is worthy of deep study and analysis.

Jewish literature, since its origin, can be assorted into nine distinct, separate divisions:

1. THE BIBLICAL DIVISION: 1800 B.C.E. to 1300 B.C.E.
2. FROM MOSES TO JUDAH: 1300 B.C.E. to 586 B.C.E.
3. POST BIBLICAL DIVISION: 586 B.C.E. to 70 C.E.

4. TALMUDIC DIVISION: 70 C.E. to 500 C.E.
5. POST TALMUDIC DIVISION: 500 C.E. to 1040 C.E.
6. THE GOLDEN AGE: 1040 C.E. to 1499 C.E.
7. LITURGICAL POETRY: 1200 C.E.
8. THE EUROPEAN DIVISION: 900 C.E. to 1500 C.E.
9. THE MODERN AGE 1500: C.E. to 1900 C.E.

THE BIBLICAL AGE of Jewish history, from the 18th to the 13th century, B.C.E., includes the Wilderness Period, the Patriarchal Age and the Exodus. It contains recorded history of the Book of Genesis where we find stories of the Patriarchs as far back as the first man, Adam (and the Garden of Eden); then the generations that follow through to Noah, then to Abraham and to Joseph. Judaic history begins with Abraham, the first man to proclaim his belief in One God. For it was to Abraham that God said unto him: ''I am God Almighty; walk before me, and be thou whole hearted. And I will make My covenant between Me and thee, and will multiply thee accordingly . . . And I will establish My covenant between Me and thee and thy seed after thee throughout their generations for an everlasting covenant; to be God unto thee and to thy seed after thee . . . and ye shall be circumcised in the flesh of your foreskin; and it shall be a token of a covenant betwixt Me and you.'' (Gen. 17:1-11)

Genesis, as a narration of historical tales, was handed down from generation to generation, from father to son, specifically for lessons of morality. Its deep ethical value underlines, even at that early age, the search for a meaning of life. It constantly stresses the radical difference between a virtuous and sinful existence and is quick to reward the godly and punish the evil doer. Every tale contains a moral and as each unfolds in a continuous progression of religious precepts, we discover the path of the Jewish caravan as it winds its way over the course of history.

The Moses to Judah Division describes an era unsurpassed in literature for sheer miraculous occurrences. It cites, in glowing terms, the Divine Revelation, through which the destiny of the entire civilization of the Israelites was transformed into a closely integrated unit as God's chosen people. We are aware of the Moses 'experience'; the story of Moses receiving the Ten Commandments on Mount Sinai, when he asked, "who God is?". The answer through the revelation states: that God is the Being One, the "I" as "Being" and the "Being" as "I", that God is the eternal "I AM", the eternal unity of "I" and "Being". In this setting, Moses said unto God: "Behold, when I come unto the children of Israel, and shall say unto them: the God of your fathers hath sent me unto you; and they shall say unto me: What is His name? What shall I say unto them? And God replied: "I AM THAT I AM"; and He said: Thus shall you say unto the children of Israel: "I AM hath sent me unto you." (EX. 3:13-14)

And Moses complied with the word of the Lord. In the third month after the children of Israel were gone forth out of the land of Egypt, on that very day came they into the wilderness of Sinai. There Israel encamped before the mount. And Moses went up unto God, and He-Who-Is called unto him out of the mountain, saying: "Thus shalt thou say to the house of Jacob, and tell the children of Israel: Ye have seen what I did unto the Egyptians, and how I bore you on eagles wings, and brought you unto Myself. Now therefore, if ye will hearken unto My voice indeed, and keep My covenant, then ye shall be Mine own treasure from among all peoples; for all the earth is Mine; and ye shall be unto Me a kingdom of priests, and a holy nation. These are the words which thou shall speak unto the children of Israel." And Moses came and called for the elders of the people and set before them all these words which He-Who-Is commanded him. And all the people answered together, and said: "All that He-Who-Is hath spoken we will do." And Moses reported the words of the people unto Him-Who-Is. (Exodus 19: I-8)

In the deepest and most religious significance, the exodus from Egypt was the beginning of the history of the Jewish existence. It denoted a significant point; that the Israelites did not just march out of Egypt on their own, the Eternal One led them out, and they had become His chosen people. The Exodus was also the covenant that God requested: the covenant of the Ten Commandments which begins with: "I am He-Who-Is thy God, who brought thee out of the land of Egypt, out of the house of bondage" (Ex. 20:2). It is with this command that future generations would celebrate this deliverance in the Passover Seders, where Jews eternally would state "Generation after generation shall consider itself as though it had gone forth from Egypt."

The Post Biblical segment of Jewish history, from the destruction of the Temple in 586 B.C.E. to 70 C.E., approximately 500 years of radical upheaval in the complex world of the Jewish caravan, was known as the era of the Prophets. They were men, deemed to be close to God, who through special revelations, were able to predict the future. The prominence of these men of vision paralleled the rise and fall of powerful nations—Babylonia, Moab, Assyria, Persia and Egypt—and their prophecies elevated them to positions of leadership. Claiming to utter God's words, interpreting His commands, offering moral and ethical precepts, they became the undisputed leaders of the Jews, who adhered to their admonitions to the letter.

After the death of Moses, the greatest prophet, whose wisdom and divinations forged the quarreling tribes back into a united nation was Samuel. He was a sage and a prophet, a brilliant writer of dictum and poetry, whose oratory made him the leader of the Jews. In the Book of Samuel, we find his bitter condemnation of the monarchy system, with a forceful denunciation of the rule of kings. He created a declaration of principles urging pure monotheism: ''This is the way of the king who will reign over you. Your sons he will take, appoint them for his horsemen, and they will run before his chariots. He will designate to his benefit, officers over thousands, and officers over fifties, to plow and harvest his harvests, and make his weapons and his chariot parts. Your daughters he will take for spice mixers, butchers and bakers. He will confiscate your fields, your vineyards and olive groves, and give them to his own servants . . . if you cry out some day against the king you yourself have chosen, God will not answer you on that day. (SAM. 8: 11-18)

Still the people insisted on a king which Samuel reported to God—and He instructed him to permit them this wish. It was at a time when a monarchy was considered as a catastrophe to Israel. In this segment of history, we find the return of the Jews to Zion, the restoration of the Second Temple, the surrender of Judah to Alexander the Great, the struggle of the Maccabees, the spread of Hellenism, the war against Rome, and the destruction of the Second Temple.

The Talmudic Age, considered to be the greatest period of achievement in literary creativity, was the culmination of the recordation of the spiritual, intellectual and ethical life of Jewish existence. Continuing for over 400 years, from the year 70 C.E. to 500 C.E., a massive compendium of literature was created in which almost 1000 years of Jewish life was defined, analyzed, debated, discussed and expounded, dating back to the Babylonian era of Jewish captivity. During this time period, the Talmud was assembled. Acknowledged as perhaps the most creative literary accomplishment of all time, the Talmud was the primary factor, during many years of Jewish tribulation, that was responsible for their survival. It is a massive collection of books containing a comprehensive analysis of the Universe in its entirety,—before Creation, during existence and after death—in which is specifically detailed the monumental conglomeration of Jewish religious experience and wisdom. The heart of the Talmud contains a mass of debates, monologues, dialogues, conclusions, suppositions and commentaries of sages, scholars, teachers and rabbis who interpreted the Torah for the teaching of law, liturgy and tradition.

The Talmud is composed of two divisions: the Mishna and the Gemara; sixty three tractates and over two and a half million words. The average cycle of study, to competently read the Talmud is seven years. The original purpose for the creation of the Talmud was the rabbis fear that the Oral Law would be forgotten in Israel. With worry over its continuity, much of that which was 'oral' was written down, but the worry continued. What the teacher had spoken was gradually recorded; thus the Oral Law, in two different time periods and in two different locations—Babylonia and Jerusalem—became two sets of books, although still a single book. The two bodies of work, the first called the Mishna (teaching) and the second called the Gemara (the continuing), when completed were called the Talmud (the learning).

The two directions of the Talmud continued throughout in a parallel vein. Both were literary works of tremendous depth and breadth and preserved the unity relationship as derived from the Bible and the Talmud. The dealing of Law, on one hand, and the treatment of the poetical, mystical and philosophical on the other hand, were related in basic meaning. This paradoxical relationship between the schools emphasized the individual and special character of the people. It is only when a man exists in both the 'Legal' sense as well as in the philosophical and poetic 'sense', can that what is most personal in his life unfold.

The Post Talmudic era, from the 6th Century C.E. to the middle of the 11th Century C.E. was the time when the Geonim flourished to their greatest degree. The Geonim, a group of remarkable men who devoted their lives to the completion of the Babylonian Talmud, produced the accepted standards for Judaic wisdom and literature. Entirely through their efforts, the Talmud became the revered Law Book of the Jews, Responsa Literature was highly developed, liturgical poetry was injected into prayer books and mysticism arose to its heights. This tremendous achievement was accomplished amidst great turmoil. Under Persian rule, Jewish persecution was being practised and the great Talmudic institutions were in a precarious state. Only the defeat of the Persians by Islam transformed the situation. Omar, the Caliph of the Arabs, grateful for Jewish assistance in his conquest, granted special privileges to the Jewish people. All restrictions against Judaism were abolished and the two Talmudic academies were reopened.

At this time, the Geonim flourished. The two academies at Sura and Pumbeditha, once again operating in full bloom, began dispersing legal decisions to Jews around the world. At the head of the Jewish community was the Exilarch, with the Gaon of Sura regarded as the supreme religious leader. One eyewitness account of installation of an Exilarch follows:

"The first homage is paid on Thursday in the synagogue, which is announced by the blowing of trumpets and everone, according to his means, sending presents. The leaders of the community and the wealthy send handsome garments, jewelry, gold and silver vessels. On Thursday and Friday, the Exilarch gives great banquets. On the morning of the Sabbath, the nobles of the community call for him and accompany him to the synagogue. Here a wooden platform, covered entirely with costly cloth, has been erected, under which a picked choir of sweet voiced youths, well versed in the liturgy, has been placed. This choir responds to the leader in prayer, who begins the service with Boruch she-mar. After the morning prayer, the Exilarch, who until now has been standing in a covered place, appears; the entire congregation rises and remains standing until he has taken his place on the platform, and the two Geonim, the one from Sura preceding, have taken seats to his right and left, each making an obeisance.

A costly canopy has been erected over the seat of the Exilarch. Then the leader in prayer steps in front of the platform and, in a low voice audible only to those close by, and accompanied by the 'Amen' of the choir, addresses the Exilarch with a benediction prepared long beforehand. Then the Exilarch delivers a sermon on the text of the week, or commissions the Gaon of Sura to do so. After the discourse, the leader in prayer recites the Kaddish, and when he reaches the words, "during your life and your days," he adds the words, "and during the life of our prince, the Exilarch." After the Kaddish, he blesses the Exilarch, the two heads of the schools, and the several provinces that contribute to the support of the academies, as well as the individuals who have been of special service in this direction. Then the Torah is read. When the Kohen and Levi have finished reading, the leader in prayer carries the Torah scroll to the Exilarch, the entire congregation rising; the Exilarch takes the scroll in his hands and reads it while standing. The two heads of the schools also rise, and the Gaon of Sura recites the Targum (translation) to the passage read by the Exilarch. When the reading of the Torah is completed, a blessing is pronounced by the Exilarch.

The Golden Age of Jewish literature existed for over 400 years, from the middle of the 11th Century C.E. to the latter part of the 15th Century C.E., when the centers of learning shifted from the Middle East to Spain. This was the Sephardic division of the Jewish diaspora, whose religious philosophy and poetry reached heights never before attained. Here the mystic philosophy of Caballah was developed and flourished along with many books on morals and ethics.

Most notable was the work of one man from Toledo. He was Joseph Caro who wrote the SHULCHAN ARUCH, a new concept for valid law, Torah and Oral Teaching. With almost mystical power, through the years, he transformed that which had value to his people into that which presented that valid law, simply and visibly, so that everyone could find and possess what they needed and wanted. Joseph Caro had in mind the many who wanted a simple way to adhere faithfully to the Torah. To make it understandable, he named the four parts of his work; the "WAY", the "HELP", the "LAW", and the "KNOWLEDGE", each accessible to those who were seeking enlightenment. This work, the SHULCHAN ARUCH (the prepared table) was written with humility in mind, and piety and humility was the reaction in those who read it.

The Caballah, a philosophy in mysticism, found its greatest acceptance during times of persecution and massacre, for within its concepts, the Jews were able to seek relief from their misery by drifting into imaginary worlds through its spells and magic rites. It contained unusual interpretations of sacred writings and called for redemption and faith in the coming of the Messiah. In the Caballah they found the will and desire to live in the midst of despair. They found a refuge outside of the world of reality; an imaginary existence free from torture and abuse. In this era Jewish literature, of all types, blossomed; morality, poetry, philosophy, ethics, mysticism and exegesis. The four centuries, ending in 1492 when the Jews were expelled from Spain, found the Sephardic culture to be one of the finest chapters in the Jewish caravan.

LITURGICAL POETRY.

During the 13th Century, many writers rose to prominence as the importance of liturgical poetry grew enormously. Entered into the prayer books, they consisted of poems in the form of prayers of repentance and supplications to God. Through the centuries, poets, many of them anonymous, submitted thousands of poems in which many were included in prayer books covering the entire sphere of Jewish liturgy. They were also assembled in special anthologies to be studied at leisure. Containing these special poems are the following: the Siddur, the Chumash, the Mahzor, the Selihot, the Haggadah, and the Zemirot. On the High Holidays, many of these liturgical poems were set to music which were chanted by the Chazzans.

Hymn of Weeping: This hymn is part of the Ne'ilah service on the Day of Atonement.

Lord, I remember, and am sore amazed
To see the cities stand in haughty state,
And God's own city to the low grave razed
Yet in all time we look to Thee and wait.

Spirit of mercy! Rise in the night! Awake
Plead to thy Master in our mournful plaint,
And crave compassion for thy people's sake
Each head is weary, and each heart is faint.

I rest upon my pillars—love and grace,
Upon the flood of ever-flowing tears;
I pour out prayer before His searching face,
And through the father's merit lull my fears.

O Thou Who hearest weeping, healest woe!
Our tears within Thy vase of crystal store;
Save us; and all Thy dread decrees forego,
For unto Thee our days turn evermore.

Highest Divinity. From the Rosh Hashanah prayers.

Highest divinity,
Throned in the firmament,
Potentate paramount,
Hand superdominant,
Lord of infinity!

Highest divinity,
Great in performing all,
Sure in decreeing all,
Stern in unbaring all,
Lord of infinity!

Highest divinity,
Speaking in holiness,
Vestured in righteousness,
Heedful of suppliants,
Lord of infinity!

Highest divinity,
Time is His dwelling place,
Goodness e'erlastingly

Spanning the firmament,
Lord of infinity!

Highest divinity,
King of the universe,
Piercer of mysteries,
Causing the dumb to speak,
Lord of infinity!

Highest divinity,
Propping, sustaining all,
Slaying, surviving all,
Seeing, unseen of all,
Lord of infinity!

Highest divinity,
Crowned with omnipotence,
Right hand victorious,
Saviour and shelterer,
Lord of infinity!

Highest divinity,
Sleeping nor slumbering,
Center of restfulness,
Awed angels chanting His praise,
Lord of infinity!

Lowly humanity,
Doomed to go down to death,
Grave-ward and lower still,
Vain is man's heritage,
Sovran of Vanity!

Lowly humanity,
Sleep is his daily end,
Deep sleep his final goal.
Darkness flows over him,
Sovran of Vanity!

Highest divinity,
Dynast of endlessness,
Timeless resplendency,
Worshipped eternally,
Lord of Infinity!

The European Division of Jewish history must be regarded as one of the darkest. Continuing almost to the end of the 18th Century, this blight on the conscience of man cannot erase the torture and degradation perpetrated against the Jews in almost every country in Europe except Holland. France, Germany and England were the worst transgressors. There, considering the Jews the enemies of God and humanity, the Church dignitaries, lodging charges of infamy and murder, provoked mass recriminations against them thereby inciting the persecution of thousands of men, women and children. In every case, government authorities cooperated with the church officials in wiping out the enemies of society—the helpless Jews.

Despite these adverse conditions, scholars, poets, teachers, moralists and visionaries continued to write and study while these horrible pogroms were going on. They could still summon the patience, strength and endurance to create a visionary ideal world where they could find peace and equality. Such was the destiny of the Jews as they continued to seek the impregnable answer to the mysterious workings of their God.

The Modern Age in the Jewish caravan, since the 16th Century, has been involved in periods of transition, transformation, enlightenment and internal crises. Traditional orthodox dogmas and tenets were transplanted by new movements and philosophies. Many new ideas flourished such as the Enlightenment movement, or the Haskala, which attempted to assimilate Jewish tradition with that of the outside world. Secondly, there arose the Hasidic movement which advocated deep piety and conviction. Another was the Maskilim in Berlin which under the tutelage of Moses Mendelssohn, urged complete adoption of modern assimilation in Jewish liturgy to bring about full acceptance and emancipation.

With all these radical measures being exerted on the Jews from within, there still remained the deep rooted animosity and discrimination from the outside world. Confined to ghettos, the Jews lived under rigid restrictions, politically immobile and economically thwarted. Regarded as outsiders and aliens, they were completely subjugated by the political parties in power.

Suddenly, a thesis by one man, Asher Ginsberg, whose vision was exemplified in his writing, gradually brought about the Zionist movement, with the accent on National Regeneration which they hoped would cope with the continuous discrimination. Originating with a small nucleus of pioneers in Palestine, it gradually blossomed into a confirmed movement with writers, teachers, educators and pioneers settling in Israel. It was at this time that Zionism was determined to be the final end and solution against Jewish persecution. During this time, and culminating in 1948, two of the greatest Jewish historical events took place. Hebrew was transformed into a modern living language, and Israel, the homeland for the Jews, became an independent and sovereign nation.

At the turn of the 19th Century, with Zionism becoming almost an obsession among the Jews in the diaspora and with a center of Hebrew literature being established in Palestine, waves of immigrants began to arrive on its shores. Called the ''Aliyah'' (Hebrew for 'going up'), thousands of writers, dreamers, pioneers, educators and political leaders arrived in Israel, determined to bring about a national rebirth of Jewish culture and tradition. With the Hebrew language as a background, a Hebrew educational system was established. Hebrew newspapers and periodicals were inaugurated and Hebrew literature, displaying its tremendous potential, finally found an outlet for survival.

MOSES MENDELSSOHN.

Moses Mendelssohn, a German Jew, born in the small town of Dessau in 1729, is credited with having initiated the thought of establishing Zionism as the only escape from the thousands of years of continuous persecution against the Jews. Through his innovative writings, Mendelssohn prophesized change; changes in the lives of the Jews never before dreamed of, let alone considered to be even remotely possible. His entire life became a symbol of emancipation, prophecies that would forever remove the walls of the ghettos. In his books and essays, Mendelssohn, at that time one of the most respected men in Germany, pleaded for his fellow Jews in the name of progress and justice. He asked for complete emancipation and integration into German life and culture and to prove his sincerity, he translated the Book of Genesis into the German language. The Berlin Academy of Sciences submitted his name as a member, a heretofore unheard of distinction for a Jew from the ghetto.

ASHER GINSBERG.

Born in the Ukraine during the reign of the czars, Asher Ginsberg, using the pen name of Ahad Ha-am, was considered one of the foremost thinkers and visionaries of the 19th Century. Writing numerous essays, which he kept hidden for fear of persecution, he was finally persuaded to submit them to Ha Melitz, the oldest Jewish publishing house in Russia.

Continuing to publish additional essays as a necessity for Jewish survival, he stressed the need for a national rehabilitation for all Jews in their ancient homeland. He emphasized that the return of the Jewish people to Palestine was a historic prerequisite, not just to combat anti-Semitism but to reinstitute the very fabric of Jewish life and culture. In time, he awakened the Jewish consciousness and the movement grew. His vision and deep insight won for him thousands of followers. Following are a few of his basic concepts:

———When a land is destroyed but the people are alive there comes Ezra or Nehemiah and rebuilds it. When a people is destroyed—who can come to help it?

———Any new idea, whether religious or moral, cannot be sustained in life unless there be a group of zealots willing and ready to dedicate their lives to it.

———The two basic elements in man, the material and the spiritual, can live together, when the spiritual part uplifts the material. Instead of the spirit's descending to the level of the material, the material should ascend to the level of the spirit.

———Immorality places the "I" first and foremost, leaving nothing for the next fellow. True justice places the "I" and the "thou" upon an equal basis.

JACOB COHEN

One of the most noted poets in Israel who died in 1960. The following poem is one of his more notable accomplishments:

The Eternal Jew.

A wandering Jew once met a man
With blood spattered clothes and an axe in his hand.
The Jew whispered ''God'' as he started aback.
The man, too, was startled, his visage grew black.
''Why are you wandering here, Jew?'' he cried.
The Jew said his word: ''God will always abide.''
The man cried in fury: ''What whisper you there?''
The Jew made reply: ''God is judge, I declare.''
He swung up his axe, smote the Jew on his head,
The falling Jew cried: ''God avenges the dead.''
Now when that same man to the seashore did go,
The Jew he beheld as he walked to and fro.
Astonished he cried: ''What, are you still alive?''
The Jew made his answer: ''In the Lord I do thrive.''
He seized on the Jew, flung him into the sea.
The Jew sank, and never a word uttered he.
Now when that same man went forth on the chase,
He found the Jew meeting him, face unto face,
He raged and he shouted: ''Alive yet are you?''
''With the aid of the Lord,'' responded the Jew.
He took him, a bullet right through him he shot,
The Jew fell; and falling, he called on his God.
That night the man dreamt, And what did he dream?
Before him the Jew stood, Alive he did seem.
He stared at him piercingly, and murmured once more;
''God sees what befalls, He is judge as of yore.''
He leapt up to clutch him, he brandished his fist,
The Jew rose in air, and he vanished in mist.
In the morning he heard him knock at his door.
In the evening he saw him still striding before.
He returned in his dreams. He returns to this day.
He troubles him dreaming and waking, they say.
What power is hid in him? What secret at call?
He has ''God'' on his lips in his rise and his fall.

MICAH JOSEPH LEBENSOHN

One of the greatest poets of the Haskala period, Micah Joseph Lebensohn lived for only twenty four years after suffering from tuberculosis. Haunted by his fear of death, his deep feelings were expressed in his poetry.

Wine.

Like an arrow shot
To Death from Birth:
Such is your lot,
Your day upon earth.
Each moment is
A graveyard board
For moments that
Come afterward.
Like brethren act:
Beneath the sky
They made their pact.
So Void and Vita
Destroy, create;
Now swallow up,
Regurgitate,
The past is past;
The future lies
Still overcast;
The present flies,
Who shall rejoice
Us, scatter woe,
Make sweet our life
And bring Death low!
My hearties, wine!
Wine scatters woe,
Makes glad the life,
And brings Death low!

THE PHILOSOPHY OF MAIMONIDES

Rules for Physical Health:

A man should never eat except when he is hungry, nor drink except when he is thirsty; and he should not delay the performance of the act of purgation. . . He should not keep on eating until his stomach is filled, but leave about a fourth part of his appetite unsatisfied. He is not to drink water during a meal, but only a little water mixed with wine. When the food begins to digest, he may drink as much as is proper; much water, however, should not be drunk even when the food is digesting. He should not eat until he is completely assured that he has no need of performing his natural functions. He should not eat until he has walked before the meal a sufficient distance for the body to begin feeling warm, or do some kind of work, ot take some other exercise. The general rule is, he should exercise his body and tire it daily in the morning, until it begins to feel warm, rest a little until he is refreshed, and then have his meal. To take a hot bath after exercise is a good thing, but then he should wait a little before eating.

One should always remain seated while eating, or recline on one's left side. One should not walk, ride, undergo exertion, or induce perspiration. One should not walk about until the food becomes digested. Whoever walks about, or exerts himself, immediately after a meal brings on himself serious illnesses.

Day and night being twenty four hours, it is enough for a person to sleep a third part thereof, viz., eight hours. These hours should be toward the end of the night, so that there are eight hours from the beginning of his sleep to sunrise, and he consequently gets up from his bed before the sun rises. It is not proper to sleep lying on one's face or back, but on the side—at the beginning of the night on the left, and at the end of the night on the right side. He should not retire to sleep immediately after a meal, but wait about three or four hours. He should also not sleep during the day.

Things which are laxative, e.g., grapes, figs, mulberries, pears, melons and all kinds of cucumbers and gurkins, one may eat as appetizers, not partaking of them together with the food, but waiting a little while and then eating his meal. Costive things, such as pomegranates, quinces, apples and Paradise pears, he may eat immediately after a meal, but should not overindulge in them.

If one wish to partake of poultry and meat at the same meal one should eat the eggs first; lamb and beef, he should give precedence to the former. A person should always partake of the lighter food first and the heavier later.

During the summer he should eat cooling things and not take too much spice; but he may use vinegar. During the winter he should eat warmth giving food, use much spice, and take a little mustard and asafoetida. He should follow these directions in cold countries and hot, in each place according to the local conditions.

There are foods which are exceedingly harmful and a person should never eat them; e.g. large, salted and stale fish, salted stale cheese, mushrooms and all fungi, stale salted meat, wine fresh from the press, and cooked food which has been standing until its flavor has gone. Likewise any food which is malodorous and excessively bitter to the body like a deadly poison. There are, on the other hand, foods which are injurious, though not to the same extent as the former; therefore it is right that a person should indulge in them sparingly and at rare intervals. He should not accustom himself to the use of them as food, or frequently eat them with his food. In this category one large fish, cheese, milk which has stood more than twenty four hours from the time of milking, meat of big bulls and rams, beans, lentils, chick-peas, barley bread, unleavened bread, cabbage, leek, onions, garlic, mustard, and radishes. All these are harmful foods of which one should eat but very little indeed, and only in winter. In summer one ought not eat them at all. Beans and lentils by themselves should not be eaten in summer or winter; gourds, however, may be eaten in summer.

There are some foods which are injurious, though not to the extent of the above mentioned; e.g., water-fowl, small pigeons, dates, bread toasted in oil or kneaded in oil, fine flour which has been so thoroughly sifted as to leave not even a particle of bran, brine and pickle. One should not overindulge in them; and the man who is wise, curbs his desire and is not carried away by his appetite, abstaining from them altogether unless he requires them as medicine.

A person should avoid unripe fruits, for they are like swords to the body. Similarly carobs are always harmful; likewise all sour fruits are bad and should be eaten only in small quantities in summer and in hot climates. Figs, grapes, and almonds are always beneficial, whether fresh or dried. One may eat of them as much as one needs, but not to excess, even though they were more beneficial than all other fruits of trees.

Honey and wine are bad for the young, but good for adults, especially in winter. One need eat in summer two-thirds of what one eats in winter.

There is another rule stated in connection with the healthy condition of the body: As long as a person works and takes plenty of exercise, does not eat in excess, and keeps his bowels regulated, no ailment will befall him and his strength keeps developing, even if he eat unwholesome food. But whoever sits idle and does no work, or retards the natural functions, or is of a costive nature, even though he eats wholesome food and take care of himself according to medical regulations, he will suffer all his life, and his strength will diminish. Excessive eating is to the body of a man like deadly poison, and is the root of all diseases. Most illnesses which befall men arise either from bad food, or from immoderate indulgence in food, even of the wholesome kind. . .

The rule about the bath is this: A man ought to enter the bathhouse each week, but he should not enter it immediately after a meal, nor when he is hungry, but when the food begins to digest. He should bathe the whole of his body in hot water, but not of a heat to scald the body. The head only is to be washed in very hot water. After that he should bathe in lukewarm water, then in water still cooler, until he finally bathes in cold water. The head, however, should not be immersed in lukewarm or cold water. One should not bathe during winter in cold water, nor take the bath until the whole body is in a state of perspiration and has been shampooed. He should not stay long in the bath, but as soon as his body perspires and has been shampooed, he should take a shower and go out. . . .

When he leaves the bath, he should dress and cover his head in the outer room, so as not to catch cold; even in summer he must be careful. After leaving the bath, he should wait a while until his body has relaxed, and the heat has departed; then he may take a meal. If he can sleep a little on leaving the bath, before his meal, this is very beneficial. He should not drink cold water when he comes out of the bath, much less drink it while in the bath; but if he is thirsty on leaving the bath and cannot resist drinking, he should mix the water with wine or honey, and drink. If he anoint himself with oil in the bath, during winter after he has had a showerbath, it is beneficial.

A person should not accustom himself to constant blood-letting; he should only be cupped in a case of emergency. He should not undergo it either in summer or winter, but a little during the spring, and a little in autumn time. After fifty years of age one should never submit to blood letting. Nor should a person be cupped and enter the bath on the same day, or go on a journey; nor should he be cupped on the day he returns from a journey. . . .

Whoever conducts himself according to the rules we have prescribed, I guarantee that he will not be afflicted with illness all his days until he reaches advanced age and dies. He will not need a physician, but will always enjoy good health, unless he was physically weak from birth, or gave way to evil habits from early youth, or some plague or drought befall the world.

Yad, Deot IV, 1-18,20

WISDOM FROM THE ZOHAR

The Zohar (Radiance) is a commentary of the Pentateuch which was the sacred textbook of the Jewish mystics of the Middle Ages. It was compiled by a 13th Century Spanish Caballist named Moses de Leon and is an interpretation of the Scriptures in purely theosophical terms. Many of its ideas were drawn from Indian literature, coming directly from the Hindu mystics:

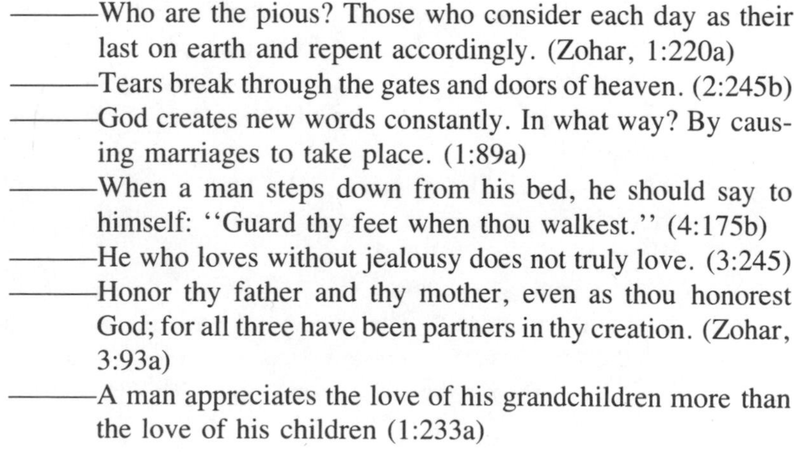

———Who are the pious? Those who consider each day as their last on earth and repent accordingly. (Zohar, 1:220a)

———Tears break through the gates and doors of heaven. (2:245b)

———God creates new words constantly. In what way? By causing marriages to take place. (1:89a)

———When a man steps down from his bed, he should say to himself: "Guard thy feet when thou walkest." (4:175b)

———He who loves without jealousy does not truly love. (3:245)

———Honor thy father and thy mother, even as thou honorest God; for all three have been partners in thy creation. (Zohar, 3:93a)

———A man appreciates the love of his grandchildren more than the love of his children (1:233a)

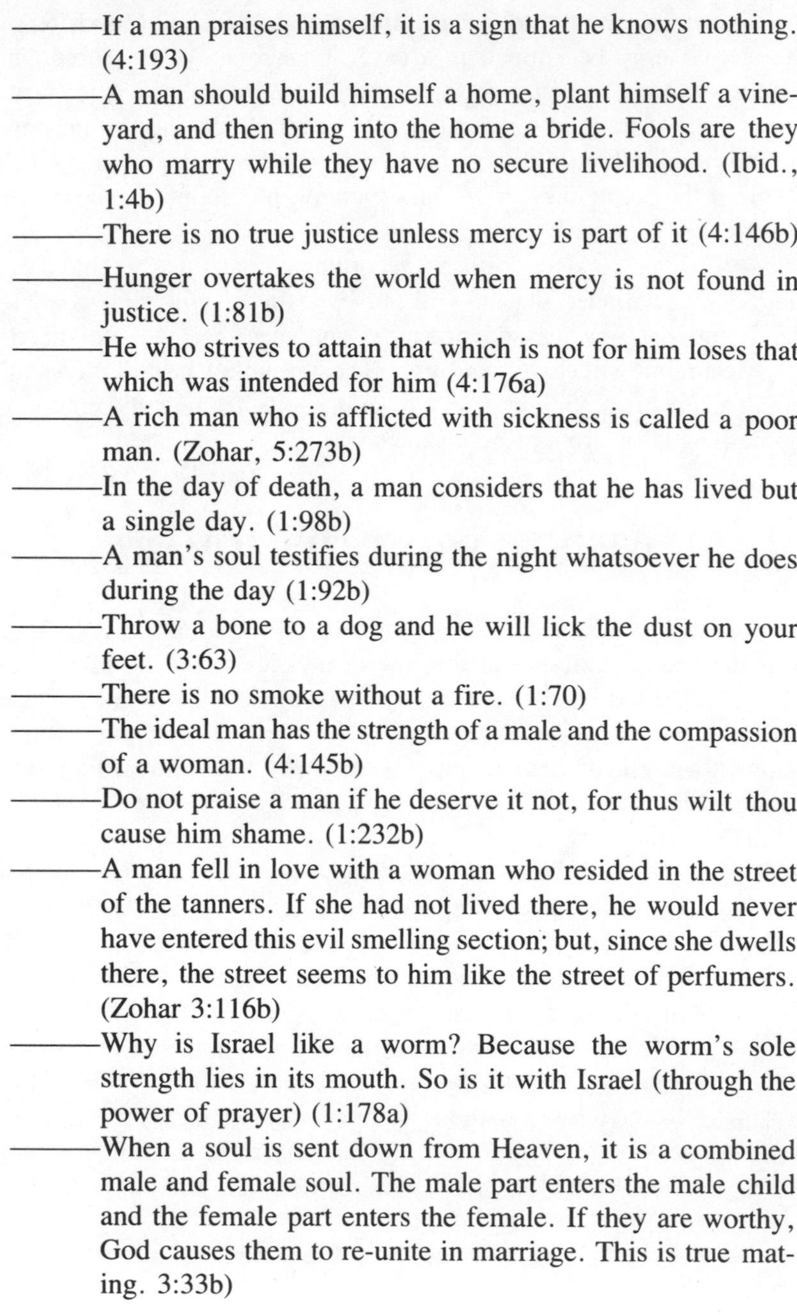

———If a man praises himself, it is a sign that he knows nothing. (4:193)

———A man should build himself a home, plant himself a vineyard, and then bring into the home a bride. Fools are they who marry while they have no secure livelihood. (Ibid., 1:4b)

———There is no true justice unless mercy is part of it (4:146b)

———Hunger overtakes the world when mercy is not found in justice. (1:81b)

———He who strives to attain that which is not for him loses that which was intended for him (4:176a)

———A rich man who is afflicted with sickness is called a poor man. (Zohar, 5:273b)

———In the day of death, a man considers that he has lived but a single day. (1:98b)

———A man's soul testifies during the night whatsoever he does during the day (1:92b)

———Throw a bone to a dog and he will lick the dust on your feet. (3:63)

———There is no smoke without a fire. (1:70)

———The ideal man has the strength of a male and the compassion of a woman. (4:145b)

———Do not praise a man if he deserve it not, for thus wilt thou cause him shame. (1:232b)

———A man fell in love with a woman who resided in the street of the tanners. If she had not lived there, he would never have entered this evil smelling section; but, since she dwells there, the street seems to him like the street of perfumers. (Zohar 3:116b)

———Why is Israel like a worm? Because the worm's sole strength lies in its mouth. So is it with Israel (through the power of prayer) (1:178a)

———When a soul is sent down from Heaven, it is a combined male and female soul. The male part enters the male child and the female part enters the female. If they are worthy, God causes them to re-unite in marriage. This is true mating. 3:33b)

ECCLESIASTES

Ecclesiastes (Hebrew for Kohelet) is an extraordinary book written approximately in the year 200 B.C., by an unknown Jewish visionary but credited to King Solomon. The word Kohelet does not have any specific meaning in Hebrew and is assumed to be the name of the author. Reflected in the book is a deep sense of resignation and a negative attitude towards life itself, wherein the author sees no purpose for life:

ALL IS VANITY.

Vanity of vanities. . .
Vanity of vanities, all is vanity!
What does a man gain from all his toil
At which he toils beneath the sun
One generation goes, and another comes,
While the earth endures forever.
The sun rises and the sun sets,
And hastens to the place where he rose.
The wind blows toward the south,
And returns to the north.
Turning, turning, the wind blows,
And returns upon its circuit.
All rivers run to the sea
But the sea is never full;
To the place where the rivers flow,
There they continue to flow.
All things are wearisome;
One cannot recount them,
The eye is not satisfied with seeing,
Nor is the ear filled with hearing.
Whatsoever has been done is that which will be done;
And there is nothing new under the sun.
Is there a thing of which it is said, 'Lo, this is new'?
It was already in existence in the ages
Which were before us.
There is no memory of earlier people;
And likewise of later people who shall be,
There will be no memory with those who are later still.

WISDOM IS VAIN.

I, Koheleth, was king over Israel in Jerusalem; and I set my mind to search and to investigate through wisdom everything that is done beneath the heavens. It is an evil task that God has given the sons of men with which to occupy themselves. I have seen everything that has been done under the sun; and lo, everything is vanity and striving for the wind.

I thought within myself thus: I am great and have increased in wisdom above all that were before me over Jerusalem; and my mind has seen abundant wisdom and knowledge. So I set my mind to knowing wisdom and to knowing madness and folly. But I am convinced that this too is striving for the wind.

For with more wisdom is more worry, and increase of knowledge is increase of sorrow.

WEALTH IS VAIN.

I said to myself: ''Come now, let me test you with mirth; so enjoy yourself.'' But this also was vanity. . .I made myself great works; I built myself houses; I planted vineyards for myself; I made myself gardens and parks. . .I bought male and female slaves and . . . gathered for myself silver and gold, the treasure of kings and provinces. . . . And nothing that my eyes desired did I withhold from them. . . . Then I reviewed all my works which my hands had made, and the toil which I had expended in making them, and lo, everything was vanity and striving for the wind, and there was no profit under the sun. . . . So I hated life, for everything that is done under the sun seemed to me wrong, for everything is vanity and striving for the wind.

LIFE IS VAIN.

For there is one fate for both man and beast . . . as the one dies so dies the other. The same breath is in all of them, and man has no advantage over the beast; for everything is vanity. All go to one place; all are from the dust, and all return to the dust. Who knows that the spirit of man goes upward and that the spirit of the beast goes downward to the earth?. . .

I considered once more all the oppressions that are practiced under the sun: for example, the tears of the oppressed, with none to comfort them, and the strength in the hands of their oppressors, with none to comfort them. So I congratulated the dead who were already dead, rather than the living who are still alive. And happier than both of them did I regard him who had never been, who had not seen the wicked work which is done under the sun.

And so I have seen wicked men carried to the tomb and praised from the holy place and lauded in the city where they had acted thus. . . . There is vanity which is wrought upon the earth, namely that there are righeous men to whom it happens in accordance with what should be done to the wicked, and there are wicked men to whom it happens in accordance with what should be done to the righteous. I say that this too is vanity.

EAT, DRINK AND BE MERRY. . .

So I commend mirth; for there is nothing good for man under the sun except to eat, drink, and be merry; for this will stay by him in his toil during the course of his life which God gives him under the sun.

Go, eat your food with gladness,
And drink your wine with a happy mind. . .
Enjoy life with the wife whom you love
All the days of your empty life,
Which He has given you under the sun;
All your empty life.(9:7,9)

BIBLICAL JURISPRUDENCE

BIBLICAL JURISPRUDENCE

There is extensive evidence written in the Talmud to verify the fact that judicial courts, administering justice throughout the land of Israel, existed from the days of Moses until the destruction of the State. This system of courts, also mentioned frequently in the Bible, was composed of Houses of Judgement (the Beth Din) and were presided over by famous biblical leaders. There were numerous Courts at various times in Israel including the Beth Din of Moses (R.H. 119), the Beth Din of Shem, Samuel and Solomon (MAK 23b), the Beth Din of Jerubbaal, etc.

The highest court, used in interpreting complex issues, was the Great Sanhedrin (the Supreme Court) where sages and scholars worked collectively through the Talmud to render decisions on complex problems that arose in reference to legal technicalities and religious interpretations. We find this mentioned in a letter from Artaxerxes to Ezra: ''And thou Ezra, after the wisdom of thy God that is in thine hand, ye shall appoint magistrates and judges, which may judge all thy people that are beyond the river; all such as know the laws of God; and teach ye him that knoweth them not. (EZRA vii, 25). In all cases, the renderings of the Sanhedrin was considered the final word.

In describing the physical characteristics of these Courts, the Rabbis stated: 'In the beginning all disputes were resolved in three different Courts: the Court of seventy-one, in the Chamber of Hewn Stone; the Court of twenty-three which were located in cities throughout Israel and the Courts of three. If a decision was required on a point of civil or religious law (the HALACHAH), the person went to a Court in his city. If the judges knew the answer they immediately informed him, however, should the judges not be able to answer him, he and an expert of the court proceeded to the Court on the Temple Mount. Should this higher court not be able to render a decision, they went to the court located in Chel. If, still, there was no solution, this court accompanied the two men to the Supreme Court (the Great Sanhedrin) which was located in the Chamber of Hewn Stones. (TOSIFTA SANH. VII I.).

THE GREAT SANHEDRIN

The Great Sanhedrin consisted of seventy-one learned men. As it was said: ''Gather unto me seventy men of the elders of Israel.'' (NUM. XI. 16). Including Moses, the total became seventy-one.

The Sanhedrin was seated in the form of semi-circle so that the members of the court could see each other. The president sat in the center and the elders (according to seniority) sat on his right hand and left. (TOSIFTA SANH. VIII I). Two secretaries of the judges stood in front of them, one on the right, the other on the left, and recorded the words of those who were for an acquittal and of those who were for a conviction. A third secretary recorded the words of those who were for acquittal and separately those who were for a conviction. Three rows of the disciples of the Sages sat in front of them, each one in an appointed place. The first row were the first ordained, as then those in the second row then moved into the first row to replace them. (Sanh. IV. 3 f).

'Although the Court in the Chamber of Hewn Stone consisted of seventy-one, there could never be fewer than twenty-three present. Should one have to leave, he must see that there were at least twenty-three present or he could not leave.

When the Great Sanhedrin was destroyed by the Roman General Gabinius in the 1st Century B.C.E., he divided Judea into five separate districts and appointed five councils to govern the Jews: one was in Jerusalem, one in Gadara, one in Hamath, one in Jericho and one in Galilee. The council in Jerusalem held the greatest prestige in religious and civil matters but began to decline in the 1st Century C.E. The Talmud refers to it in this manner: 'The Great Sanhedrin suffered ten removals; from the Chamber of Hewn Stone to the trading station, from the trading station to Jerusalem, from Jerusalem to Jabneh, from Jabneh to Usha, from Usha back to Jabneh, then back to Usha and then to Shaphraam, from Shaphraam to Beth Shearim, from Beth Shearim to Sapphoris and from Sapphoris to Tiberias. (R.H. 31a,b)

THE CRIMINAL COURTS

All criminal charges were decided by a Court of twenty-three. To avoid the court being equally divided, one was added to make it an odd figure. 'A town to qualify having a Sanhedrin of its own, must have at least two hundred and thirty people, so that each member of the Court would be a 'ruler of ten' (EXOD XVIII 21)
With the end of civil autonomy for the Jews, the authority of the criminal courts came to an end.

Some of the cases decided by the Sanhedrin were described thusly: ''A person having unnatural intercourse with an animal, and the animal, are tried by the court of twenty-three, as it was said: ''Thou shalt kill the woman and the beast'' (LEV. XX 16) Whether an ox which has gored a person is to be stoned is decided by a Court of twenty-three; as it is said, 'The ox shall be stoned, and his owner shall be put to death' (EXOD. XXI 29). Likewise, with the wolf, lion, bear, leopard, hyena and snake, their death is decided by a Court of twenty-three. In ancient times, the trials of animals were common proceedures.

THE CIVIL COURTS

Civil cases were decided by a Court of Three, (local Beth Dins) who sat on certain fixed days, usually Mondays and Thursdays, in towns and cities throughout Palestine. Falling under their jurisdiction were the following classifications of cases: larceny, bodily damage, rape, seduction and slander. The trial of slander, in many cases was referred to the Court of twenty-three because there were times it involved the death sentence; e.g. When a rabbi's daughter is slandered as to her moral character. If the charge were true, she suffered death by burning (Lev. XXI 9); consequently, by Biblical Law, if the accuser made a false charge, he must suffer death.

(Deut. XIX. 19)

Most civil cases were decided by a Court of Three. Each party in the litigation selected one judge and they jointly appointed the third. Each party could reject the third judge by bringing proof that they were related to the litigants. However, if such proof was not forthcoming, they could not be disqualified.

(SANH. III 1)

The litigants had to sign a document in which they agreed to abide by the decision of the three judges. This document was called 'compromissa'.

(p.m.k. 82a)

A very important function of the Beth Din was the regulation of the calendar. At that time, the months were not determined by calculation but by observation, and witnesses who had seen the new moon had to appear before the court to substantiate the validity of their evidence.

JUDGES

There were strict regulations governing the qualifications of judges. Usually, all Israelites were qualified to try civil cases but only Rabbis, Levites and Israelites who can give their daughters in marriage into the priesthood and who were of pure Israelitish descent, could try criminal cases. (SANH. IV 2)

Whoever is qualified to judge criminal cases can try civil cases but those qualified to try civil cases cannot try criminal cases. Whoever is qualified to judge is qualified to give evidence but there are some qualified to give evidence that are not qualified to judge. (p JUMA 43b).

A judge must have physical, moral and intellectual perfection. It should not be undertaken solely for the honour attached to it. Some of the guiding rules are: "Be deliberate in judgement", "Be very searching in the examination of witnesses and be heedful of thy words, lest through them they learn to falsify." "Say not, 'Accept my view' for the choice is theirs and it is not for you to compel.". (SANH. 17a)

WITNESSES

There are many references in the Talmud regarding witnesses and their qualifications to be a witness. To be a witness and assist in the dispension of justice was considered a sacred duty. "Three persons does the Holy One, blessed be He, hate: who speaks one thing with his mouth and another thing in his heart; who knows evidence in connection with his fellow man and does not testify for him; and who sees something unseemly in his fellow man and testifies against him singly." (PES113b) Furthermore, the witnesses must know against Whom and before Whom they testify, and Who will exact punishment of them. (SANH. 6b)—The perjurer testifies against God, because by means of false evidence justice is perverted SANH. 8a).

Those disqualified from acting as either judge or witness are "the dice player, lender of money on interest, the flyer of doves (wagerers on races), and who traffics on produce on the Sabbath. Others disqualified are: robbers, herdsmen, and extortioners. No women or minors are qualified. If a witness accepts pay, his evidence is disallowed. Any relation to either party is disqualified. Also a friend and an enemy.

The Bible states that at least two witnesses are required to establish a case. A single witness who is uncorroborated is not believed. (R.H. III I). Circumstantial evidence, however convincing, was not accepted. A witness was only allowed to testify who actually saw the crime committed. The following is an example: "We saw the accused run after a man with a sword in his hand; the man who was pursued entered a shop on account of him and the accused entered the shop after him; there we saw the man slain and the sword, dripping with blood, in the hand of the murderer." (TOSIFTA SANH. VIII 3) It follows therefore, that no charge could be sustained unless the actual crime was seen by two men of repute.

Perjury was harshly dealt with. "If anyone believed to have borne false witness, let him, if convicted, suffer the very same punishment which he, against whom, he bore witness, would have suffered. (Antiq. IV VIII 15).

THE TRIAL

During the course of a trial, strict regulations were laid upon judges to treat all parties to a suit equally and to never display the slightest partiality. Some of the rules were: "It is the duty of both litigants to stand during the trial. If the judges wish to permit both to be seated they may do so; but it is forbidden to permit one to sit and the other to stand. Nor is it allowed for one to speak at length and the other to be told to be brief. If a scholar and an ignoramus have a suit, the former may not enter the court in advance of the other and take a seat, because it might appear he was arranging the case in his favor. If one party appears in tatters and the other is wearing an expensive robe (to impress the judges), the latter is told, either dress like him or clothe him in a manner similar to yourself.

There are different procedures in civil and criminal cases. Civil cases are tried by a Court of three; criminal cases by a Court of twenty-three. Civil cases open with the defense or the claim; criminal cases must open with the defense. In civil cases a majority of one is sufficient to find for the defendant or the plaintiff; in criminal cases, a majority of one acquits, but two are needed for a conviction. In civil cases all the judges may argue either for the defendant or the plaintiff; in criminal cases they may all argue for an acquittal but not for a conviction. In civil cases of ceremonial impurity or purity, the judges express their opinions beginning with the seniors; in criminal cases, they begin with the juniors, to prevent the juniors from being unduly influenced by that of the elders (SANH. IV If).

When a trial involved capital punishment the witnesses are cautioned and impressed with the gravity of the case. This reads: ''Perhaps the evidence you are about to give is based on conjecture or hearsay, or something said by another witness, or a statement made by another person. Perhaps, also you are unaware that we shall subject you to a searching cross-examination. Take note that criminal cases are not like civil cases. In the latter a man forfeits his money and makes atonement but in criminal cases, the responsibility of his blood and the blood of his seed rests upon him until the end of the world. (GEN. IV. 10)

PUNISHMENT

The punishment of criminals, according to rabbinical records, had many ramifications depending largely on the severity of the crime and the conditions involved. The crime of murder which has been proven has one of two sentences passed against the condemned person! If death was caused by an accident not due to culpable negligence, the person is banished to a city of refuge; if it was deliberate homicide, the punishment is death.

However, when the Court found that the homicide was deliberate and sentence of death was passed; there was great reluctance to carry it out.

A death sentence took one of four forms: Stoning, burning, decapitation, or strangulation. In stoning, the prisoner was taken outside the Court. One man stood at the entrance with a flag in his hand, another was mounted on a horse a short distance away. When they reach a distance about ten feet from the place of stoning, they say to the condemned man. "Confess, since it is the way of all who are condemned to death to confess. Whoever confesses will have a share in the world to come." If he does not know how to confess, they tell him to say. "May my death be an atonement for all my sins."

When he was four feet away from the place of stoning, they remove his garments. In the case of a man, they leave a covering in front; in the case of a woman, both before and behind.

The person condemned to burning is sunk in manure up to his knees; a twisted scarf of coarse material is placed within soft cloth and twined around his neck; one witness pulls it at one end and the second at the other end until he opens his mouth; the executioner lights a wick and throws it into the mouth so that it enters and burns his entrails.

In decapitation, this was performed by striking off the head with a sword, after the manner of the Romans. Strangulation was carried out by sinking the condemned person in manure up to his knees; a twisted scarf of coarse material is placed around his neck; two persons pull at each end of the cloth until the criminal chokes to death.

The agonies of execution were alleviated for the condemned person by his being given a drink which produced a state of stupefaction. He is given a grain of frankincense in a cup of wine, that his senses should become numbed; as it is said, "Give strong drink unto him that is ready to perish, and wine unto the bitter in soul" (Prov. XXXI. 6)

THE AMERICAN SANCTUARY

THE AMERICAN SANCTUARY

The continued presence of physical and emotional extremes has been the lifestyle and the social design for Jews throughout their long and painful history. With their very existence always dependent on the benevolence of a local ruler, the Jews in the Diaspora alternated between being tolerated to being persecuted. The latter reached its ultimate level in the form of the Holocaust. Nowhere in the annals of mankind has this consistency of subjugation against a minute portion of world civilization ever been duplicated and its cause lay, not in the ignorance and sadism of the persecutor, but in the moral conflict and defeatism of the Jew himself.

Grasping the crumbs of assimilation during the rare moments of his acceptance in societies that tolerated his presence, the Jew meekly submitted to conversion and absorption in order to identify himself with that society. In the end, regardless of stature, position and ability, the inevitable cycle of disillusionment and despair repeated itself with tragic regularity. The complacent Israelites became slaves of the Romans, the influential Marranos were crucified on the cross in Spain and the austere, wealthy German Jews became fuel for the furnaces.

In modern times, after Hitler, Jewish leaders and analysts began to doubt whether it was possible for Judaism and the Jewish people to survive and whether Jewish culture and tradition had any significant relevance on the international stage. "As modern science and technology begins to penetrate the complex facade of Jewish life," states a contemporary historian, "Jewish religious principles and institutions will fall further and further into a state of disuse."

One must analyze this transition with respect to the tremendous impact of modern society on the international Jewish community. In the early 1800's, many Jews were occupied in the matter of survival by eking out a living by being peddlers, merchants, hotel keepers, and barterers; living in poverty and remaining apart from their non-Jewish neighbors. With the rapid growth of America and the influx of millions of Europeans upon the scene, a complete transition took place with a vast number of Jews becoming involved in industry, international trade and governmental positions. With this metamorphosis came a greater interdependence between the Jew and the non-Jew; a more secular relationship induced by the mutual interest of both parties. Simultaneously, this condition created a situation where in Jewish religious principles, institutions, education of the young and dedication to the spirit of Judaism became progressively weaker and weaker. Considering the fact that they were always in the minority, with the stigma of persecution constantly present, this situation had a more drastic effect on the Jews than on other religious factions.

As America prospered and its influence on the international scene grew into tremendous proportions, the religious and political emancipation of the Jews gathered momentum around the globe. They attained complete religious freedom in the United States in 1787, in France in 1791, and in Holland in 1796. Throughout the 19th Century the struggle continued with Marx, Lassalle and Rieser leading the way, and with the signing of the Treaty of Versailles, Jews in Central and Eastern Europe were emancipated. Tragically however, along with this new born freedom, they moved further and further away from Judaism.

This condition remained until the rise of a new form of anti-Semitism; a realization that complete assimilation into modern society by Jews was almost an impossibility. This new version of anti-Semitism, composed of small cells of Jaw-baiting minorities, with unlimited funds behind them, proceeded to exhort the fact that Jews were alien in culture, ethics and lifestyle, which immediately brought about a reaction of hatred and contempt.

The Jewish reply was not long in coming. Their inherent instinct of self-preservation brought about a new Jewish consciousness that created a closeness of spirit and forced them to rely upon their own resourcefulness. From their memory of past persecution, a determination to survive enabled them to stem the swift current of assimilation and once again, become a Jew. This transmutation was particularly strong among the poor and the working class but its effect took root in all social and economic levels. They were forced to revert to their ancient history and tradition to prevent complete destruction. Several movements arose to combat their accusers. They realized that to exist in the modern world they must re-evaluate Judaism and bring it up to date by re-establishing the Jewish religion as a humanistic culture and establishing Jewish life into the spirituality of Jewish mysticism.

Although a portion of the Jews, particularly those in the United States, supported inclusion into the national culture of their country, the majority insisted that Western culture be incorporated into Jewish life by the creation of Jewish Nationalism. With this declaration, the Zionist movement, advocating the establishment of a Jewish homeland in Palestine, came into being. It was then that world Jewry was rent asunder. They became sharply divided and lost much of their social autonomy, but, nevertheless, they retained the strength and togetherness from the memory of past suffering.

It was during this time that the Jewish international caravan began to move westward. Since the Nazi Holocaust, the Russian persecutions and the discrimination of Jews in many European and Mid-Eastern countries, an Americanization process was inaugurated. Half of the Jews in the world now live in North and South America. Six million live in the United States where, since its origin in 1492, the Jews have made many contributions to its development.

In 1948, with practically the entire Jewish population exterminated by the Nazis, a new breed of Jew evolved from the ashes; a Jew who fought against insurmountable odds for his future survival. It was this type of Jew, who faced an enemy that outnumbered them by a hundred to one, and overcame them to establish a Jewish homeland for the first time in 2000 years. This feat was accomplished by only one realization—he had no place else to go.

Since its discovery in 1492, the United States of America, the Gan Eden for persecuted Jews from every corner of the earth, has been the only place on the globe where they have found their God given right to live and worship in peace. Driven by cruel and sadistic governments, forced to flee into unchartered lands, they had come to America with only their hopes and prayers as an assurance of survival.

The Jewish presence in the United States is a saga of unbelievable proportions. They arrived from every country under the sun for the same reason as did the Quakers and Pilgrims; as refugees from religious persecution. As Mary Antin, a Jewish immigrant, once wrote:

'Every immigrant ship is another Mayflower and Ellis Island is just a new name for Plymouth Rock.'

The first Jews to arrive were the Marranos from Spain and Portugal. Since 1492, when they had become fugitives from a vehemently anti-Semitic Catholic regime, they were searching for a place to be able to live without fear. Occasionally, a few came from England and Germany but until 1815, the vast majority of Jews were those who arrived from Spain.

In the early 1850's, a flood of Jewish refugees swept in from Germany and other Eastern European countries to escape the bitter pogroms in those areas. It was a time of great poverty and distress in Germany and once again they fled, seeking a life free from fear.

During the 1880's, subjected to persecution from the Czarist regime in Russia, thousands of Jews, along with other minorities, fled from that area all searching for a deliverance from tyranny.

After the Revolutionary War in 1776, there were 3000 Jews in America. In 1840 there were 15000; in 1881, 250,000; and in 1928 there was a total of 4,200,000 Jews. In breaking down their origination, the first 15,000 to arrive were the Sephardim from Spain and Portugal. The next 3,500,000 were the Jews from Central and Eastern Europe; the largest group coming from Poland and Russia.

Prior to their exodus to the United States, many Marranos from Spain settled in Brazil. In 1631, the Jews who were living secretly in Recife, later called Pernambuco, helped their friends, the Dutch, capture Recife from Portugal, thus giving them the opportunity to openly return to Judaism. It was at this time that the first Jewish community was created on American soil. During this era, the Jews of Recife blossomed. They formed a congregation, called the Kahal Kodesh, built fine homes, established planations and initiated extensive trade with Holland and other foreign countries.

In 1653, just as their freedom seemed most secure, the war between Holland and Portugal took a different turn. Again, the Jews, utilizing all of their wealth and efforts, were unable to turn the tide of battle and in 1654, when Recife fell to the Portuguese, they were ordered to leave the country immediately under threat of death. Their wanderings began once again. Many went back to Holland; others to Curacao, Surinam and some to New Amsterdam, which later became New York.

It was in September of 1654, that 23 Jewish men, women and children entered the harbor of New Amsterdam from Cape St. Anthony in Brazil. When Peter Stuyvesant, the Dutch Governor of New Amsterdam asked that they be turned away, the directors of the Dutch West Indies Company voted against him. This was the charter of the first Jewish settlement in the United States and the beginning of religious freedom for them.

In the ten years that followed they acquired a Jewish cemetery near what is now the Bowery. Only a portion of that cemetery remains today with a few tombstones upon which can be seen Spanish surnames. The inscriptions are in both Hebrew and Spanish.

When New Amsterdam became New York, the Jews were still merely tolerated and not accepted as full citizens. It was not until 1682 that they finally rented a small house which they converted into a synagogue. One must remember that beside being Jews, these people were pioneers along with the rest of the inhabitants. They finally built their first synagogue in 1683.

Forty five years later, in 1728, they organized their first congregation, called Shearith Israel, the (Remnant of Israel). This congregation exists to this day and is the oldest Jewish congregation in the United States. Its present location is on Central Park West. It is still Orthodox and observes the Sephardic ritual and liturgy as it did 250 years ago.

It was at this time that the Jewish population and wealth increased. Much of their dealings were in foreign trade and in 1711, when donations were being subscribed for the steeple of the Trinity Church in New York, several wealthy Jews were among the donors. In addition, they donated money for a Christian church building fund.

During the latter half of the 18th Century, the leading Jew on the scene was Hyman Levy, who traded with the Indians, buying their furs in return for other products. One of his many employees was John Jacob Astor, who later became the greatest merchant in New York and one of the wealthiest men in the country. When Astor worked for Hyman Levy, he received one dollar a day for beating and pelting furs.

The most liberal area where the Jews established a colony was in Newport, Rhode Island. This colony, led by Roger Williams, a bold and courageous clergyman, made no distinction between his church and the House of Israel. It was in Newport, in 1658, that the Jewish group began the Masonic Order in the United States. The tiny synagogue built there in 1763 still exists. Henry Wadsworth Longfellow, the immortal poet, utilizing his knowledge of Jewish life and culture wrote the following poem about: 'The Jewish Cemetery in Newport'.

Gone are the living, but the dead remain
And not neglected; for a hand unseen
Scattering its bounty, like a summer rain
Still keeps the graves and their remembrance green.

How came they here? What burst of Cristian hate?
What persecution, merciless and blind,
Drove o'er the sea—that desert desolate—
These Ishmaels and Hagars of mankind?

Pride and humiliation, hand in hand,
Walked with them through the world, where'er they went,
Trampled and beaten were they as the sand,
And yet unshaken as the continent.''

The Jewish Caravan Through the Colonies.

Once again, as in the countries from which they had escaped, the Jews discovered that prejudice and discrimination also existed in the New World. It appeared in various places, at different times, and in all instances, the Jews would get up and move to new locations that were available in the vast expanse of this newly discovered country. It began in New Amsterdam under the leadership of Peter Stuyvesant. From there, small colonies of Jews moved to Massachusetts, Connecticut, Pennsylvania and parts of the South. The first Jewish settlements in this search for a life without fear are recorded as follows: Newport, 1677; New Haven, 1759; Philadelphia, in 1726; Lancaster, in 1730; Richmond in 1790 and Savannah in 1732.

These facts distinctly point out the similarity of the flight of the Jews in this country to their wanderings throughout their long and perilous history. Either as single pioneers or in small colonies of merchants, the Jews wandered from one area to another throughout the Eastern seaboard, searching for a place to call home. In Pennsylvania, under the Quaker, William Penn, they found moderate freedom; in Maryland, they were merely tolerated; in Virginia, they were forbidden to enter; South Carolina's constitution advocated toleration for 'Jews, heathens and dissenters'; and in Georgia, they were defended by General Oglethorpe who offered them an opportunity to settle in that state.

During all this time, more and more Jews were arriving from England, Portugal and Spain. In Savannah, in 1734, the Portuguese Jews founded their first congregation. In 1775, during the timc of the Revolution, five congregations existed in the areas that were most tolerant of the Jews. They were New York, Newport, Charleston, Savannah and Philadelphia. In all the colonies, at this time, there was a total of 2500 Jews, practically all of them Sephardic and most of them living in seacoast towns.

THE PURITANS

In England, during the time of Oliver Cromwell, the Puritans were in control of the country both physically and spiritually. It was at this time that the Jews enjoyed their greatest measure of freedom for the Puritans founded their religion and philosophy on the Old Testament. They were deeply interested in the Jewish Bible and Jewish law and their aversion to kings and other rulers was based on the fact that the perfect government must be a government by God. They believed that the end of the world was coming and before it happened, the Jews had to be brought together from the four corners of the earth.

In New England, the same views existed. Many Puritans studied Hebrew and as early as 1655, Hebrew was taught at Harvard College. They taught that the Old Testament and Jewish biblical laws should be established at the very beginning of life in the New World of America. The Puritans combined their demand for freedom and respect for the law in the same ways the Jews had observed this way of life throughout their history. Using the feast of Succoth as a model, they established the feast of Thanksgiving as a celebration for the harvest and as an offering of thanks to God, the Giver of the harvest.

The most famous founding fathers: Thomas Jefferson, Benjamin Franklin, Thomas Paine, John Adams and James Madison were

Deists, or free thinkers, who believed in a God of nature rather than a personal God. In his autobiography, Benjamin Franklin pointed out: ''The existence of God; that he created the world and governed it by His Providence; that our souls are immortal; and that all crimes will be punished and virtue rewarded, either here or hereafter.'' When the Jewish congregation Mikveh Israel of Philadelphia once appealed for aid, Franklin headed the list of donors.

In Rhode Island, Roger Williams, a devout minister and a student of Hebrew, fought for freedom and equal rights for all religions. This was contrary to the European theory which declared that the State should advocate the true religion. Williams was joined in his declarations by Thomas Hooker, the liberal head of state in Connecticut. When designs for a seal of the United States were being proposed, Thomas Jefferson, Benjamin Franklin and John Adams suggested the motif of Israel crossing the Red Sea with Pharoah in pursuit. The motto was to be, ''Rebellion of Tyrants is Obedience to God.'' It was a matter of history that in most cases the early Protestant forerunners in the battle for civil rights derived their principles and motivation from the Old Testament. It was also a common belief among the settlers that the structure of the infant republic was being founded not on the British Constitution but on the way of life of Israel in ancient Palestine.

The Beginning of Religious Freedom.

At the present time, Americans accept the principle of religious freedom as a normal and natural fact. However, there was a time when this principle was in jeopardy and it took the moral courage of great men, whose liberal philosophies proved to be decisive during the birth of this new nation, to bring about the accomplishment of religious freedom. Through the constant efforts of Jefferson and Paine, who were able to sway the undecided members of the various sects in individual states, did the adoption of religious liberty become a reality.

The thirteen colonies were settled by pioneers from all parts of Europe. Each one brought over his own idea and the majority opinion was that the government should establish the 'true' religion. However, there were complex and complicated problems. The people from England and Germany advocated Protestantism, those from France,

Spain and Portugal insisted on Catholicism and the Quakers and Baptists demanded to worship God in their own way. Then there were the Jews who refused to accept any of these dogmas for fear of future persecution as had happened in the past. The conflict and indecision became unbearable. In New England, they established theocracies, founded on the laws of ancient Israel but adopted Protestantism as their religion. In Massachusetts, Connecticut and New Hampshire, the Congregational Church became the official church. Virginia, North and South Carolina, retained the Church of England. In Maryland, they established the Catholic religion and in New York and New Jersey, the Dutch Reformed Church was "official." Only in Georgia, which advocated religious freedom for all religions, did the Jews enjoy complete liberty.

With this constant bickering going on, it is unbelievable that the final priveledge of complete religious freedom for the Jews even came to pass as it did in the New World. The decisive battle took place in Virginia on two occasions, in 1776 and in 1785, two years before the Constitution was adopted. The primary problem of finding a solution was that in the original thirteen states any changes in the Bill of Rights could only be enacted with the consent of the people in each individual state.

In 1785, Thomas Jefferson authored the 'Virginia Law to Establish Religious Freedom'. Special clauses permitting Jews to worship God in their own way were injected by James Madison and George Mason. When the law was being presented for passage, Thomas Jefferson was in France as the United States Ambassador and James Madison was its principle advocate in the legislature.

There was much opposition to the law. Patrick Henry led the opposition to its passage. After a six year struggle it was finally approved and became part of the law of the state. Soon the other colonies adopted the law that gave religious freedom to all people.

In 1808, a Jew, Jacob Henry was elected to the state legislature. When a political opponent attempted to have him unseated because of an old Constitutional provision, Jacob Henry arose and spoke up. The speech he gave was later entered in a collection called "The American Orator." One of the points he brought out was, "that conduct alone should be subject to human laws and that man should suffer civil disqualification for what he does, and not for what he thinks or believes in."

The American Revolution.

Having been deprived of religious freedom during their entire existence, the majority of Jews in America were jealously in favor of the struggle against England. Aware of continued recrimination under the yoke of the British, they lent their support and wealth in the battle for self rule. The Revolution was basically a struggle against tyranny with many opposing factions joining together for the common cause.

In Philadelphia, nine prominent Jews were among the signers of the Non-Importation Resolution against British imports in 1765. Although there were only a few thousand Jews in all the colonies, the majority of those who were physically able fought under George Washington and distinguished themselves in the cause of liberty. They came from every city in the thirteen colonies but the largest group came from South Carolina where every healthy male was already a member of the state militia. In this company, commanded by a Captain Lushington, twenty six Jews served with distinction and the command was often referred to as the "Jews" company.

Those Jews who were not actively fighting for the cause contributed in many other ways. Large sums of money were given to the government to purchase supplies, pay the troops, and sustain the war. The leading contributor was a Polish Jew who came to America in 1772. He was Haym Salomon of Philadelphia who was imprisoned as being a sympathizer of the Revolution.

In prison, due to his knowledge of many languages, Salomon was made an interpreter which gave him the opportunity to escape. His official title was 'Broker to the Office of Finance' and in this capacity he freely spent thousands of dollars, accepting in return doubtful notes of exchange. When he died in 1785, he was bankrupt. Many prominent Americans, including James Madison were kept solvent by loans from Haym Salomon. In 1850, sixty years after his death, the 30th Congressional committee officially recorded the following: "The committee from the evidence before them are induced to consider Haym Salomon as one of the truest and most efficient friends of the country at a very critical period of its history."

When George Washington was elected as our first president, he wrote to various Jewish congregations thanking them for their assistance. To the Jews in Georgia, he wrote: "May the same wonder-working Deity, who long ago delivered the Hebrews from their Egyptian oppressors, planted them in the Promised Land, whose providential agency has lately been conspicuous in establishing these

Seventeenth-century sea trader Michael Gratz, from Philadelphia; helped open the Allegheny Mountains to settlement and trade. (portrait by Thomas Sully—American Jewish Archives).

Rebecca Gratz (1781-1869), model for Walter Scott's Rebecca, in Ivanhoe, founded the first Hebrew Sunday School Society in America. (portrait by Thomas Sully—American Jewish Archives)

United States as an independent nation, still continue to water them with the dew of heaven and make the inhabitants of every denomination participate in the temporal and spiritual blessings of that people whose God is Jehovah."

The Post Revolution Period.

When the American colonies achieved their independence from England in 1776, the pulse and heartbeat of the Jewish communities resided in the synagogue. All Jewish activity revolved around the

Uriah Phillips Levy (1792-1862), Commodore, United States Navy. Commander of the Mediterranean Fleet; abolished corporal punishment in the Navy. Restored Thomas Jefferson's estate and willed it to the federal government. (American Jewish Archives)

August Bondi, German-born abolitionist; fought with John Brown in the Missouri-Kansas border wars (American Jewish Archives)

synagogue and every Jew was a member. Built in colonial motifs, they were constructed for orthodox services with the readers platform in the center and a gallery separating the women. One of the first things they inaugurated was the establishment of Jewish education for the young. As early as 1731 the New York congregation, the Shearith Isreal, began a daily school where the rabbi taught Hebrew and English. As the population increased and public schools were being built, the Jewish children enrolled in those schools and attended the Hebrew schools on Sundays or in the evenings.

The first Jewish Sunday school was founded in 1838 by Rebecca Gratz, an outstanding Jewish woman with great vision. Noticing that the Christians established religious schools for their children one day a week, she initiated the same system for the Jewish children which was the beginning of Jewish training for young Jews. They were taught Hebrew, Jewish religion, customs and worship. The idea quickly spread to every part of the New World.

In this new and unsettled world, the Jewish presence had a

fascinating development. Either singly or in small groups, the pioneering Jews would appear in one city, then suddenly in another city hundreds of miles away. As these individual groups were strengthened by new arrivals, a congregation was immediately established. In this manner, the great Jewish community of America took its roots. The original pioneer Jews were all fearless and religious men. In Richmond, it was Isaiah Isaac; in South Carolina there was Jacob Cohen; in Baltimore, Maryland, the earliest known Jew in 1773 was Jacob Levy, a merchant, who was authorized by Congress to sign bills of credit: in New Orleans, in 1802, the first Jewish settler was Judah Touro. He was followed by Jews from England, Holland and Germany as well as Jews from other parts of America. As the pioneers began to move westward, the Jews were among them. Jewish settlements were founded in Louisville in 1814; in St. Louis in 1816; Cincinnati in 1817; and in Cleveland in 1837.

In the war of 1812, the Jews once again shared in the battle. Though small in number, 43 Jews served in the Armed Forces. Three Jews distinguished themselves by attaining high military rank. They were Commodore Uriah P. Levy; Captain John Ordroneaux of New York, who captured a number of enemy vessels, and Captain Mordecai Myers. The most prestigious of these men was Uriah P. Levy. Bold, stubborn, adventurous and extrovertish, Levy, who was born in Philadelphia, led a charmed life. Court martialed six times for

Levi Strauss, the inventor of Levi's pants. His idea, to use tent canvas for work pants, made him one of the most successful of all the "merchant princes." (American Jewish Archives)

Adam Gimbel, a Bavarian immigrant who peddled his wares along the banks of the Mississippi River. His success as a peddler led to the founding of Gimbel's Department Store. (American Jewish Archives)

Michael Goldwater, grandfather of Senator Barry Goldwater, came to Arizona in the late 1860's. As a freighter, army supplier and merchant, he laid the foundation for the Goldwater influence. (American Jewish Archives)

insubordination, he died a Commodore just after the Civil War, the highest rank in the United States Navy. Levy was such an admirer of Thomas Jefferson that he donated a statue of him which still stands in Washington, D.C. He also owned Monticello, which is now a United States shrine as the Jefferson memorial. His nephew, Congressman Jefferson Levy was a subsequent owner of Monticello, eventually he turned it back to the government for use as a national shrine.

By far, the bulk of the Jewish pioneers in America were notably Sephardim from Spain, who by 1840 numbered 15,000. From that time until the latter part of the century, during the 1880s, the number of Jews increased to over 250,000; the majority being German Jews who left a bitterly poor country with little hope for the future. After the Napeoleonic War, the stringent laws against the Jews once again came out into the open. Germany became militaristic and severe restrictions, both political and religious, forced the Jews to migrate. In Bavaria specifically, the Jews were restricted. They were prohibited from becoming citizens, burdened with heavy taxes, forced to live in ghettos and their marriages curtailed.

The German Jews who arrived in America were radically different from the Spanish Jews. In comparison to the Sephardim, who were proud and wealthy, the majority of German Jews were poor and uneducated. They were, however, enterprising and hard working. Usually starting out by peddling with a small pack, they saved their money and bought a horse and wagon. As the savings increased they rented a store and started a business. Many of these businesses eventually became so successful that they still remain to this day as some of the largest department stores in the country. One example is the head of the Strauss family who arrived in 1852. He peddled through Georgia with a horse and wagon, then opened a store and sent to Germany for his family. From this humble beginning evolved Macy's Department Store in New York City.

This was typical of the character of the German Jews who had migrated to America. They were smart, hard-working, possessed a keen business sense, and had the ability to organize and set into operation means for expanding their operations. Tremendously resourceful and ambitious, they gave their children the finest education and put great effort into building up the Jewish Community in America. As new immigrants continued to arrive from Germany they scattered to every important city in the new country. They established communities in Chicago in 1837, one year after the city was incorporated. They helped settle Cincinnati in 1823 and were among the earliest pioneers in California during the gold rush. The same took place in dozens of other cities; Portland, Memphis, Indianapolis, St. Louis, St. Paul and many others. Wherever they went, they immediately built a cemetery and a synagogue. Following that, they founded a society to take care of the sick and the education of their children. In this manner the great Jewish Community of the United States was begun. This was the time the B'nai B'rith had its greatest growth, the Hebrew Union College was founded, and many organizations were created to help the immigrants and the poor.

The Civil War.

As the Civil War matched brother against brother, so it pitted Jew against Jew. Listed in the Union Army were over 6000 Jews. In the Confederate forces there were 1500. Twenty three Jews attained the rank of officer. These included David de Leon, Surgeon General of the Confederacy; A.C. Meyers was Quartermaster General; Brigadier General Frederick Knefler; and Colonels Leopold Blumenberg from Baltimore, Philip Joachinson of New York, and Edward Solomon from Chicago. Seven Jews received the Congressional Medal of Honor for distinguished bravery. Of the casualties, 336 were killed and 316 were wounded in battle. For the first time in American history, rabbis were appointed as Chaplains in the Army, an act which required a special decree from President Abraham Lincoln.

Reform Judaism.

Until 1824, the entire Judaic presence in America followed the orthodox teachings of their ancestors. Many of these early pioneers knew very little about the ancient laws and customs of Judaism but they believed implicitly that those laws contained the important truths and principles of the manner in which life should be lived. This feeling among the early Jews created a life of piety and steadfast devotion to the religion of their parents and grandparents whom they knew to be wise and good people. They believed in the Thirteen Articles of Maimonides, the belief in One God, the teachings of the prophets and in the coming of the Messiah. These tenets are still upheld by many Jews to this day; however, subtle changes for modernization were taking place at that time. These changes, bringing about a system of reform, was to become one of the most important transitions of Judaism, the creation of the Reform Movement.

The origin of Reform Judaism began in 1818 in Hamburg, Germany, where the earliest reformers decided to make the Jewish liturgy and services more modern and beautiful. There was great opposition to the movement but it also had strong backing from many influential persons. One of these, Leopold Zunz, the historian, showed them that new ideas, laws and prayers had been injected into Judaic culture on several occasions in the past.

In America, the first mention of reform occurred in 1824 in Charleston, South Carolina. The congregation at that time was Beth Elohim which was founded by the Sephardim but contained a majority of German Jews. A committee of younger members drew up a set of petitions to inject changes in the services, such as shortening the prayers, reading some of them in English and interpreting some of the Hebrew liturgy into English so that it could be understood by all the members.

When this was rejected by the elders, the petitioners withdrew from the congregation and formed their own group with a cadre of fifty members. They called themselves 'The Reformed Society of Israelites' and conducted services without a rabbi. Due to tremendous opposition from the orthodox shul, the new society lasted eight years then disbanded and re-entered the temple. However, the seeds of reform had taken root and when the Temple was destroyed by fire, then rebuilt, reformed changes were made, including the installation of an organ. The bitterness continued until eventually the Orthodox minority receded from the congregation and founded a congregation of their own. This wide breach existed until after the Civil War.

It was not long until Reform Judaism spread to many other cities: Baltimore in 1842, Albany in 1846, New York in 1845, Cincinnati in 1854, Philadelphia in 1855, Chicago in 1858 and many others. All of the Reform rabbis were German born, liberal in thinking and determined to spread the modern and progressive methods of Judaic thought. The man, most responsible for its growth was Isaac M. Wise, a Bohemian, who arrived in America in 1846 from Czecho-Slovakia with his wife and baby. He pioneered the construction of Reform temples and introduced progressive ideas, one of which was that rabbis should be Americans who could speak English. He founded an English newspaper in Cincinnati called the 'Israelite' and wrote a new prayer book called the Minhag America (the American custom). Zealously writing sermons, histories, novels and plays, he also traveled around the country expounding his theories of reform. In time, he became nationally renowned and respected, and his following grew larger and more enthusiastic. In 1880, when German immigration was cut off, Isaac Wise's labor began to bear fruit and the Union of American Hebrew Congregations was born. Its offshoot, the Hebrew Union College began with thirteen students. Today, there are hundreds of students in the graduating classes, most of whom serve in Jewish synagogues and/or in educational institutions.

The Russian Migration.

In the latter part of the 19th Century, from 1880 to the early 1900's, the Jewish population in the United States soared from 250,000 to well over 3,500,000 due to tremendous waves of immigrants from Eastern Europe. The vast majority coming from Czarist

Russia and Poland, they were part of the most concentrated body of Jews anywhere in the world, which ran from the Baltic to the Black Seas. Poor and oppressed almost beyond belief, deeply pious and intensely devoted to Judaism, they endured discriminations, were forced to live in ghettos, and could not own or rent land of their own.

While in Russia, the Jews never felt that they were a part of the country. They lived their secular and religious lives within their own Jewish communities. They rarely spoke to or had dealings with other Russians, except in an official capacity as when taxes had to be collected. When the pogroms started in the 1880's the Jews were blamed for the miserable conditions and persecuted. It was when these outbreaks of violence continued throughout Russia that the Jews finally packed their few belongings and fled to America. During their lives in Russia, practically all of these Jews spoke Yiddish, a language which was primarily based on German and other Eastern European languages and reconstructed into an idiomatic and colloquialized tongue. Although they established religious schools and taught their children to read Hebrew, which is the language of the Bible, the families and communities continued to converse in Yiddish.

Hester Street, on New York City's East Side in 1895. Thursdays and Fridays were the bargain days as people pushed and jostled one another.

These Ashkenazic Jews brought to America a new culture. They were simple people possessing virtues of piety, close and devoted family ties and a deep dedication to their faith. The transition from the Russian autocracy to American democracy filled them with awe and gratitude and they immediately founded a multitude of organizations and societies to help them cope with this new way of life. From the medieval conditions of Russia, where there was no freedom of thought and expression, to the modern atmosphere of America was a tremendous leap and the adjustment, though slow and gradual, finally took place.

The Jewish peddler on New York City's East Side in 1895. Two barrels support a plank upon which his wares are displayed. Peaches were two cents a quart; eyeglasses, ten cents a pair.

The majority of Russian Jews settled on the Eastern seaboard, primarily in the New York area where they plied the same trades as they did in Europe. Thousands went to work in the garment factories where they were overworked and underpaid. By 1910, there were almost 2,000,000 Jews in New York City.

The years that followed brought about great changes. Having been helped by the German Jews when they first arrived, the Russian immigrants, when acclimated to their new surroundings, founded their own secular culture, unlike the German or American secularism.

A group of children from an Orthodox Jewish family from Passaic, New Jersey in 1915.

They started Yiddish newspapers, theatres, labor unions and community centers. They became American citizens and sent their children to universities; they entered politics and became active Americans yet, with it all, they retained their Jewish culture and tradition, the same as they had done in the old country.

Zionism.

Unlike the German Jew, who considered himself an adherent of a particular religious faith, the Russian Jews adhered to the fact that they represented a Jewish nationality. They came from a land where they did not share equally with other men and while living in Russia, they felt that Russia was their enemy. It was as living in exile and a deep longing persisted for a return to the land of their ancestors in Palestine. The German Jew, on the other hand, felt that America was their promised land. Their motto, repeated numerous times, stated: ''This country is our Palestine, this city our Jerusalem, this house of God, our Temple.'' They were like all other Americans except for their religion and felt that the life of a Jew in America

A Bar Mitzvah boy reads his Haftorah while his friends watch attentively.

was everything that they had hoped for. Except for their religion, they identified themselves completely with other Americans in every aspect of the 'American way of life'.

The Russian Jews, shaped by the oppressive conditions of their past, felt that religion without a national homeland would not preserve the Jews as a people in the modern world, and with this feeling, the new theory of Zionism took root and found support when it was propounded. In 1896, Theodore Herzl, reporting on the Dreyfus trial in France, described how a Jew was hounded even in a liberal country and wrote that he was convinced that the Jews required a national homeland. He published the book, "Der Judenstat", (the Jewish State) and called together the first Zionist Congress at Basle, Switzerland in 1897. The aim of this congress was the establishment for the Jewish people of a publicly and legally assured home in Palestine.

The movement was immediately approved by the Russian Jews in America and a convention was called. Rabbi Stephen A. Wise was its first secretary. Zionist organizations were immediately founded which included the 'Young Judea' and the 'Hadassah'. Famous Americans took up the call; Judge Julian Mack, Justice Louis D. Brandeis of the Supreme Court, and Louis Lipsky. In 1917, the British government issued the Balfour Declaration, which endorsed a Jewish National Home. In 1922, the United States Congress passed a resolution endorsing this same program. The establishment of the State of Israel in 1948 was the culmination of this movement.

Two young pupils in a Hassidic Hebrew school in Brooklyn study the Torah portion for the upcoming Sabbath.

THIRTY YEARS OF CONFLICT

A venerable Hassidic teacher instructs his young pupil in the language of the Bible.

THIRTY YEARS OF CONFLICT

On November 29, 1947, after some 65 years of Jewish immigration into Israel, greatly increased during the era of Nazi persecution, the United Nations General Assembly voted to abolish the 1920 British Mandate and partition Palestine into Jewish and Arab states. The Arabs rejected this plan and civil strife was fomented.

Since then, the history of Israel's relationship with its Arab neighbors has been one of war, unending distrust and attempts by other nations both to exploit and to end those disputes. Following are a list of the major events since that time:

May 14, 1948

The British withdraw. The chief Zionist groups proclaim the new state of Israel, occupying 5,500 square miles of Palestine granted them by the U.N. The next day, troops from seven Arab states invade Palestine.

January 7, 1949

The war of attrition ends with Israel having gained 30% more territory than originally allocated to it. Transjordan annexes the West Bank. Some 750,000 Arab refugees have fled from Israel to neighboring states.

July 26, 1956

Under the leadership of Gamel Abdel Nasser, Egypt nationalizes the Suez Canal. An agreement with the Soviet Union has already provided Egypt with large quantities of arms. Nasser repeatedly threatens Israel.

October 26, 1956

Operating under a secret pact with Britain and France, Israeli armies overrun the Sinai Peninsula. Franco-British forces move in to 'protect' the Suez Canal. Under U.S. and Soviet pressure, Britain

A young rabbinical student sits in a Succoth in the Mea Serim section of Israel, a concentrated community of highly orthodox Jews who live much in the same manner as their European ancestors.

and France soon withdraw and Israel pulls out nearly a year later. A United Nations force is installed to guard the Egyptian-Israeli border.

May 19, 1967

After convincing the U.N. that it should withdraw its force from the Sinai, Egypt blockades the Gulf of Aqaba, closing a key Israeli shipping route and moves its troops to the Israeli border.

June 5-10, 1967

Fearing an attack, Israel strikes first. In just six days, it seizes the Sinai Peninsula, Syria's Golan Heights and all of the West Bank, including East Jerusalem.

November 22, 1967

The U.N. Security Council unanimously adopts Resolution 242, calling for recognition of Israel's sovereignty but also for withdrawal of Israeli troops from occupied territory and for settlement of the Palestine problem. Israel holds onto conquered lands.

July 1972

Anwar Sadat, who became Egyptian President after the death of Nasser in 1970, clashes with the Soviets and ousts 20,000 Russian ''advisers''.

October 6, 1973

Egypt attacks across the Suez Canal on Yom Kippur while Syrian troops attack the Golan Heights. Israel counter-attacks and reaches to within 20 miles of Damascus and across the Suez into Egypt. Heavy losses on both sides. The oil producing states announce a cutoff of exports to nations supporting Israel and oil prices soon escalate. Secretary of State Henry Kissinger finally negotiates a cease fire on November 11.

September 4, 1975

Two years of negotiations marked by Kissinger shuttling between capitals finally produce a true agreement signed in Geneva that results in Israeli withdrawals from a strip of the Sinai.

Orthodox Jews at prayer in the modern Jeshurun Synagogue in Jerusalem.

May 17, 1977

Menachem Begin, a former guerrilla leader, wins a victory over the long dominant Labor Party and forms a conservative coalition government.

November 19, 1977

Sadat flies to Jerusalem and tells the Knesset that Egypt is ready to make peace, but that Israel must return Arab lands.

September 17, 1978

The Camp David Conference, called by President Carter, ends after 13 days. The three leaders sign an agreement on a framework for peace.

March 5, 1979

President Carter announces that he will fly to the Middle East in search of Peace.

STAGES OF PARTITION OF PALESTINE

Peel Commission, 1937

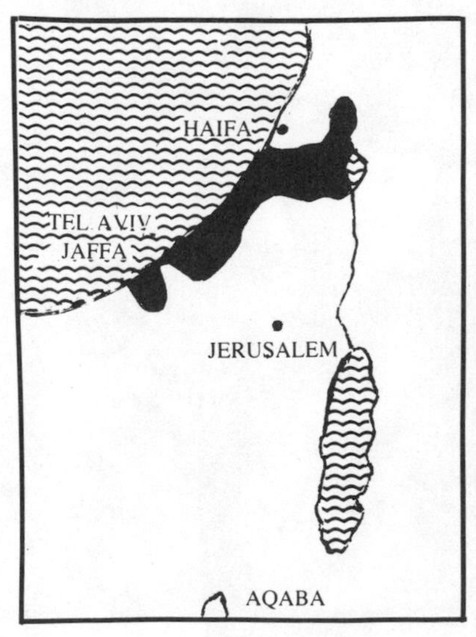

Woodhead Commission, 1938

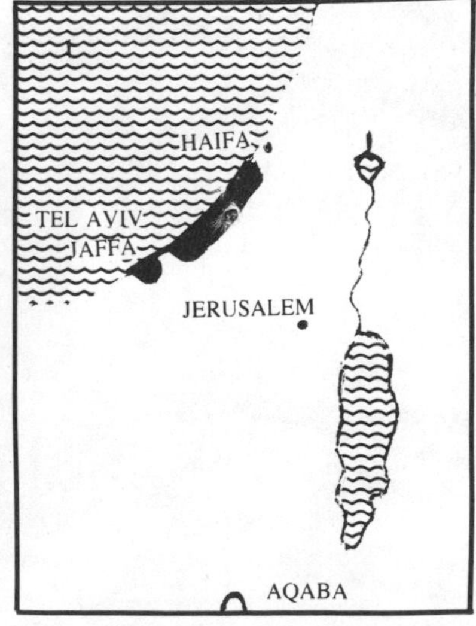

Benching licht (lighting of the candles). Children in a nursery school in Tel Aviv are encouraged to follow the traditions of Judaism by practicing the lighting of the candles to herald-in the Sabbath.

UNO Proposal, 1947

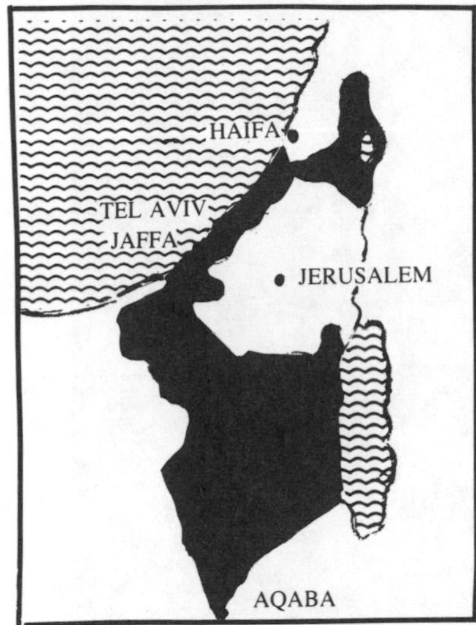

Armistice lines, 1949

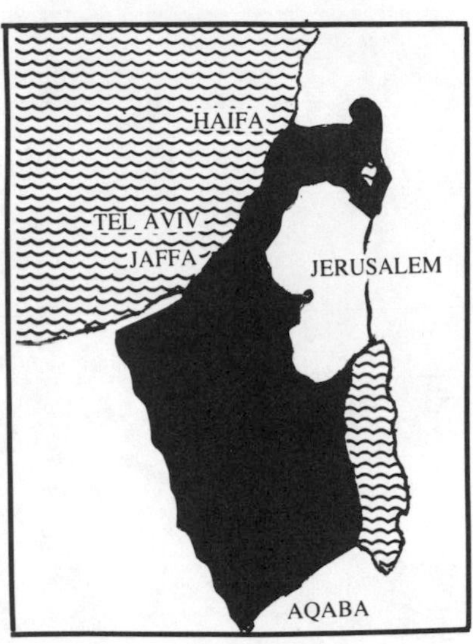

THE 126TH PSALM

At the signing of the Israeli-Egyptian Peace Treaty in Washington on March 26, 1979, Prime Minister Menachem Begin recited the 126th Psalm which was written two millenia and 500 years ago, when the Jewish forefathers returned from their first exile to Jerusalem and Zion.

> "When the Lord turned again the captivity of Zion, we were like them that dream. Then was our mouth filled with laughter, and our tongue with singing: Then said they among the heathen, "The Lord hath done great things for them." The Lord hath done great things for us; whereof we are glad.
>
> Turn again our captivity, O Lord, as the streams in the south. They that sow in tears shall reap in joy. He that goeth forth and weepeth, bearing precious seed, shall doubtless come again with rejoicing bringing his sheaves with him."

The Book of Books
Psalm 126

An old bronze candelabra of the 17th Century. One of the many treasures in the "Alta" synagogue in Prague, Czechoslovakia.

ENGLISH TO YIDDISH COMMON USAGES BY CATEGORY

ENGLISH TO YIDDISH COMMON USAGES BY CATEGORY

DAYS OF THE WEEK

SUNDAY	ZOONtik
MONDAY	MAUNtik
TUESDAY	DINStik
WEDNESDAY	MITvauch
THURSDAY	DAWnershtik
FRIDAY	FREItik
SATURDAY	SHAbbas

MONTHS OF THE YEAR

JANUARY	YAHnooahr
FEBRUARY	FEBrooahr
MARCH	MARTZ
APRIL	ahPRIL
MAY	MY
JUNE	YOOnee
JULY	YOOlee

AUGUST	auGOOST
SEPTEMBER	sepTEMbehr
OCTOBER	awkTAWbehr
NOVEMBER	nawVEMbehr
DECEMBER	deTZEMbehr

SEASONS OF THE YEAR

SPRING	FREElingg
SUMMER	ZOOmehr
FALL	HAHRbst
WINTER	VINtehr

THE NUMERICAL SYSTEM

1	AINTZ	20	TZVANTZIK
2	TZVAY	21	AIN UN TZVANTZIK
3	DRY	22	TZVAY UN TZVANTZIK
4	FEEYER	23	DRY UN TZVANTZIK
5	FINF	24	FEEYER UN TZVANTZIK
6	ZEX	25	FINF UN TZVANTZIK
7	ZIBN	26	ZEX UN TZVANTZIK
8	ACHT	27	ZIBN UN TZVANTZIK
9	NIEN	28	ACHT UN TZVANTZIK
10	TZEHN	29	NIEN UN TZVANTZIK
11	ELLF	30	DRYTZIK
12	TZVELF	40	FEHRTZIK
13	DRYTZN	50	FOOFTZIK
14	FEHRTZN	60	ZECHTZIK
15	FOOFTZN	70	ZIBITZIK
16	ZEXTZN	80	ACHTZIK
17	ZIBITZN	90	NIENTZIK
18	ACHTZN	100	HOONDEHRT
19	NIENTZN	200	TZVAY HOONDEHRT

1000 TOYZNT 2000 TZVAY TOYZNT

1980
NIENTZN HOONDEHRT UN ACHTZIK

THE FAMILY

MOTHER	MAHmeh
FATHER	TAHteh
WIFE	FROY
HUSBAND	MAHN
DAUGHTER	TAUCHtehr
SON	ZOON
GRANDMA	BAUbeh
GRANDPA	ZAYdeh
BROTHER	BROOdehr
SISTER	SHVEStehr
AUNT	TANteh
UNCLE	FETTEHR
NIECE	pliMENitzeh
NEPHEW	pliMENik
COUSIN	keZINI
SON IN LAW	AYdim
GRANDCHILD	AINikil
GREAT GRANDPA	ELTER ZAYDEH
GREAT GRANDMA	ELTER BAUBEH
GREAT GRANDCHILD	UR-AINikil
FATHER IN LAW	SHVEHR
MOTHER IN LAW	SHVIGER
BROTHER IN LAW	SHVAUgehr
SISTER IN LAW	SHVEGerin
DAUGHTER IN LAW	SHNOOR

HOLIDAYS

NEW YEARS	ROSH HASHANAH
FAST OF GEDALIAH	TSOM GEDALIAH
DAY OF ATONEMENT	YOM KIPPUR
TABERNACLES	SUCCOTH
REFOICING OVER THE LAW	SIMCHAS TORAH
FEAST OF DEDICATION	CHANUKAH

FEAST OF LOTS	PURIM
PASSOVER	PESACH
FEAST OF WEEKS	SHEVUOTH
FEAST OF AB	TISHA B'OV
CHRISTMAS	NIT'L
EASTER	PAHSKEH

JEWISH NAMES

ANNA	CHAHNEH
REBECCA	RIVKA
SAMUEL	SHMUEL
JOSEPH	YUSSL
MOLLIE	MAHLKEH
BERNARD	BERREL
JACOB	YAHKOV
JOHN	YIENKEL
MORRIS	MUTTL, MOISHE
HYMAN	CHAIM
JULIUS	YUDL
ROSE	RAUCHEL
ISAAC	YITZCHOK
HARRY	HERSHEL
LOUIS	LAIBEL
GERTRUDE	GITTEL
DAVID	DAUVID
WILLIAM	VOLVIL
FANNIE	FAHNEY
NATHAN	NAUCHEM,NAUSSN
ABRAHAM	AVRUM,AVROOM
ISRAEL	YISHROEL
RACHEL	RAUCHEL
MOSES	MOISHE
DEBORAH	DVORA
MEYER	MAYER
MICHAEL	MICHEL
HANNA	CHANA
FREIDA	FREDA
CHARLES	CHAIM

ISADORE	ITZIK, YITZCHOK
IRWIN	ITZIK
IRVING	ITZIK
ALAN	AVRUM
ALBERT	AVRUM
JACK	YAHKOV, YAHNKL
ZELDA	INDI
FAYE	FAYGIL
GOLDE	GOLDEH

AUTOMOBILE PARTS

ACCELERATOR	aktzeleRAHtaur
BATTERY	bahTEHRyeh
BOLT	SHROYF
BRAKE	TAURmauz
HEADLIGHT	fauNAR
HORN	trooMAYT
NUT	MOOtehrkeh
SPRING	sproonTZINeh
STARTER	STAHRtehr
STEERING WHEEL	KEHrevehr
TAIL LIGHT	HEENteshehr LEMpil
TIRE	RAYF
SPARE TIRE	zahPAHSrayf
WHEEL	RAWD

WINDSHIELD WIPER	FENTZterveeshehr
AUTO	OYtaw
GAS	gahzauLEEN
GARAGE	gahRAHZHSH
CHAINS	KAYtin
JACK	OONterhaybehr
KEY	SHLEEsil
TIRE PUMP	BAYFpaumpeh

TOOLS

HAMMER	HAHmehr
PLIERS	TZVAHNGG
SCREWDRIVER	SHROYfintzeehr
WRENCH	MOOtehrdrayehr
NAILS	NAUGlen

HOUSEHOLD WORDS

APARTMENT	DEEreh
BATHROOM	VAHnetzeemehr
BED	BET
BEDROOM	SHLAUFtzeemehr
BLANKET	KAULDreh
BUREAU	KAUMAUD

CARPET	TEHpech
CEILING	STELyeh
CELLAR	KEHlehr
CHAIR	SHTOOL
BELL	GLEHkil
COFFEE POT	KAHvehnik
COOK	KEHchin
CURTAINS	FAURhahngg
DINING ROOM	ESStzeemehr
DISHES	KAYlim
DOOR	TEER
ELECTRIC BULB	ehLEKtrisheh LEMpil
FAN	venteeLAHtor
FLOOR	pahdLAUgeh
FURNITURE	MEHBil
GARDEN	GORtin
GAS METER	GAZmestehr
GAS RANGE	GAZpleeteh
HALL	kaureeDAUR

IRON	PRESsil
KEY	SHLISSL
KITCHEN	KEECH
LAMP	LAUMP
LINEN	dos VESH
LIVING ROOM	VOYNtzeemehr
MATTRESS	mahtRAHTZ
MIRROR	SHPEEgil
MURSERY	KINdehrtzeemehr
OVEN	OYVN
PAN	FAHN
PANTRY	SHPIZkahmehr
PILLOW	KEEshin
QUILT	PEHrehneh
REFRIGERATOR	freejeeDEHR
RENT	DIRehgelt
ROOF	DACH
ROOM	TZIMehr
SAUCEPAN	FENdil
SILVERWARE	ZILbervarg

TEA KETTLE	TZHIYnik
WALL	VAHNT
WINDOW	FENTZtehr

BREAKFAST FOOD

BUTTER	Pootehr
CEREAL	KAHsheh
CREAM CHEESE	KREMkez
EGGS	AYEHR
JUICE	ZAHFT
ORANGE	foon mahRAHNtzin
PRUNE	foon FLOYmen
TOMATO	foon tawMAHten
LOX	LAHX
TOAST	TAUST
BREAD	BROYT
BAGLES	BAYgil
ROLLS	BOOLkes
GRAPEFRUIT	GRAYPfroocht
MELON	mehLAWN

SOUPS

BORSCHT	BORSHT
BARLEY SOUP	pehrilGROYpen zoop
CHICKEN SOUP	YOYCH
with NOODLES	mit LAUKshen
MATZO BALLS	KNAYDlech
SCHAV	SHAHV
SPLIT PEA	AHRbes zoop
POTATO	kahrTAWfil zoop
VEGETABLE	GREENsin zoop

VEGETABLES

BEANS	fahSAULyes
BEETS	BOOreekes
CARROTS	MEHrin
CAULIFLOWER	kahleefYAUrin
CELERY	sehLEHRyeh
CUCUMBERS	ooGEHRkes
LETTUCE	sahLAHT
MUSHROOMS	SHVEMlech
ONIONS	TZIBehles
PEAS	AHRbes

PEPPERS	FEHfehrs
POTATO	kahrTAWfel
RADISHES	REHteklekh
SPINACH	shpeeNAHT
TOMATOES	tauMAHten

APPETIZERS

FILLED FISH	gehFILteh fish
PICKLED HERRING	mahreeNEERteh HEHring
CHOPPED HERRING	gehHAHKteh HEHring
CHOPPED LIVER	gehHAHKteh LEHbehr
GREEK SALAD	GREEkheeshehr sahLAHT
SAUERKRAUT	ZOYehreh KROYT
SMOKED FISH	gehREYcherteh fish
DILL PICKLES	ZOYehreh OOgehrkes

ENTREES

ROAST BEEF	gehBRAWteneh RINdehrins
BOILED BEEF	gehKAUCHTeh RINdehrins
CORNED BEEF	GEPEHkilt flaysh
BLINTZES	BLINtzes
BOLOGNA	VOORSHT

STUFFED CABBAGE	HAUloobtzes
CARP	KAHRP
ROAST CHICKEN	GehBRAWtenen HOON
BOILED CHICKEN	GehKAUCHTeh HOON
CHICKEN FRICASSEE	gehHAHKteh HOON
COLD CUTS	OYFshnit
STUFFED DERMA	KISHkeh
DUCK	KATSHkeh
GOOSE	GANDZ
GOULASH	GOOlahsh
KNISHES	K'NISHes
KREPLACH	KREPlach
KUGEL	KOOgel
LAMB	SHEPsen flaysh
LIVER AND ONIONS	LEHbehr mit TZIBehles
NOODLE PUDDING	LAUKshen KOOgel
OMELETTE	AUMlett
PANCAKES	LAHTkes
POT ROAST	RAWool flaysh

TONGUE	TZOONG
TURKEY	INdik
VEAL CHOPS	KELbehrneh KAUTleten
WHITE FISH	VIsehr fish

SEASONINGS

GARLIC	K'NAUbel
CHICKEN FAT	SHMAHLTS
HORSERADISH	CHRAYN
KETCHUP	KETSHoop
MUSTARD	ZEHneft
OIL	BOYmel
PEPPER	FEHfehr
SALT	ZALTZ
VINEGAR	EHsik

FRUITS

APPLE	EHpil
BANANA	bahNAHneh
BERRIES	YAHGdes
CHERRIES	KAHRshen
FRUIT	OYPS

GRAPES	VYNtoyben
PEACHES	FEHRSHkes
PEARS	BAHRnes
PINEAPPLES	ahnahNAHsen
PLUMS	FLOYmen
PRUNES	gehTRIKenteh FLOYmen
RAISINS	RAWzhinkes

NUTS

ALMONDS	MAHNDlen
FILBERTS	VAHLDnisLECH
NUTS	NIS
PEANUTS	EHRDnislech
PECANS	peeKAHNEN
WALNUTS	VEHleesheh NIS

BEVERAGES

COFFEE	KAHveh
COCOA	kahKAHaw
LEMONADE	leemawNAHD
MILK	MILCH
ORANGEADE	awrahndZHAYHD

SELTZER	SELtzehr vahsehr
SODA	SAWdeh
TEA	TAY

DESSERTS

BAKED APPLE	gehBAHkehnehr EHpil
CHEESE CAKE	KEZkoochin
COFFEE CAKE	KAHVEH koochin
HONEY CAKE	HAWnik lehkech
SPONGE CAKE	tawrt
COOKIES	KEEchehlech
STEWED FRUIT	kawmPAWT
ICE CREAM	IZkrem
PASTRY	gehBEKS
PIE	pi
RICE PUDDING	RYZKOOgel
SHERBET	FROOCHT iz
STRUDEL	SHTROOdel

SCHOOL SUBJECTS

ARITHMETRIC	ahritMEHtik
ART	KOONST
CHEMISTRY	CHEMyeh

ECONOMICS	ehkawNAWmik
ENGLISH	ENGGlish
HISTORY	gehSHICHteh
LANGUAGES	SHPRAHchen
MUSIC	mooZIK
PHILOSOPHY	feelawSAWFyeh
PHYSICS	feeZIK
READING	LAYehnen
SPELLING	OYSLayg

PROFESSIONS

ACTOR	ahktYAWR
ACTRESS	AHKTriseh
ARTIST	KINSTlehr
BROKER	MEKlehr
BANKER	bahnKEER
DANCER	TAHNtsehr
DENTIST	TZAWN dawkterh
DOCTOR	DAWKtehr
ENGINEER	inzhehNEER
JOURNALIST	zshoornahLIST

LAWYER	ahdvawKAHT
MUSICIAN	MOOseekehr
OCULIST	OYgin dawktehr
OPTOMETRIST	AWPteekehr
PHARMICIST	ahpTAYkehr
PRINTER	DROOkehr
SCIENTIST	VISENshahftlehr
SURGEON	kheeROORG
TEACHER	LEHrehr

JOBS—BUSINESS

APPRENTICE	LEHren yingle
BAKER	BEHkehr
CARPENTER	STAWLyehr
CUTTER	TZOOshnydehr
DESIGNER	MAWDEHlen tzaychehnehr
EMPLOYEE	AWNgehshteltehr
EMPLOYER	AHRbetgehbehr
ELECTRICIAN	ehLEKtreekehr
EXPERIENCE	PRAHKtik
FOREMAN	OYFsehehr

HELPER	gehHILF-HELFEHR
MECHANIC	mehCHAHneekehr
PLUMBER	REHrenshlawsehr
SALARY	SCHREEres
SALESMAN	fahrKAYFehr
STOREKEEPER	KREHmehr
TAILOR	SHNYdehr
TECHNICIAN	TECHneekehr
TRADE	FAHCH
UNION	FAHRAYN
WAGE	LOYN
WORK	AHRbet
WORKER	AHRbetehr

BANKING

ACCOUNT	KAWNteh
BANK	BAHNK
BEARER	BRENgehr
BONDS	awbleeGAHTSyes
BRANCH	feelYAHleh
CASH	mehZOOmen

CASHIER	kahSEErehr
CHECK	TZEERtehr-TCHEK
CREDIT	krehDIT
DEBIT	DEHbit
DEBT	CHOYV
DRAFT	TRAHteh
ENDORSE	tshehREEren
EXCHANGE	OYSByt
IOU	VEKsel
INTEREST	prawTZENT
LOAN	HahlVAUeh
NOTE	VEKSEL
SECURITY	gahRAHNTyeh
SHARE	AHKTZyeh
SIGNATURE	OONtehrshrift
STATEMENT	KAWNtehoystsoog
STOCKBROKER	MEKlehr

BUSINESS ADMINISTRATION

ADVERTISING	rekLAHmeh
AGENT	ahGENT

BILL	CHESHbin
BILL OF LADING	LAWDtzetel
BILL OF SALE	farKOYFtzetel
BOOKKEEPER	boochHAHLtehr
BUILDING	BINyen
BUSINESS	gehSHEFT
BUYER	AYNkoyfehr
CANCELLATION	ahnooLEEroong
CATALOGUE	kahtahLAUG
COMMERCE	MEESChehr
COMPANY	gehZELshaft
CONFERENCE	bahRAHtoong
CONTRACT	kaunTRAHKT
CONSIGNMENT	SHEEkoong
COPY	KAUPyeh
CREDIT	krehDIT
DELIVERY	TZOOshtel
DEPARTMENT	AUPtayl
DISCOUNT	hahNAUcheh

DOCUMENT	dawkooMENT
DRAFT	TRAHteh
ELEVATOR	LIFT
ESTIMATE	SHAHtzoong
EXPERT	exPEHRT
EXPORT	exPAURT
FINANCIAL	feenahnzYEL
FIRM	FEERmeh
FREIGHT	FRACHT
IMPORT	imPAURT
INDUSTRY	inDOOStreeh
INSURANCE	fahrZEEkhahroong
INVOICE	CHESHbin
JOBBER	fahrMITlehr
LAWYER	ahdvauKAHT
MANAGER	fahrVAHLtehr
MESSENGER	shauLEEach
MODEL	mauDEL
MORTGAGE	heepauTEK

NOTARY	nauTAHR
NOTE	VEKsil
OFFICE	beauRAU
OPTION	AUPteerrecht BRAYREH
POWER OF ATTORNEY	FOOLmacht
PRICE	PRYZ
PROFIT	REHvach
RETAIL	KHAUdim-LACHDIM
SALE	fahrKOYFIN

CLOTHING

APRON	FAHRtech
BLOUSE	BLOOzeh
BRASSIERE	STAHnik
COAT	MAHNtil
COLLAR	KAULnehr
CUFFLINKS	SHPAUNkes
DIAPERS	VINdehlech
DRESS	KLAYD
GIRDLE	kaurSET
GLOVES	HENCHkes

HAT	HOOT
JACKET	ZSHAHket
NECKTIE	SHNIPS
OVERCOAT	AYbehrmahntil
PAJAMAS	peeZSHAHmeh
PANTIES	oonTER-HAYZlech
ROBE	chahLAHT-SHAHL
SCARF	SHAHRfil
SHIRT	HEMD
SHOES	SHEECH
SKIRT	KLAYdil
SLACKS	HOYZin
SOCKS	skahrPEHtin
SUIT	kaustYOOM
SWEATER	SVEHtehr
VEST	VEStil

COLORS

LIGHT	HEL
DARK	TOONkil
BLACK	SHVAHRTZ

BLUE	BLOY
BROWN	BROYN
CREAM	KREM
GRAY	GROY
GREEN	GRIN
ORANGE	auRAHNZSH
PINK	RAUzehveh
PURPLE	LEElah
RED	ROYT
WHITE	VYSS
YELLOW	GEL

BOOKS & STATIONERS

BOOK	BOOCH
BLOTTER	LESHpahpeer
CARBON PAPER	KAHLkeh
DICTIONARY	VEHRTERbooch
ERASER	MEHkehr
INK	TINT
MAGAZINES	ZSHoorNAHlin
PENCIL	BLIeln

CARDS	KAURtin
STRING	SHTRIK
TISSUE PAPER	ZYDpahpeer
SCOTCH TAPE	KLEPTZEHlaufahn
POSTCARDS	PAUSTkahrtlech

DRUG ITEMS

ADHESIVE TAPE	FLAHStehr
ALCOHOL	AHLkauhaul
ANTISEPTIC	ahnteeSEPtik
ASPIRIN	ahspeeREEN
BANDAGES	bahnDAHzSHIN
BORIC ACID	BAURzyehrs
EPSOM SALTS	BITehrzahltz
GARGLE	SHVENKechts
GAUZE	MEHRleh
ICE BAG	IZzahk
IODINE	YAUDI
CASTOR OIL	RITsnayl
COLD CREAM	HOYTkrem
COMB	KAHM

COTTON	VAHteh
LAXATIVE	AUPfeerechts
LIPSTICK	LIPinshtift
MOUTHWASH	SHVENKechts
NAIL FILE	NEGenfyle
PEROXIDE	SOOpehraukSEED
POWDER	POOdehr
RAZOR	GAUlehr
ROUGE	SHMINkeh
SHAMPOO	SHAHMpoo
SOAP	ZAYF
THERMOMETER	tehrmauMEHtehr
TOOTHPASTE	TZAUNpahsteh

BEAUTY AIDS

BARBER	SHEHrehr
SHAMPOO	SHAHMPOO
FACIAL	bahHAHNDloong foon PAUnim
MANICURE	mahneeKOOR
MASSAGE	mahSAHZSH
CHIROPODIST	FOOSdauktehr

TURKISH BATH	SHVITSbaud

AILMENTS

APPENDICITIS	ahpendeeTZEET
A BITE	ah BIS
A BLISTER	AH PENchehr
A BOIL	Ah GESHVEER
A BURN	ah BREN
CHILLS	TZITehrin
A COLD	ah fehrKEEloong, KAHLT
CONSTIPATION	fahrSHTAUpoong
A COUGH	ah HOOST
A CRAMP	ah KRAHMP
DIARRHOEA	SHILshil
DYSENTERY	deesenTEHRyeh
EARACHE	OYehrvaytik
FEVER	HITZ
HOARSENESS	HAYsehrlk
INDIGESTION	BOYCHvaytik
NAUSEA	nitGOOTklyt
PNEUMONIA	LOONgenauntzeendoong

SORETHROAT	HAHLZvaytik
SPRAIN	OYSleenkoong
TYPHOID FEVER	FLEKteefoos
VOMIT	OYSbrechin

PARTS OF THE BODY

ANKLE	KNEHchil	FOOT	FOOS
APPENDIX	BLINdeh-KISHkeh	FOREHEAD	SHTEHrin
ARM	AUrem	HAIR	HAUR
BACK	PLAYtzeh	HAND	HAHNT
BLOOD	BLOOT	HEAD	KAUP
BONE	BAYN	HEART	HAHRTZ
BREAST	BROOST	HEEL	PEEYAHteh
CHEEK	BAHK	HIP	LEND
CHEST	BROOST	INTESTINES	INgehvayd
CHIN	KIN	JAW	KINbayn
EAR	OYehr	JOINT	gehLENK
ELBOW	EHLinboy-gen	KIDNEY	NEER
EYE	OYG	KNEE	K'NEE
FACE	PAUnim	LEG	FOOS
FINGER	FINgehr	LIP	LIPF

LIVER	LEHbehr	SKIN	HOYT
LUNG	LOONG	SKULL	SHAHRbin
MOUTH	MOYL	SPINE	ROOkinbayn
MUSCLE	MOOSkil	STOMACH	MAUgen
NAIL	NAUgil	THIGH	DEECH-PAULKEH
NECK	NAHkin	THROAT	HALDZ
NERVE	NEHRV	THUMB	GRAUberFINgehr
NOSE	NAUZ	TONGUE	TZOONG
RIB	RIP	TONSILS	MAHNDlen
SHOULDER	AHKsil	WRIST	HAHNTGEHlenk

TIME EXPRESSIONS

DAY	TAUG
NIGHT	NACHT
MIDNIGHT	HAHLbehNACHT
YESTERDAY	NECHtin
LAST NIGHT	NECHtinbahNACHT
TODAY	HIYNT
TONIGHT	HIYNTbahNACHT
TOMORROW	MORgen
LAST YEAR	fahr ah YAUren

LAST MONTH	LESTIN CHOYdesh
NOON	MITTAUG
EVENING	AUvent
MORNING	INDER FREE
TWO O'CLOCK	TZVAY dehr ZAYgehr
IT IS HALF PAST. . . .	ESS IZ HAHLB nauch
QUARTER PAST.	FEHRtil nauch
QUARTER TO.	FEHRtil tzoo
HOUR	SHTOONdeh
MINUTE	minNOOT
MONTH	MAUNAT-CHOYDESH
YEAR	YAUR
LIFETIME	AH LEBEN

ARTICLES

ASHTRAY	AHSHtehtzil
BOTTLE OPENER	FLAHSHehfenehr
BOX	KEStil

BULB	LEMpil
CAN OPENER	kahn ehfenehr
CLOTH	TOOCH
CLOCK	ZAYgehr
CORK	KAUrik
CUSHION	KEEshin
DOLL	LAHLkeh
CHEWING GUM	KYgoomeh
HOOKS	HEKlech
JEWELRY	TZEEroong
LOCK	SHLAUS
MIRROR	SHPEEgil
NEEDLE	NAUdil
NOTEBOOK	NAUTITZ (HEFT)
PAIL	EHmehr
PIN	SHPILKEH

PURSE	BIYTIL
RADIO	RAHDYAW
SCISSORS	SHEHR
SCREW	SHROYF
SILK	ZIYD
SUITCASE	chehmauDAHN
THREAD	FAUdem
UMBRELLA	SHEErem
VASE	VAHzeh
WOOL	VAUL
ZIPPER	BLITZshlesil

LEXICON
ENGLISH TO YIDDISH
DICTIONARY

LEXICON
ENGLISH TO YIDDISH
DICTIONARY
A

ABLE —— KEHN
Are you able to stand?
Kehnt ir shtayn?
KEHNNEN
Mir kehnnen dos taun.
We can do it.
KEHN NISHT —— Cannot.
(also means) To know.
Do you know him?
Ir kehnt ehm? or Du kenst ehm?

ABOUT —— ahROOM
He walks about the house.
Ehr gayt ahroom dehm hoiz
(also means) Around.

ABOVE —— IBEHR *(also means: Over)*
He's flying over the ocean.
Ehr flit ibehr dem yahm.
She's looking him over.
Zie kookt ehm ibehr.

ABSCESS —— gehSHVEER
He has an abscess
Ehr haut ah gehshveer.

ABSENT —— NishTAU
They arc absent.
Zey zahnen nishtau.
(also means:) No reason.
No reason, why not.
Nishtau fahrvos.

ACCEPT —— NEHmin
You can accept the money.
Du kenst nehmin die gelt.
(also means) Take.
Take it away.
Nehm dos aveck.
geNOOMehn — Took, taken.

ACCIDENT —— OOMglick
His death is an accident.
Zyne tayt is ahn oomglick.
(also means) Tragedy.

ACCOUNT —— KAUNteh
Put money in your account.
Layg gelt in dyneh kaunteh.

ACHE —— VEYtaug or Toot vey
I have a tooth ache
Ich haub ah tzaunveytaug
My feet hurt.
Myneh fis toot vey.

ACTOR —— ahktYAUR
He is a good actor.
Ehr iz ah gootehr ahktyaur.
ACTRESS: Ahktriseh

ADDRESS —— AHdress
What is your address?
Vos iz dyn ahdress?

ADMISSION —— ahRYNtzugeyn
Admission is one dollar.
Ess kaust ah tollehr ahryntzugeyn.
Ahrein: In
Inevaynik: Inside.

ADVERTISING —— rekLAHmen
The best way to sell is in advertising.
Dehr bester vegg tzu fahrkeyfin iz tzu rekLAHmen

AFTER —— NAUCH
Come after me.
Koom mir nauch
(also means)
He's following me.
Ehr gayt mir nauch.
What else?
Vos nauch?
Once again.
Nauch ah mohl.

AGAIN —— NAUCH A'MOHL
Again and again.
Nauch a'mohl un tahkeh nauch a'mohl.
Do it again.
Tu dos nauch a'mohl.

AGENT —— AHgent.
He is an agent for the company.
Ehr iz ahn ahgent fahr die fihrmeh.

AID —— HILFF
I need help or aid.
Ich darff hilff
Help me!
Hilff mir!

AIR —— LOOFT
He's flying in the air.
Ehr fleeht in der looft.

AIRMAIL —— LOOFTpaust
Send it by airmail.
Shick daus mit dehr looftpaust.

AIRPORT —— FLEEplahts
The airport is busy.
Dehr fleeplahts is farnoomin.

AJAR —— AUfin
The door is ajar
Die tier iz aufin.
(also means) Open.

ALCOHOL —— BRAUNfin, SHNAPPS or Alkohohl
Would you like a little whiskey?
Vilt ihr a bissil shnapps?

ALL —— AHleh
All children are beautiful.
Ahleh kinder zahnen shayn.
AHLemin: Everybody, Everyone.

ALL TOGETHER —— Ahleh tzuzamen.
We are all together.
Mir zahnen ahleh tzuzamen.
tzuZAHMEN — together.

ALLOW —— LAUzin
Will you allow me to go?
Vestu mich lauzin gayn?
Let me go.
Lauz mir gayn.

ALMONDS —— MAHNDlin
Almonds are the best nuts.
Mahndlin zahnin di besteh niss.

ALONE —— ahLAYN
I'm alone.
Ich bin ahlayn.

ALSO —— OYCHit or OYCH
He is also coming.
Ehr koompt oychit.

ALWAYS —— AHleh maul or SHTENdik
He is always good.
Ehr iz ahleh maul goot.

AM —— BIN
I am forty years old.
Ich bin fehrtzik yaur ahlt.
Vu bistu?
Where are you?

AMBULANCE —— AHMboolahns
They took him in the ambulance.
Zey hauben ehm genoomen in dehm ahmboolahns.

AMEN —— auMAYN
Used in all religions at the end of a prayer to denote affirmation.
Also used as a response for 'May God Will it.'

AND —— UN
Ten and Six are sixteen.
Tzen un Zex macht zechtzin
Fifty five
Finf un fooftzik.

ANGRY —— BROYgis
He is very angry.
Ehr iz zeyer broygis.

ANIMAL —— beHAYmeh
He looks like an animal
Ehr kookt oys vie ah behaymeh.

ANKLE —— KNECHil
He broke his ankle.
Ehr haut tzubrauchin zyn knechil

ANTIQUE —— ahnTIK
The table is an antique.
Dehr tish iz ahn ahntik.

ANTISEPTIC —— ahnteSEPTik
The antiseptic will help it.
Die ahnteseptik vett dos helfin.

ANYONE —— EHMitzehr
Is anyone coming?
Vett ehmitzehr koomen?

APPLE —— EHpil
This is a red apple.
Dos iz ah royter ehpil.

APPENDIX —— BLINdeh Kishkeh
They have to take out his appendix.
Zoy darfen aroys nemmin zyne blindeh kishkeh.

APPOINTMENT —— tzuNOYFtref.
Have you an appointment?
Haustu ah tzunoyftref?

APPRENTICE —— LEHRENyingil
He is only an apprentice.
Ehr iz naur ah lehrenyingil.

APRON —— FAHRtech
The apron is dirty.
Dehr fahrtech iz shmootzik.

ARM —— AWRem
He broke his arm.
Ehr haut tzubrauchin zyne awrem
(also means) Poor
He is a poor person.
Ehr iz ahn awremehr mensh.

ARRIVE —— AWNkoomen
They will arrive at two o'clock.
Zay vellen awnkoomen tzvay a'zaygehr.

ART —— KOONst
KINSTLEHR: Artist
AH KINTZLEHR: A bunco artist.

ASH —— AHSH (sing. and plur.)
You left the ashes on the table.
Du haust gehlauzen die ahsh ahffen tish.

ASK —— FREHGG
Ask me a question!
Frehgg mich ah frageh!
What are you asking?
Vos fregstu?

ASPIRIN —— ahspiRIN
Take an aspirin for your headache.
Nehm ahn ahspirin fahr dyn kaupvaytik.

AUTHOR —— meCHAHber (writer: SHREIbehr)
He is the author of this book.
Ehr is die mechahber foon dehr booch.
TZU SHRYBIN: To write.

AUTOMOBILE —— OYtaw
This is a beautiful automobile.
Dos iz a sheyneh oytaw.

AUTUMN —— HAHRbst
Autumn is the nicest time of the year.
Hahrbst iz dehr shehnsteh tzyte foon yaur.

AVENUE —— EHvenyoo
They live on Third Avenue.
Zey voynen oyf dehr dritter ehvenyoo.

AWAY —— AHveck.
Go away!
Gay ahveck!

B

BACK —— tzuRIK
Go back!
Gay tzurik!
BACK (n) Playtzeh
My back hurts.
My playtzeh toot vay.

BAD —— shlECHT
These things are bad.
Die zahchin zahnen shlecht.
(also means) Evil.
He is an evil man.
Ehr iz ah shlechter mensh.

BAGEL —— BAYgil
A very popular doughnut shaped roll, usually eaten with lox and cream cheese.

BAG —— ZAHK
Give me a bag of potatoes.
Gitt mir ah zahk kahrtaufil.

BAGGAGE —— bahGAHZSH
Where is my baggage?
Voo iz myn bahgahzsh?

BAKE —— BAHK
Will you bake the meat?
Vestu bahken die flaysh?
BAKED: Gebahken
BAKER: Behkehr

BALCONY —— bahlKAWN
He's speaking from the balcony.
Ehr rhet foon dehm bahlkawn.

BALLET —— bahLETT
I'm going to the ballet.
Ich gay tzu dem bahlett.

BANANAS —— BahNAHNes
Bananas are fruit.
Bahnanhnes zahnen froocht.

BANDAGE —— bahnDAHZSH (as in montage)
The cut needs a bandage.
Dehr shnitt darff ah bahndahzsh.

BANK —— BAHNK
Put your money in the bank.
Layg dyn gelt in dehr bahnk.
Banker: Bahnkeer
Bankrupt: Bahnkrawt
Banknote: Bahnknawt.

Bar (Soap) —— Shtik zayf

BARBER —— SHEHrehr
The barber is cutting his chair.
Dehr shehrehr shnyte zeineh hawr.
Barber shop: Shehrenryh

BARGAIN —— Metzeeyeh
It's a real bargain.
Dos iz takeh ah mehtzeeyeh

BARLEY —— pehrelGROYpen
Do you like barley soup?
Ir glycht pehrelgroypen zoop?

BARTENDER —— BAHRshenker
The bartender will give you a drink.
Dehr bahrshenker vett eych gebben ah troonk.

BASEBALL —— BAISbahl
We're going to a baseball game.
Mir gayen tzu ah baisbahl shpill.

BATH —— VAHneh or BAUD
Take a bath.
Nehm ah vahneh.
STEAMBATH: Shvitz baud.
BATH ROOM: Vahnehtzeemehr
Bathing suit: Baud kaustyoom.

BE (to) —— Zyne (tzu)
Will you be there?
Vestu daurten zyne?
To be or not to be.
Tzu zyne tzu nisht tzu zyne.

BEACH —— PLAZSH
It's a beautiful beach.
Dos iz a shayneh plazsh.

BEANS —— fahSAULyes
Baked beans.
Bahbahkeneh fahsaulyes.

BED —— BEHT
This is a soft bed.
Dos iz ah veycheh beht
Bedspread: Behtgevahnt.

BEER —— BIER
Have a glass of beer.
Haub ah glauz bier.

BEETS —— BOORehkiz
Red beets.
Reyteh boorehkiz.

BEFORE —— FAHRn or Freeyer
Before evening.
Fahrn auvent

BEHIND —— HINtehr
The wood is behind the stove.
Die holtz iz hintehr dehm oyvin.

BELL —— GLEHkil
Ring the bell.
Kling dehr glehkil.

BELT —— GAHRtil
The pants comes with a belt.
Die hoyzin koompt mit ah gahrtil.
(also means:) Garter
Garterbelt: Zaukinbehdil

BEND —— shTOOP (also means) PUSH (also:) BAYG
Bend down: Bayg Zich
Push: Shtoop zich.
Push it in: Shtoop dos aryne.

BESIDE —— LEHbin
The child is beside her mother.
Dehr kind iz lehbin eer mammeh.
(Also means) Near — Nauent

BEST —— BESTer
A is better than B but C is the best.
A iz bessehr vee B auber C iz der bester.
Better: Bessehr.

BILL —— CHESHbin (hard CH)
The bill is very high.
Dehr cheshbin iz zayer tyer

BIRD —— FAYgel
The bird flew away.
Dehr faygel iz aveck gefloygn
Little bird: Faygelech
Also used colloquially to denote homosexuality
He is a fairy.
Ehr iz ah faygehleh.

BIRTHDAY —— gehBOORStaug.
Today is his birthday.
Hynt iz zyn gehboorstaug

BITE —— BYSS (as in MICE)
Don't bite the hand that feeds you.
Byss nit die hahnt vos git dir essen.
BITTEN: Gebissen
BITE (N) Biss (as in KISS)

BLACK —— shVARTZ
Black is not white
Zhvartz iz nisht vyhss

BLANKET —— KOLdreh
The blanket is warm.
Die koldreh iz vahrehm

BLIND —— BLIND (as in SINNED)
He is blind.
Ehr iz blind.

BLISTER —— POOcheer or BLOOter
I have a blister on my foot.
Ich haub ah poocheer auf myn foos.

BLOOD —— BLOOT
He lost a lot of blood.
Ehr haut fahrlauren ah sach bloot.
BLOODY: Blootick
BLEEDING: Geyt bloot
BLEED: Blootikin

BLOND —— BLAUNdeh
She has blond hair.
Zie haut blaundeh hawr.

BLOTTER —— LASHpahper or KLEHker

BLOUSE —— BLOOzeh or BLOYz
Her blouse is green.
Eer bloyz iz grin.

BLUE —— BLOY
The sky is blue.
Dehr himmel iz bloy.

BOAT —— SHIFF
We're going by boat.
Meer gayen mit ah shiff.

BOIL —— geSHVEER or BLAUtehr. (ailment)
The boil hurts.
Dehr geshveer toot vay.

BONE —— BAYN
He has a bone in his throat.
Ehr haut ah bayn in hahldz

BOOK —— BOOCH (hard CH)
Did you read this book?
Haustu gelezzin dehm booch?
BOOKKEEPER: Booch-hahl-tehr
Book Store: Beechehr kraum

BORROW —— BAURG (as in Morgue)
May I borrow the sugar?
Khen ich baurgen die tzukehr?
BORROWED: Gehbaurgen

BOTHER —— TCHEHpeh
Don't bother me.
Tchehpeh mich nisht.

BOTTLE —— FLAHSH
A bottle of liquor.
Ah flahsh brahnfin.

BOX —— KEStil
A box of apples.
Ah kestil ephil.

BREAD —— BROYT
Die broyt iz nisht frish
The bread is not fresh.

BREAK —— tzuBRECH
Break the door down.
Tzubrech die teer.
BROKEN: Tzubrauchen

BOY —— YINgil
The boy goes to school.
Dehr yingil gayt in shooleh.
YOUNG MAN: Yoong
He is a healthy young man.
Ehr iz a gezundtehr yoong.
(Term of endearment) Yingeleh.

BREAKFAST —— FRISHtik
Eat a good breakfast.
Ess ah gootin frishtik.

BREAST —— BROOst
The breast of the chicken.
Die broost foon die hoon

BRING —— BREYNG
Bring him in.
Breyng ehm ariyn.
BROUGHT: Gehbrahcht.

BRIDE —— KAHlleh
The bride is beautiful.
Die kahlleh iz zayer shayn.

BROKER —— MEKlehr (as in Heckler)
He is the broker for the house.
Ehr iz dehr meklehr fahr die hoiz.

BROTHER —— BROODehr
He is my older brother.
Ehr iz mye elterehr broodehr.

BROWN —— BROYN
A brown horse.
Ah broineh fehrd.

BRUSH —— BAHRsht
Brush your teeth.
Bahrsht dyneh tzaynehr.

BUILDING —— BINyen
The building is of stone.
Dehr binyen iz foon shtayn.

BULB —— LEMpil
This bulb gives off a lot of light.
Die lempil git ah sach licht.

BUM —— TRAUMbenik
He was always a bum.
Ehr iz ahleh mauhl gehvehn ah traumbenik

BUREAU —— kauMAUD
Put the things in the bureau.
Layg die zachen in dehr kaumaud.

BURN —— BREHN
The fire is burning strong.
Dehr fiyehr brehnt shtark
BURNT: Gebrehnt

BURST —— gehPLATZT
BUS —— BOOS
The bus is coming.
Dehr boos koomt
BUS STATION: Boos stahntzyeh
BUS STOP: Boos aupshtell

BUSINESS —— gehSHEFT
How is business?
Vie iz dehr gesheft?

BUSY —— fahrNOOmen
He is very busy.
Ehr is zayer fahrnoomen.

BUT —— AUbehr (also means) 'Either'
BUTCHER —— KAHtzev
He is a kosher butcher
Ehr iz ah kaushehrehr kahtzev.

BUTTER —— POOtehr
This is sweet butter.
Dos iz zisseh pootehr.

BUY —— KOYF
Don't buy the shoes.
Koyf nitt die shich.
SELL: Fahrkoyf
BUYER: Einkoyfer
BOUGHT: Gekoyftt

C

CAFE —— KAHFeh
I'll see you in the cafe.
Ich'll dier zehn in dehr kahfeh

CAKE —— KOOchin
I want a white cake
Ich vil ah vysen koochin
Honey Cake: Lehkach

CALAMITY —— OOMglik
This is a terrible calamity.
Dos iz ah shlechtehr oomglik.

CALL —— ROOPHF
Call a policeman!
Roophf ah pawlitzyahnt!

CAMERA —— ahpahRAHT
The camera takes a good picture
Dehr ahpahraht nempt ah gootin bild.

CAN —— KEHN
Can you come with me?
Kehn ir koomen mit mir?
CANNOT: Kehn nisht.

CANCELLATION —— ahNOOleeroong
Call for a cancellation
Roophf fahr ahn ahnooleeroong

CANDY —— tzuKEHRkeh
Children like candy
Kinder glychin tzukehrkeh.

CAP —— HITil
He's wearing a cap
Ehr traukt ah hitil

CAPTAIN —— kahpeeTAHN
The captain is a handsome man.
Dehr kahpeetahn iz ah shayner mahn.

CAR —— OYtaw
The car goes very fast.
Dehr oytaw gayt zayer shnehl.

CARDS —— KAURtin
Do you want to play cards?
Vilstu shpielin kaurtin?
BUSINESS CARDS: Handil Kartlech

CAREFUL —— AWPgehheet
Be careful.
Zyte awpgehheet

CARPENTER —— STAWLyehr
He's a good carpenter
Ehr iz ah gooter stawlyehr

CARPET —— TEHpech
Walk on the carpet.
Gay ahffin dehr tehpech.

CARROT —— MEHrin
The carrots are fresh.
Die mehrin zahnen frish.

CARRY —— TRAUGG
Carry the shoes over here.
Traugg die shich ahhehr

CASH —— GELT
How much cash do you have?
Viffehl gelt haustu?

CAT —— KAHTZ
The cat caught a mouse.
Die kahtz haut gehchahppt ah moiz
KITTEN: Kehtzahleh

CATALOGUE —— KAHTahlaug
Send me a catalogue.
Shick meer ah kahtahlaug.

CAULIFLOWER —— KAHeefYAWrin
The cauliflower is green.
Dehr kaheefyawrin iz grin.

CEILING —— STELyeh
The ceiling is very high.
Die stelyeh iz sayer hoych.

CELEBRATION —— SIMchah
It's a great celebration
Ess iz a groyseh simcheh

CELERY —— sehLEHRyeh
The celery is very green.
Die sehlehryeh iz zayer grin.

CELLAR —— KEHlehr
The things are in the cellar.
Die zachin zahnen in dehr kehlehr.

CENTER —— TZENtehr
This is the center of the world.
Dos iz dehr tzentehr foon dehr veldt.

CEREAL —— KAHsheh
Do you want cooked cereal?
Vilt eer eingehkauchteh kahsheh?

CHAINS —— KAYtin
They have him in chains.
Zey hahlten ehm in kaytin.

CHAIR —— SHTOOL
Sit on the chair.
Zitz auffin shtool.

CHANGE —— OYSbytin
I'll take the change.
Ich'll nemin die oysbytin.

CHARGE —— AWPtzawl
I'll charge the clothes.
Ich'll awptzawlin die klaydehr.

CHEAP —— BILLick
The price is cheap.
Dehr priyz iz billick

CHEEK —— BAHK
She has red cheeks.
Zie haut rayteh bahkin
CHEEKS: Bahkin
SMALL CHEEKS: Bekahlach

CHEESE —— KEZ (as in Fez)
This is cheese cake.
Dos iz ah kezkoochin

CHECK —— TSHEK or KHESHbin
His check is good.
Zyhn tshek iz goot.

CHERRIES —— KAHRshin
These cherries are sweet.
Die kahrshin zahnen ziss

CHEST —— BROOST
(also means) Breast

CHICKEN —— HOON (female) Heen
It's a soft chicken.
Dos iz ah vaycheh hoon.
ROOSTER: Hoon

CHILL —— Kelt or TZITehr
He has the chills.
Ehr tzitehrt mit kelt.
(also means) Shiver

CHILD —— KIIND (as in win)
She is a smart child.
Zie iz ah kloogeh kiind.
CHILDREN: Kinder (as in Hinder)
CHILD's PLAY: Kindershpeel
CHILDLIKE: Kinderish
SMALL CHILDREN: Kinderlach

CHIN —— GAUMBEH or KIN
He has a double chin.
Ehr haut ah taupele gaumbeh

CHIROPODIST —— FOOSdauktehr
I'm going to the chiropodist.
Ich gay tzu dehm foosdauktehr.

CHOP —— HOCK
He's chopping the wood.
Ehr hockt die holtz.
CHOPPED: Haut gehockt

CIGAR —— TZIgahr
Do you want a cigar?
Wilstu ah tzigahr?
CIGARETTE: Pahpeerausin

CITY —— SHTAUT
It's a big city.
Dos iz ah grayseh shtaut.
VILLAGE: Shtet'l

CLAP —— KLAHP or PAHTCH
Clap your hands.
Pahtsh mit die hent.
(colloquial)
Hit your head against the wall.
Klahp sich kaup in vant.

CLASS —— KLAHSS
First class.
Ehrshteh klahss

CLEAN —— RAYN (as in Drain)
This is a clean house.
Dos iz ah rayneh hoiz.

CLERK —— fahrKOYfehr
They have five clerks here.
Zey hauben finf fahrkoyfehrs daw.

CLOCK —— ZAYgehr
The clock is fast
Dehr zaygehr gayt shnell.
What time is it?
Viefihl iz dehr zaygehr?
It's six o'clock
Ess iz zex dehr zaygehr.

CLOSE —— fahrMACH
Close the door.
Fahrmach die teer.

CLOTHES —— KLAYdehr
He has nice clothes
Ehr haut shayneh klaydehr
CLOTH: Shtuffin or Gevant

COAT —— MAHNtil
This is a warm coat.
Dos iz ah varehmehr mahntil

COCOA —— kaKAHwau

COFFEE —— KAHveh
This is strong coffee.
Dos iz shtarkeh kahveh

COLD —— KAHLT
It is cold, not hot.
Ess iz kahlt, nisht hais
It's a cold night.
Ess iz ah kahlteh nacht

COLLAR —— KAWLnehr
This collar is tight
Der kawlnehr iz engir

COLLEGE —— KAHledzsh
I go to college.
Ich gay in kahledzsh

COLOR —— KAWLyehr
The color is red.
Dos iz ah rayteh kawlyehr

COMB —— KOOM
Comb your hair!
FerKahm (v) dyneh hawr!

COME —— KOOM
Come here
Koom ahehr.
COMING: Koomin
HAD COME: Haut gehkoomen

COMFORTABLE —— bahkVEHmeh
This is very comfortable
Dos iz zayer bahkvehmeh.

COMMERCE —— MIScher or KAUMertz

COMPASSION —— rachMAUNis
Have compassion!
Haub rachmaunis!

CONCERT —— kaunTZEHRT

CONFERENCE —— baRAHtoong
It's an important conference.
Die barahtoong iz vichtik.

CONFUSED —— FAHTchadit, or Tzumisht
He is very confused
Ehr iz zayer tzumisht.

CONGRATULATIONS —— MAZEL TOV

CONSIGNMENT —— SHEEkoong
He bought it on consignment.
Ehr haut dos gehkayft aun sheekoong

CONSTIPATION —— fahrSHTAUPoong

CONSUME —— ESS (also means) Eat
They've consumed everything.
Zey hauben ahlis gegessen.
Eat my child.
Ess miy kind.

CONTAIN —— LIKT
This package contains clothes
In dem pehkil likt klaydehr.

CONTRACT —— KAWNtrackt
Read the contract.
Lehz dehm kawntrackt.

CONVERSATION —— SHMOOess

COOK —— KAUCH
Cook the meat.
Kauch die flaysh.
COOKED: Gehkaucht
A COOK: Ah Kehchin

COOL —— KEEHL
This is a cool night.
Dos iz ah killeh nahcht.
COLD: Kahlt

COPY —— KAUPyeh
Make only one copy.
Mahch naur ayn kaupyeh.

CORK —— KAWrik
Put the cork in the bottle.
Shtik dem kawrik in dehr flahsh

CORNER —— RAWG
Take the second corner
Nehm dehr tzvaytin rawg.

COST —— PRIYZZ
How much does it cost?
Viffil iz dehr priyzz?

COTTON —— VAHteh
The dress is of cotton.
Dos klayd iz foon vahteh.

COUGH —— HOOST
He has a bad cough
Ehr haut ah shlechten hoost.

COW —— KOO
The cow gives milk.
Die koo git milch

COZY —— HAYmish (also means) Friendly.
This house is cozy
Die hoiz iz haymish.
He is a friendly person.
Ehr iz ah haymisheh mensh.

CRAFTSMAN —— balmaLOCHeh
He is really a good craftsman.
Ehr iz tahkeh ah gooter balmalocheh

CRAMP —— KRAHMP
I've got a cramp in my leg.
Ich haub ah krahmp in myn foos.

CREAM —— SHMAHNT or KREMM
I take cream in my coffee
Ich nehm shmahnt in myn kaveh.
SOUR CREAM: Smetehneh
CREAM CHEESE: Krem Kez

CREDIT —— KREHdit
He has no credit.
Ehr haut kayn krehdit.

CRAZY —— miSHOOgeh
He's crazy.
Ehrz mishoogeh.
A CRAZY PERSON: Mishoogenehr
A CRAZY IDEA: Mishoogahss

CRY —— VAYN
Don't cry for him.
Vayn nitt fahr ehm.
Why are you crying?
Fahrvos vainstu?

CUCUMBERS —— ooGHEHRkis
These cucumbers are very sweet.
Die ooghehrkis zahnen zeyer ziss.

CUFF LINKS —— SHPAUNkis
He has golden cuff links.
Ehr haut gauldineh shpaunkis.

CURTAIN —— farHAHNGG
The curtain is dirty.
Die farhahngg iz shmootzik.

CUSHIN —— KEEshin
I sleep without a cushion.
Ich shlauff aun ah keeshin.

CUT ——(v) SHNEYD (as in — bride)
Don't cut the cloth
Shneyd nit di vahreh
A CUT: SHNITT (n)
A TAILOR: Shniyder
ALREADY CUT: Shoyn geshnitten
TO CUT WITH A SCISSOR: Shehr.

D

DAIRY —— MILchick
Milk is a dairy product.
Milch iz ah milchickeh prodook

DANCE —— TAHNtz
I can dance all night.
Ich ken tahntzin ah gahntzen nacht.
DANCED: Tahntzt
DANCING: Tahntzin

DARK —— FINstehr
The sky is dark
Dehr himmil iz finstehr.

DATE —— DAHteh
The date is tomorrow
Die dahteh iz morgin

DAUGHTER —— TAUCHtehr
I have a daughter and a son.
Ich haub ah tauchtehr un ah zoon.

DAY —— TAUG
This is a warm day.
Dos iz ah varimehr taug.
DAYS: Tegg

DEAD —— TAYT
He is dead twenty years.
Ehr iz shoyn tayt tzvantzik yawr.

DEAF —— TOYB
He is entirely deaf
Ehr iz ingahntzen toyb

DEAR —— TYehr
It is too expensive (dear)
Ess iz tzoo tyehr
She's a dear person.
Zie iz ah tyehreh mensh.

DEBT —— CHOYV
Pay your debts.
Bahtzaul dyneh choyves

DECK —— DEK
Get up on deck
Gay aroof aufen dek.

DELIVERY —— TZUshtell
The delivery is late.
Dehr tzushtell iz shpet

DEMON —— TYvil

DENTIST ——TZAWNdawktehr
I'm going to the dentist.
Ich gay tzu dehm tzawndawktehr.

DEPARTMENT —— AUPtayl
This is the shoe department.
Dos iz dehr shich auptayl

DESK —— SHRYBtish
He is sitting at the desk.
Ehr zitzt aufen shrybtish.

DEVIL —— malchuMAUvis (Angel of death)
He's a devil
Ehrz ah malchumauvis

DIAPERS —— VINdlech
The diapers are wet
Die vindlech zahnen nahss

DIARRHEA —— SHILshil
His diarrhea makes him sick.
Zyn shilshil macht ehm krahnk

DIFFERENT —— AHNdersh
The two horses are different.
Die tzvay fehrd zahnen ahndersh.

DIM —— TOONkil
The lights are dim.
Die licht zahnen toonkil

DINE —— EHSS
We will dine at home.
Meer vellin ehssin in dehr haym
DINING ROOM: Esstzimmer
DINNER: Mitaug

DIRT —— SHMOOTZ
Don't bring the dirt into the house.
Brayngg nitt die shmootz in dehm hoiz
DIRTY: Shmootzik

DISCOUNT —— hanAUCHes
Do I get a discount?
Kreehg ich ahn hanauches?

DISHES —— KAYlim
Don't break the dishes.
Tzubrech nitt die kaylim.

DISTRIBUTE —— fahrTAYlin or OYStaylin
Distribute the food.
Fahrtayloys dos essin

DITCH —— GRAWbin
It's a wide ditch
Dos iz ah brayter grawbin.

DIVORCE —— GETT
They're getting a divorce.
Zey kriggin ah gett.

DO —— Tu or Tawn
Do me a favor.
Tu meer ah toyveh.
What can you do?
Vos kenstu tawn?

DOCTOR —— DAWKtehr
Call a doctor.
Rooff ah dawktehr.

DOG —— HOONT
He's a big dog
Ehrz ah grayser hoont.

DOLL —— LAHLkeh
It's a beautiful doll
Dos iz ah shayneh lahlkeh.

DOLLAR —— TAHlehr
Let me have change of a dollar.
Gibb mir klayn-gelt fahrin tahlehr.

DOOR —— TEER
Close the door.
Fahrmach die teer

DOUBLE —— TAWpil
I'm seeing double
Ich zeh tawpil

DOUGH —— TAYG
Make a sweet dough
Mach ah zeessin tayg.

DOWN —— OONtin (also means) Under
or'Ahraup'
Go under the house.
Gay oonin dehm hoiz

DOZEN —— TOOTS
Twelve rolls make a dozen
Tzvelf zemmil maacht a toots

DRAFT —— VEHsil
Get me a bank draft
Krig mir ah veksil

DRESS —— KLAYD
It's a pretty dress
Ess iz ah shayn klayd
CLOTHING: Klaydehr or Klaydung

DRINK —— TROONK
I'll have a drink of water
Ich'll haubin ah troonk vassehr.

DROP —— TRAWpin
It's only a drop
Dos iz nawr ah trawpin

DRUGS —— MEHDitzin
This drug is for my cold.
Die meditzin iz fahr myn kahltt

DRUNK —— SHICKehr
He's a drunk
Ehrz ah shickehr

DRY —— TROOKin
Dry the dishes
Trookin oys die kaylim

DUCK —— KAHTCHkeh
The duck is very good.
Die kahtchkeh iz zeyer goot.

E

EACH —— YEDder
Each one
Yedder aynehr

EAR —— OYehr
He can't hear out of one ear.
Ehr kennit hehrin auf ayn oyehr
EARACHE: Oyehrvaytik

EARLY —— FREEH
Come early.
Koom freeh
EARLIER: Freehehr

EARRINGS —— Oyringlech
Golden earrings
Goldeneh oyringlech

EAST —— MIZrach
We live in the East.
Mir voynen in der mizrach

EAT —— ESS
Eat, my child
Ess, miyn kindd.
FOOD: Essen
HAS EATEN: Haut gehgessin
GULP: Shlingen

ECONOMICS —— eecoNOMik

EDUCATE —— LEHRenn

EGGS —— AYehr
The eggs are very fresh
Die ayehr zahnen zayer frish

ELBOW —— EHLinboygin
He has a broken elbow
Ehr haut ah tzubrauchenehm ehlinboygin

ELECTRIC —— ehLECtrish
This is an electric light
Dos iz ahn ehlectrishe lamphil

ELEVATOR —— LIFFT
It's a fast elevator
Dos iz a shneller lifft

EMPLOY —— AWNshtehlin
EMPLOYEE: Awngehshteltehr
EMPLOYER: Ahrbetgehbehr

EMPTY —— POOST
The house is empty
Dehr hoiz iz poost.

END —— ENDeh
It's the end of the story.
Dos iz die endeh foon die gehshichteh

ENDORSE —— zshiRIRhern
Endorse the check
zshirirhern dehm check

ENGINE —— MAWtaur
ENGINEER: Inzshenir

ENGLISH —— AYNglish
Do you know how to speak English?
Vaystu vie tzu reddin Aynglish

ENJOY —— geNEEsin or farBRACH
I enjoy all music
Ich genees alleh muzik

ENOUGH —— gehNOOG
That's enough
Shoyn gehnoog

ENTRANCE —— AREYENkoomin or Arayngang
The door is the entrance.
Die tier iz dehr araynkoom
ENTER: Koom ahryne

ENVELOPE —— kaunVEHRtin
Send it in an airmail envelope
Shick dos in a looftpaust kaunvehrtin

ERASER —— MEHkehr

ESTIMATE —— SHAHtzoong
The estimate is high
Die shahtzoong iz tyehr

EVENING —— AUvent
It's nice in the evening.
Ess iz shayn in auvent

EVERY —— AHleh
I go there all the time.
Ich gay daurtin ahleh mohl
Every child is good.
Ahleh kinder zahnen goot.
EVERYTHING: Ahles
EVERY ONE: Yedder ayner

EXCHANGE —— OYSbyte
Exchange the shoes.
Bytoys die shick
This is an exchange.
Dos iz ahn oysbyte

EXCUSE ME —— ahntSHOOLdikt mir
EXIT —— ahROYSgang
This door is the exit.
Die teer iz dehr ahroysgang

EXPECT —— Richtin zich
Don't expect him
Richt zich nit auf ehm.

EXPENSIVE —— TYehr
The house is very expensive
Dos hoiz iz zayer tyehr

EXPERIENCE —— PRAHKtic
EXPERT: Expehrt

EXPLODE —— OYFrysin
EXPORT —— EXpaurt
We only export
Mir expaurteerin naur

EYE —— OYG
EYES: Oygin
EYEBROWS: Brehmehn
EYELASHES: Veeyehs
EYELIDS: Oygin lendil

F

FACE —— PAUnim
He's got a nice face.
Ehr haut ah shaynim paunim

FADE —— OYSblankeerin
FAINT —— CHALlishin
He has fainted.
Ehr haut gehchallisht

FAIR —— SHAYN
It is a fair day
Ess iz ah shayner taug
She is pretty
Zie iz shayn

FALL —— FAHLL
Don't fall
Fahll nisht
FELL: Gehfahllin

FAMILY —— mishPAUcheh
This is my family
Dos iz myn mishpaucheh

FAN —— venteeLAHtaur
The fan makes it cool
Die venteelahtaur macht dos kihll

FAR —— VIYT
Don't go far
Gay nisht viyt
FURTHER: Viytehr
VERY FAR: Zeyer viyt

FARE —— FAURgelt
How much is the fare?
Veefil iz die faurgelt?

FAST —— GICH or SHNELL
He is very fast
Ehr iz zayer shnell
Go fast
Gay gich
Go faster
Gay gichehr

FAT (n) —— SHMALTZ
The meat has too much fat.
Die flaysh haut tzu fihl shmaltz

FAT (adj.) —— GRAWB
He is very fat.
Ehr iz zayer grawb.

FATHER —— TAHteh
He is my father
Ehr iz myne tahteh

FAULT —— SHOOLD (also means) Blame
It is not his fault
Ess iz nitt zyn shoold
He is not to blame.
Ehr iz nitt shooldik

FEMALE —— FROY
Females can work here.
Froyin kennen dau ahrbehtin

FERRY —— PRAUM
Take the ferry
Nehm die praum

FEVER —— HITZ
He has a fever
Ehr haut hitz
(also means) Heat

FEW —— VAYnik or Vintzik
There are very few people here
Ess zennen zayer vaynik menshehn dau
LESS: Vintzikehr
VERY FEW: Ah bisseleh or Zayer vaynik

FILL —— OYSFILLIN or Aunfillin
FILLED: Oysgefilt
TOOTH FILLING: Plawnbeh

FILBERTS —— VAULDnishlech

FILM —— FEHLM
This film is no good
Die felm iz nisht goot

FIND —— gehFIN
Find my shoes
Gehfin myneh shich
FOUND: Gehfoonen
FOUND MONEY: Gehroonen gelt

FINGER —— FINgehr
A hand has five fingers.
Ah hahnt haut finf fingehrz

FINISHED —— GE-EHNdikt or Fahrtik
The work is finished
Die ahrbit iz farehndikt

FIRE —— ah FYER (also means) Burn (Flahm)
It's on fire.
Ehs brehnt
BURNT: Fahrbrehnt

FIRM —— FEERmeh
It is a big firm.
Ess iz ah grayseh feermeh

FIRST —— EHRshteh
This is the first time
Dos iz dehr ehrshteh maull

FISH —— FEESH
This is a fresh fish
Dos iz frisheh feesh
CATCHING FISH: Chahpehn feesh

FIT —— PAHST
The pants do not fit
Die hoyzen pahst nitt.

FLAT —— FLACH or PLAHTchik
The tire is flat
Der rayf iz flach

FLOOR —— GAWrin
He's on the first floor
Ehr iz oyf dehm ehrstin ga-wrin

FOLLOW —— NAUCHgayn
Follow me
Gay mir nauch

FOOD —— ESSENvahrg
This is good food
Dos iz gooteh essenvahrg

FOOL —— GAYlem or NAHR
He is a fool
Ehr iz ah nahr
FOOLISHNESS: Nahrishkiyt
OUTWITTED: Oysgenahrt

FOOT —— FOOS
My left foot hurts
Mye leenkeh foos toot vay
FEET: Fees
FOOTBALL: Foosbaul

FOR —— FAHR
This is for you
Dos iz fahr dier

FORHEAD —— SHTERrin
He has a large forehead
Ehr haut ah groyser shterrin

FORWARD —— fauROYS
Go forward
Gay fauroys

FOREMAN —— OYFzeyer
He is the foreman
Ehr iz dehr oyfzeyer

FORGET —— fahrGEHSS
Don't forget
Fahrgehss nitt
HAD FORGOTTEN: Haut fahrgehssin

FORK —— GAWpil
A fork and a spoon
Ah gawpil un ah leffil

FREE —— FRYE
It's good to be free.
Ess iz goot tzu zyne frye.
FREEDOM: Fryekyte

FREIGHT —— FRACHT
Send it by freight
Shick dos mit der fracht

FRET —— GRIZshen Zich
All he does is fret
Naur ehr grizshet zich

FRY —— PRAYgil
Fry the meat
Praygil dos flaysh
FRIED: Gepraygilteh

FRIEND —— FRYNT
He's a good friend
Ehr iz ah gooteh frynt

FROM —— FOON
He comes from America
Ehr koomt foon Ahmehrike

FRONT —— FAURENT
Walk in front.
Gay faurent

FROZEN —— gehFROYRIN
His hands are frozen
Zyneh hehnt zahnen gehfroyrin

FRUIT —— FROOCHT
This is a lot of fruit.
Dos iz ah sach froocht

FUNERAL —— leVYeh
It's a long funeral
Dos iz ah lahngeh levyeh

FUNNY —— KAWmish
Tell me a funny story
Dertzayl mir ah kawmishe gehshichteh

FURNITURE —— MEHbil
The house has no furniture
Dos hoiz haut nitt kayn mehbil.

G

GALLON —— GAHlaun
I want ten gallons of gas
Ich vill tzen gahlaunen gahzawleen

GARAGE —— gahRAHZSH
Take me to a garage
Nehm mich tzu ah gahrahzsh

GARDEN —— GORtin
What a big garden.
Ahzah groyser gortin

GARLIC —— KNAUbl
I'll have some garlic salami
Ich'll haubin a shtikl knaubl voorsht

GARTERS —— ZAWkinbendlech

A pair of garters
Ah paur zahkinbendlech

GASOLINE —— GAHzawleen
I don't have any gas.
Ich haub nitt kayn gahzawleen

GENTILE —— GOY (male) Shaygitz
He's a gentile.
Ehr iz ah shaygitz

GENTLE —— AYdil
She is very gentle
Zie iz zayer aydil

GATE —— TOYehr
Open the gate
Effen dehm toyehr

GET —— KRIGG
What are you going to get?
Vos krigstu?
Did you get it?
Haustu dos gehkraugin?
WILL GET: Vett kriggen

GIFT —— mahTAWneh
I have to buy a gift.
Ich darff kayfin ah mahtawneh

GIRDLE —— GAURsett
The girdle hurts me
Die gaursett toot mir vay.

GIVE —— GIB or GHIT or GHIST
What are you giving him?
Vos ghistu ehm?
HAVE GIVEN: Haut gehgebben

GLAD —— tzuFRIDDin
I am glad
Ich bin tzufriddin

GLASS —— GLAUZ
Give me a glass of water
Gibb mir ah glawz vassehr

GLOVES —— HENSHkes
A pair of black gloves
Ah pawr shvartzeh henshkes

GO —— GAY
Go away!
Gay aveck!
Where are you going?
Voo gaystu?
GONE: Aveckgegangen
WENT: Gehgahngen

GOLD —— GAULD
A gold ring
Ah gauldeneh fingehril

GOOD —— GOOT
Good enough
Goot gehnoog
It's not good.
Ess iz nisht goot.

GOODBYE —— SHALOM or AH GOOTIN TAUG

GOOSE —— GANDZ
A tasty goose
Ah gehshmahkeh gandz

GOSSIP ——(n) YACHneh or YENteh
An old gossip
Ah yenteh tehlibendeh
TO GOSSIP: bahREDin

GOULASH —— GOOlahsh
Hungarian Goulash
Hoongarishen Goolahsh

GRANDFATHER —— ZAYdeh
His grandfather is old.
Zyne zaydeh iz ault

GRANDMOTHER —— BAUBeh
GRANDMOTHER'S TALE: Baubeh Myseh

GRAPES —— VYNtroybin
What sweet grapes!
Ahzelche zisseh vyntroybin

GRAPEFRUIT —— GRAYPfroocht
A sour grapefruit
Ah zoyereh graypfroocht

GRAY —— GROY
The sky is gray
Dehr himmil iz groy

GREEN —— GRINN
A green hat
Ah grinneh hoot.

GRIND —— KRITZIN
He's grinding his teeth
Ehr kritzt mit zyne tzayn.

GROCERY —— SHPYZkraum
Buy it in the grocery.
Kayf dos in dehr shpyzkraum

GUIDE (n) —— FEErehr
I need a guide.
Ich darff ah feerehr

H

HAIR —— HAURR
She has black hair
Zie haut shvartzeh haurr.
HAIR BRUSH: Haurr barsht
HAIR STYLE: Freezoor
HAIRNET: Haurnett

HALF —— HAHLB
I'll take a half
Ich'll nehmen ah hahlb

HALL —— KAUReedawr or Zahl
Don't talk in the hall
Rehd nitt in dehr kaureedawr

HAMMER —— HAHmehr
I need a hammer
Ich darff ah hahmehr

HAND —— HAHNT
Give me your hand
Gibb mir dyne hahnt
HAND TOWEL: Hahntach

HANDLE —— bagGAYTin
Handle it carefully.
Bahgayt zich faurzichtik

HANG —— HEHNG
Hang it up.
Hehng dos ahroof

HAPPY —— FRAYlich
This is a happy day.
Dos iz ah fraylicher taug
HAPPINESS: Fraylichkyte or Glick

HARASS —— MOOTsheh
Don't harass me.
Mootsheh mich nisht.

HARD —— HARDT
He has a hard head.
Ehr haut ah hardten kaup

HARDWARE —— EYZINvargg
I need more hardware.
Ich darff mehr eyzinvargg.

HAT —— HOOT
He's not wearing a hat.
Ehr traukt nitt ah hoot.
CAP: Hittil

HAVE —— HAUB
What do you have?
Vaus*s hau*stu?
I don't have it.
Ich *haub d*auss nitt.
I had it yesterday.
Ich *haub d*os gehaht nechtin.

HEAD —— KAUPP
He's got a big head.
Ehr haut ah grayser kaupp

HEALTH —— geZOONDT
He is very healthy
Ehr iz zayer gezoondt.
Have a healthy year.
Haub ah gezoondten yawr

HEAR —— HEHRRN
We can't hear it.
Mir kennen dos nitt hehrrn.
Did you hear it?
Haustu dos gehehrt?
What do you hear?
Vos hehrstu?

HEART —— HAHRTZ
She has a good heart.
Zie haut ah gooteh hahrtz.
HEARTACHE: Hahrtzvaytik

HEAT —— HITZ
The heat is bad.
Die hitz iz shlecht.

HEAVEN —— HIMML
The heaven is blue
Dehr himml iz bloy

HEAVY —— SHVEHR
It is too heavy to lift.
Ess iz tzu shvehr tzu haybin.
HEAVIER: Shvehrehr

HEEL —— pyAHTeh
She's wearing high heels.
Zie taukt hoycheh pyahtehs

HELL —— DREHRD

HELP —— HELFF
Help me!
Helff mir!
HELPER: Helffehr

HERE —— DAW or AHhehr
Come here
Koom ahhehr.
Place the things here.
Layg die zahchin daw.

HIGH —— HAYCH
The tree is very high.
Dehr baym iz zayer haych
HIGHER: Hehchehr
HIGHEST: Hechsti

HIP —— LEND
He broke his hip.
Ehr haut tzubrauchen zyne lend.

HIRE —— DINGG
Hire me a car.
Dingg mir ahn oytaw

HISTORY —— gehSHICHteh
This is the history of the Jews
Dos iz die gehshichteh foon die Yiddin.

HIT —— SHLAUG
Don't hit him.
Shlaug ehm nisht.
PAST TENSE: Gehshlaugn

HOARSE —— HAYzehrick
I'm hoarse.
Ich bin hayzehrick

HOLD —— HAHLT
Hold this for me.
Hahlt dos fahr mir.
HELD: Gehahltin

HOLE —— LAUCH
He's got a hole in his shoe.
Ehr haut ah lauch in zyne shooch.
HOLES: Lechehr

HOLIDAY —— YAWNtiff
Have a good holiday.
Haub ah gootin yawntiff

HOLY —— HAYlick
This is a holy day.
Dos iz ah haylickehr taug.

HOME —— HAYM
Go home.
Gay ahhaym

HONEY —— HAUnik
This is a honey cake.
Dos iz ah haunik lehkehch

HONOR —— KAUVID
He is very honored
Ehr haut ah sahch kauvid.

HOPE —— HAUFFnung
She has a lot of hope
Zie haut ah sahch hauffnung
TO HOPE: Tzu hauffn

HORSE RADISH —— CHRAYN
The horse radish is strong.
Der chrayn iz shtahrk

HOSPITAL —— SHPEEtaul
They took her to the hospital
Zy hauben zee genummen tzu dehm shpeetaul

HOT —— HAYSS
This is a hot day
Dos iz ah haysser taug

HOTEL —— HAUtel
I'm staying at the hotel
Ich shtay in dehm hautel

HOUR —— SHTOONdeh
I'll wait one hour
Ich'll vahrtin ayn shtoondeh

HOUSE —— HOIZ
It's a pretty house.
Dos iz ah shayneh hoiz

HOW —— VEE
How do you feel?
VEE feelstu?
HOW MUCH: Vee feel?

HUNGRY —— HOONgehrik
I'm hungry.
Ich bin hoongehrik

HURRY —— GICH or SHNELL (also means) Fast
Hurry up!
Mach shnell!
Go in a hurry.
Gay shnell.

HURT —— TOOTVAY
My tooth hurts
Myn tzaun toot vay.

HUSBAND —— MAHN (also means) Man
Husband and wife.
Mahn un froy

I

I —— Ich
I can't go.
Ich kehn nisht gayn

ICE —— EIZ
Put ice in my drink
Tu eiz in myn troonk

IF —— OYB
If you come I'll see you.
Oyb ir koomt, Ich'll dich zehn

ILL —— KRAHNK
He's very ill.
Ehr iz zayer krahnk
SICKNESS: Krahnkyht

IMMEDIATELY —— TAYkef or YETZT
I want you immediately
Ich vill dich taykef.
COME NOW: Koom yetzt.

IMPORTANT —— VICHtig
This is important.
Dos iz vichtig

IMPROVE —— FAHRBESSern
Improve the story.
Fahrbessern die gehshichteh.

IN —— IHN or IN
Go into the house.
Gay ariyn in hoiz.

INDIGESTION —— BOYCHvaytik
I have indigestion
Ich haub ah boychvaytik

INJURE —— fahrVOONdik
Don't injure him.
Fahrvoondik ehm nisht.
INJURED: Fahrvoondikt

INK —— TINT
I write with blue ink.
Ich shrybe mitt bloyeh tint.

INSANE —— miSHOOgeh
He is insane.
Ehr iz mishoogeh
INSANITY: mishehGAHSS
INSANE MAN: Mishoogenehr

INSIDE —— INVAYnik
Go inside.
Gay invaynik

INSUFFICIENT —— VAYnik
This is insufficient.
Dos iz vaynik

INSURANCE —— fahrZEEchehroong
You have to have insurance.
Du darfst haubin fahrzeechehroong.

INTEREST —— PRAUtzent
You have to pay interest.
Du darfst bahtzaulehn prautzent

INTERPRETOR —— EEbehrzehtzehr
He's an interpretor
Ehr iz ahn eebehrzehtzehr

INTRODUCE —— FARshtehlin
Let me introduce my wife.
Lauz mich faurshtehlin myn froy.

IODINE —— YAUD
Put iodine on the cut.
Layg tzu yaud oyfin shnitt.

IOU —— VEKsil
I'll give you an IOU
Ich'll dir gebben ah veksil

IRON (n) —— PREHsil
The iron is hot.
Dos prehsil iz hayss
IRONING BOARD: PRESbret

J

JACKET —— ZSHAHket
It's a warm jacket.
Dos iz ah vahrehmehr zshah-ket

JAW —— KINbayn
His jaw is broken.
Zyne kinbayn iz tzubrauchin

JELLY —— EYNgehmahchtz

JEWELRY —— TZEEroong
The jewelry is expensive.
Die tzeeroong iz zayer tyehr.

JOB —— SHTEHleh
This is a good job.
Dos iz ah gooteh shtehleh.
JOBBER: fahrMITlehr

JOINT —— gehLENK
This is my knee joint.
Dos iz myn k'nee gehlenk

JOY —— SIMcheh or FRAYD
This is really a joy.
Dos iz takeh ah simcheh.

JUICE —— ZAHFTT
A glass of prune juice.
Ah glauz floymin zahftt.
JUICY: Zahftik

JUST —— NAUR
I am only five years old.
Ich bin naur finf yaur ahlt.

K

KEEP —— HAHLT (also means:) Hold
Hold this for me.
Hahlt dos fahr mir.

KETCHUP —— KETCHoop
May I have some ketchup?
Kehn ich haubin ah bissil ket-choop?

KEY —— SHLISSil
I've lost my key.
Ich haub fahrloyrin myn shlis-sil.

KIDNEY —— NEER
My kidneys are bad.
Myne neerin zahnehn shlecht

KILL —— gehHAHRgehnen
He will kill him
KILLED: Gehahrgeht

KINDLY —— ZYTE ahzoy goot (also means) Please
Kindly show me the way.
Zyte ahzoy goot tzygt mir dem vegg.

KISS —— KOOSH
Kiss me.
Koosh mir.

KITCHEN —— KICH
It's a small kitchen.
Dos iz ah klayneh kich.

KNEE —— K'NEE
His knee is broken.
Zyn k'nee iz tzubrauchin

KNIFE —— MESSehr
I need a knife and a spoon.
Ich darff ah messehr un ah leffil

KNOW —— KENNEN or VISSIN
What do you know?
Vos vaystu?
They know everything.
Zay vaysin alles.
I know him.
Ich kenn ehm
KNEW: Gehkent or gevoost
Did you recognize him?
Haustu ehm gehkent?

L

LADY —— FROY
She's a good lady.
Zie iz ah gooteh froy
(also means) Wife and woman

LAMB —— SHEPsil

LAMP —— LAUMP
The lamp is dim.
Dehr laump iz toonkil

LAND —— AUNkoomen
He will land in one hour.
Ehr vett aunkoomen in ayn shtoondeh.
LAND(n) LAHND or EHRD

LANGUAGE —— SHPRACH
He speaks only one language
Ehr rehd naur ayn shprach

LARGE —— GROYSS
This is a large house.
Dos iz ah groyseh hoiz
LARGER: Grehssehr

LAST —— LESTEH
This is the last time.
Dos iz die lesteh maul
LAST YEAR: Fahr ah yaurin.

LATE —— SHPETT
You are late
Du bist shpett.
LATER: Shpettehr
TOO LATE: Tzu shpett

LAUNDRY —— VEHSH
He has a lot of laundry.
Ehr haut ah sahch vehsh
LAUNDER: Oysvahshin

LAVATORY —— VAHSHtzimer
I'm going to the lavatory
Ich gay tzu dehm vahshtzimer.

LAWYER —— AHDvaukaht
You need a lawyer.
Ir darfst ahn ahdvaukaht.

LAY —— LIGG or LAYG
Lie in bed.
Ligg in bett.
Where did you lie?
Voo haustu geliggin?
The chicken laid two eggs.
Dehr hoon haut gelaygt tzvay ayehr.

LEAD —— FEERin
Lead the way.
Feehr dehm vegg.

LEAK —— RINNEN
It's leaking
Ehs rinnt

LEARN —— LEHrin
Learn how to dance
Lehrin sich vie tzu tahntzin
How can I learn Yiddish?
Vie kenn Ich lehrinin Yiddish?

LEATHER —— Lehdehr
LEAVE —— LUHZ
Leave it alone.
Luhz dos ahlayn.
They don't leave me alone.
Zey luhzzin mir nitt alayn

LEFT —— LEENKEH
This is my left hand.
Dos iz myn leenkeh hahnt.
Go left: Gay links

LEG —— FOOS (also means:) Foot
His leg hurts
Zyne foos toot vay.
Two left feet.
Tzvay leenkeh fiss.

LEMON —— LImau or LImine
LEMONADE: Limaunahd

LENGTH —— LEHNGG
Two feet in length
Tzvay fiss lahng

LESS —— VEYnickehr
That's a lot less.
Dos iz ah sahch veynickehr.

LETTER —— BREEV
Send him a short letter
Shick ehm ah koortzin breev

LETTUCE —— sahLAHT
I don't eat lettuce.
Ich ess nisht kayn sahlaht

LET'S —— LAWZmeer
Let's go to the restaurant.
Lawzmeer gayn tzu dehm restawrahn

LIBRARY —— bibleeAUtek
The book is in the library.
Dehr booch iz in dehr bibleeautek.

LIE —— AH LIGgin
Don't tell a lie.
Zaug nisht ah liggin.
Don't lie.
Ligg nisht

LIGHT —— LICHT or HEL
It is a strong light.
Dos iz ah shtahrkeh licht.
TOO LIGHT: Tzu lichtig

LIKE —— GLYCH
I like him.
Ich glych ehm.
Do you like him?
Glychstu ehm?

LINEN —— VESH
BED LINEN: Betgehvahnt
TOWELS, ETC.: Hahntehchehr

LIP —— LIPP

LIQUID —— FLEEseekyt
WATER: Vahsehr

LIQUOR —— SHNAPPS or BRAUNfin
A glass of liquor
Ah glauz shnapps

LISTEN —— HEHR
Listen to me.
Hehr mir oys.

LITTLE —— BISSil or KLAYN
Give me a little.
Gib mir ah bissil.
She's a little girl.
Zie's ah klayneh maydil

LIVE —— VAYN
Where do you live?
Voo vaynstu?
They live here.
Zey vaynen dau.
LIFE: Lehbin

LIVER —— LAYbehr
Chopped liver
Gehhakteh laybehr.

LOAN —— BAURG
Loan me a little sugar?
Baurg mir ah bissil tzukehr?

LOCK —— farSHLEEHS or Fahrshlauss
Lock the door.
FahrSHLEEHS die tier.
LOCK (n) Ah shlauss

LONG —— LAHNG
How long is the way?
Vie lahng iz dehr vegg?
LONGEST: Lahngist

LOOK —— ZOOCH or KOOK
Look for him
Zooch ehm oys.
What are you looking for?
Vos zoochstu?
LOOKED: Gezoocht

LOOSE —— LOYZ or SHITtehr
The pudding is too loose.
Dehr kugel iz tzu shittehr.

LOSE —— fahLEERehn
Don't lose the money.
Fahleer nisht die gelt.
LOST: Fahlaurin

LOW —— NEEDehrik
LOWER: Neederiker

LUNCH —— LAUNSH
We'll eat lunch together.
Mir vellen essen launsh tzuzahmin

LUNG —— LOONG
He has a bad lung.
Ehr haut ah shlechteh loong.
LUNGS: Loongen

M

MAGAZINE —— MAHGahzeen
Buy me a magazine.
Koyff mir ah mahgahzeen.

MAID —— DEENST
The maid is coming this morning.
Die deenst koomt hynt indehrfree

MAKE —— MAHCH
Make me two
Mahch mir tzvay
MADE: Gehmahcht
MAKING: Mahchin

MALE —— MAHN (also means) Man
MALES: Mehnnehr (also MEN)

MANAGER —— fahrVAHLtehr
He's the manager
Ehr iz dehr fahrvahltehr

MANICURE —— mahneeKOOR
I need a manicure
Ich darff ah mahneekoor

MANUFACTURE —— fahbreeTZEERin
Can you manufacture it?
Kenstu dos fahbreetzeerin?

MANY —— ah SAHCH
I need many of them.
Ich darff ah sahch foon zay

MAP —— KARteh
This is a map of my city.
Dos iz ah karteh foon myn shtaut

MASSAGE —— mahSAHZSH
Give me a message
Gibb mir ah mahsahzsh

MATCH —— SHVEHbehleh
Have you a match?
Haustu ah shvehbehleh?

MATCHMAKER —— SHAHTchehn
She's a good matchmaker.
Zee iz ah gooteh shahtchen

MATTRESS —— MAHtrahtz
This is a soft mattress
Dos iz ah vaycheh mahtrahtz.

MAY —— KEHN
May I come?
Kehn ich koomin?

ME —— MEER
Help me
Helfft meer.

MEAL —— MOOHLtzyhtn
The meal is good.
Der moohltzyhtn iz goot.

MEASURE —— MAUS
Give me a good measure.
Gibb meer ah gooter maus.

MEAT —— FLAYSH
Is the meat fresh?
Iz die flaysh frish?
MEATY (opposed to dairy)
FLAYSHIDIK

MECHANIC —— meCHAHNeekehr
The car needs a mechanic.
Die oytaw darff ah mechahneekehr.

MEDICINE —— mehdeeTZEEN
The medicine is bitter.
Die mehdeetzeen iz bittehr.

MEDIUM —— MITtil
This is a happy medium
Dos iz ah mittlpoonkt

MEETING —— fahZAHMloong
The meeting is tomorrow
Maurgin iz die fahzahmloong.

MELON —— MEHlaun
This is a sweet melon.
Dos iz ah zeessehr mehlaun.

MEN —— MEHNNEHR
There are many men.
Daw zahnnen ahsahch mehnnehr.

MEND —— fahrREECHtin
Will you mend my shirt?
Vett ehr fahrreechtin myn hemd?

MENU —— mehnYOO
What is on the menu?
Vos iz auf der mehnyoo?

MESS —— MISHmahsh
This is a mess.
Dos iz ah mishmahsh.

MESSENGER —— shelEEach or LOYfer
Send it with a messenger.
Shick dos mitt ah sheleeach

MIDDLE —— in MITtin
He's in the middle
Ehr iz in mittin

MIDNIGHT —— HAHLbeh NACHT

MILD —— MILder

MILK —— MILCH
Milk is a dairy product.
Milch iz ah milchiker prodookt.

MIND —— SHTEHrin
Would you mind. . . .?
Zee veht ehs eych shtehrin. . .?

MINE —— MIYNneh or MYN
This is mine.
Dos iz miyneh.

MINUTE —— MINOOT
Wait a minute.
Vahrt ah minoot.
The minutes fly by
Die minootin fleeyehn.

MIRROR —— SHPigil
Look in the mirror.
Kook in dehr shpigil.

MISS (v) —— fahrZAHMen
Don't miss the train.
Fahrzahm nisht die bahn.
MISSED: Fahrzaumt or Fahrfehlt
MISSING: FEHLN

MISTAKE —— ah TAWes or Fehler

MODEL —— MAUdehl
She is a model.
Zie iz ah maudehl.

MOMENT —— REHgeh
Wait a moment.
Vardt ah rehgeh.

MONEY —— GELT
This is a lot of money
Dos iz ah sahch gelt.

MONTH —— MAUniyt
Four weeks make a month.
Feer vauchen is ah mauniyt.

MOON —— lehVAUneh
It's a full moon
Ess iz ah gahnseh lehvauneh

MORE —— MEHR
I need more.
Ich darff mehr
MANY: Ah sahch
TOO MANY: Tzufeel

MORNING —— MAURgin
Good morning
Ah gootin maurgin

MORSEL —— PITsil or Bissn
It's only a morsel
Ess iz naur ah pitsil

MOTHER —— MAHMMEH
How old is your mother?
Wee ahlt iz dyn mahmmeh?

MOUTH —— MOYLL
She's got a big mouth.
Zee haut ah groyseh moyll

MOVE —— REERin
I can't move.
Ich kehnit reerin sich

MOVIE —— KEEnaw or FILM
We're going to the movies.
Meer gayehn tzu der keenaw.

MUCH —— Ah SAHCH
MORE: MEHR
LESS: VAYNEEKEHR
TOO MUCH: TZU FEEL
FEW: VAYNIK

MUD —— BLAWteh
This is a lot of mud.
Dos iz ah sahch blawteh.

MUSCLE —— MOOSkil
He's got big muscles.
Ehr haut grayseh moosklen.

MUSEUM —— mooZAY
This is a fine museum
Dos iz ah finehr moozay

MUSHROOMS —— SHVEMlech
I want one pound of mushrooms
Ich vil ayn foont shvemlech

MUSIC —— MOOzik
The music is beautiful.
Die moozik iz zayer shayn
MUSICIAN: Moozikehr

MUST —— MOOZ
I must go.
Ich mooz gayn.

MY —— MYNEH or MIY
This is my house
Dos iz myn hois

N

NAKED —— NAHkitt
They are naked.
Zay zahnehn nahkitt

NAIL —— NAUgil
It needs a new nail.
Ehs darft ah nyehr naugil
NAILS: Nehgil

NAME —— NAUmehn
What is your name?
Vos iz dyn naumehn?

NARROW —— SHMAUHL
This is too narrow.
Dos iz tzu shmauhl

NATIVE —— AURteeker
NATIVE ART: Aurteekeh koonst

NAUSEA —— nitGOOTkyte
He is nauseous.
Ehr haut ah nitgootkiyt

NAVEL —— POOpik
Her navel shows
Eer poopik tzygt zich.

NEAR —— NAUNT
She lives near me.
Zie voynt naunt tzu meer.
NEAREST: Nauentzteh

NECK —— NAHkin or HAHLDZ
He's got a thick neck
Ehr haut ah grawben nahkin.
NECKTIE: SHNIPPS

NEED —— DARFF
What do you need?
Vos darffstu?

NEEDLE —— NAUdil
NERVE —— NEHRV or CHOOTZPEH
He's got a lot of nerve
Ehr haut ah sahch nehrv.

NEW —— NYEH
This is a new car.
Dos iz ah nyeh oytaw
What's new?
Vos iz nye?
NEWEST: Nyesteh

NEWSPAPER —— TZYtoong
Is this today's newspaper?
Iz dos ah hyntike tzytoong?

NEXT —— KOOmendeekin
The next stop.
Dehr koomendeekin aupshtel

NIGHT —— NAHCHT
Good night
Ah gootin nahcht.

NO —— NAYN
NOT: Nitt.
NOTHING: Gornisht
NO MORE: Nisht mehr

NOISE —— TOOMIL
There's a lot of noise.
Ess iz ah sahch toomil
NOISY: Toomildik

NOON —— MITaugtzyte
NORTH —— TZAWfin
Go to the north
Gay tzu dehr tzawfin

NOSE —— NAUZ
His nose is bleeding.
Zyhn nauz blootikt

NOW —— ITZT
I'm coming now.
Itzt koom ich.

NUMBER —— NOOmehr
What is the number of your house?
Vos iz dehr noomehr foon dyn hoiz?

NURSE —— KRAHNkinshvestehr
She needs a nurse.
Zee darff ah krahnkin shvestehr.

NUTS —— NISS

O

OBSTINATE —— fahrBISSin
She is very obstinate.
Zee iz zayer fahrbissin

OBTAIN —— KRIGG
Where can I obtain a key?
Voo ken ich kriggin ah shlissil?

OCULIST —— OYgin dawktehr
You need an oculist
Ir darft ahn oygin dawktehr.

OF —— FOON
I'll take one of each.
Ich'll nemmin aynehm foon yeddin

OFFICE —— byooRAW
OFFICER: aufeetzeer
Official; Behamter

OIL —— AYL
The car needs oil
Dehr oytaw darfft ayl.

OLD —— AHLT
How old are you?
Vie ahlt bistu?
OLD PERSON: Ahlter

OMELETTE —— AUMleht
I'll have an omelette.
Ich'll haubin ahn aumleht.

ON —— OYF
Put your cards on the table.
Layg dyneh kaurtin oyf dem tish.

ONE —— AYNS
One at a time.
Ayns auf ah maul

ONION —— TZIbilleh
I like onions.
Ich glyche tzibillehs

ONLY —— NAUR
This is only for you.
Dos iz naur fahr deer.

OPEN —— AUFfin
The door is open
Die teer iz auffin.
TO OPEN: Tzu ehffenen.
OPEN UP! Ehffin oof.

OPERA —— AUpehreh
We're going to the opera.
Meer gayehn tzu dehr aupehreh.

OPTION —— aupTEERrecht or Brayreh
You have an option.
Du haust ahn brayreh

OPTOMETRIST —— AUPteekehr

ORANGE —— mahRAHNtzin
What beautiful oranges!
Vos shayneh mahrahntzin!

ORCHESTRA SEAT —— pahrTEHRplahtz

ORDER —— bahSHTEHL or Bahfehl
This is an order!
Dos iz ah bahfehl!

OTHER —— AHNdehr
OTHERS: Ahndehreh
This is another thing.
Dos iz ahn ahndehreh zahch.

OUR —— OONzhehr.
This is our house.
Dos iz oonzhehr hoiz.

OUT —— OYS
Out of bread.
Oys brayt.
OUTSIDE: foon DROYsin.
WITHOUT: AUHN
GET OUT!
Gay aroys!

OVEN —— OYvehn
This is a hot oven.
Dos iz ah hayser oyvehn.

OVER —— EEbehr
I'll think it over.
Ich'll dos daynkin eebehr.
OVERPAID: Eebehrgetzault
UNDERPAID: Oontehrget-zault.

OVERALL —— eeberAHLTZ
He's wearing overalls
Ehr traukt eeberahltz.

OWE —— KOOMT (also) Zyne shooldik
What do I owe you?
Vaus koomt eych?
(also)
Veefeel bin ich shooldik?

P

PACK —— PAHK
A pack of cigarettes.
Ah pahk pahpeerawsin
SMALL PACK: Pehkil

PACKAGE —— PEHkil
What's in the package?
Vos iz in dehm pehkil?

PAID —— bahTZAULT
The rent is paid
Dié deerehgelt iz shayn bahtzault.

PAIL —— EHmehr
Get me a pail of water.
Krigg meer ahn ehmehr vahssehr.

PAIR —— PAURR
I want a pair of shoes.
Ich vill ah paurr shich.

PAJAMAS —— peeZSHAHmehs
He's wearing pajamas.
Ehr traukt peezshahmehs.

PAL —— CHAHvehr
He's a good pal.
Ehr iz ah gooter chahvehr.
PALS: Chahvayrim

PAN —— FEHNdil
Deh fehndil iz shmootzik
The pan is dirty.
SAUCEPAN: Behkn

PANCAKES —— LAHTkes
I want three pancakes.
Ich vil driy lahtkes.

PAGE —— BLAHT
SMALL PAGE: Blehtil
PAGES: Bletlehch

PANTRY —— SHPYZkahmer
Look in the pantry.
Kook aryne in die shpyzkahmer.

PANTS —— HOYzin
His pants have a hole.
Zyne hoyzin haut ah lauch.

PAPER —— pahPEER
I want white paper.
Ich vil vyseh pahpeer.

PARK —— PAHRK
Play in the park.
Shpeel zich in pahrk.

PART —— SHTIKil (also means) Piece or Portion
A piece of salami.
Ah shtickil voorsht.

PASS —— derLAHNG
Pass the sugar.
derlahng die tzukehr

PAST —— NAUCH
It is half past ten.
Ess iz hahlb nauch tzehn.

PASTRY —— TZOOKEHR gebeks
The pastry is delicious.
Die tzookehr gebeks iz geshmahk

PAVED —— oysbrooKEERtehr
The road is paved.
Der vegg iz oysbrookeertehr.

PAY —— bahTZAUL
Pay the man.
Bahtzaul dehm mahn
PAYABLE: Oystzaulin

PEACH —— FEHRSHkeh

PEAS —— AHRbehs
The peas are sweet.
Die ahrbehs zahnen zees.

PEANUTS —— EHRDnislech or Fistahshkes

PEARS —— BAHRnehs

PECANS —— peeKAHNEN

PENCIL —— BLYehr
Write with the pencil.
Shryb mitt dehm blyehr.

PENKNIFE —— MEHsehril
The penknife is sharp.
Der mehsehril iz sharff.

PEPPER —— FEHfehr
Salt and pepper.
Zahltz un fehfehr.

PERCENT —— PRAWtzent
I want ten percent.
Ich vill tzen prawtzent.

PERFUME —— pahrFOOM
The perfume smells good.
Der pahrfoom shmehkt goot.

PERHAPS —— EFFshehr
Perhaps he may come.
Effshehr vet ehr koomen

PERMISSION —— dehrLOYbenish
You have to get permission.
Du dahrfst kriggin dehrloybenish.

PERMIT —— PAHSS

PEROXIDE —— soopehrAUKseed
Put peroxide on the cut.
Layg tzu soopehraukseed oyfin shnitt.

PERSON —— MENSH
Who is this person?
Vehr iz der mensh?

PEST —— NOODnik
He's a pest.
Ehr iz ah noodnik.

PETTICOAT —— OONtehrklayd
She's wearing a petticoat.
Zie traukt ahn oontehrklayd.

PHARMACY —— ahpTAYk

PHILOSOPHY —— feelauSAUFyeh

PHYSICS —— FEEzik

PICKLE —— OOGEHRkes
This is a sour pickle
Dos iz ah zoyehreh oogehr-keh.

PICTURE —— BILD
She takes a good picture.
Zie nemt ah shayneh bild.

PIE —— PYH
The pie is fresh.
Die pyh iz frish.

PIECE —— SHTIK
Give me a piece of bread.
Gibb meer ah shtik broyt.
SMALL PIECE: Shtikil

PIG —— CHAHzehr
He's a pig.
Ehr iz ah chahzehr.

PILL —— PIIL
I have to take a pill
Ich darff nehmen ah piil.

PILLOW —— KISHin
This is a soft pillow
Dos iz ah vaycher kishin.

PIN —— SHPILkeh
BROACH: BRAUSH

PINEAPPLE —— anahNANS

PINK —— RAUzeh
She's wearing a pink dress.
Zie traukt ah rauzeh klayd.

PIPE —— liYOOLkeh

PIPSQUEAK —— SHMENdrick
He's a real pipsqueak.
Ehrz ah richtehker shmen-drick.

PITY —— rachMAUNes
Have pity.
Haub rachmaunes.

PLACE —— PLAHTZ
This is the right place.
Dos iz dehr richtehker plahtz.

PLAGUE —— MAHkeh

PLANE —— EHRaupplahn
I'm going by plane.
Ich gay mit dehm ehraup-plahn.

PLATE —— TEHlehr
The plate is broken
Dehr tehlehr iz tzubrauchin

PLAY —— SHPEEL
Play with the children.
Shpeel mitt die kindehr.
CHILDSPLAY: Kindersh-peel.

PLEASE —— Zyh ahzay goot.
Will you be good enough to. . . . . .

PLIERS —— TZVAHNG

PLUMS —— FLOYmin

PLUMBER —— REHRINshlausehr

PNEUMONIA —— LOONGenauntzeendoong.

POINT —— VYST AUN
Point the way.
Wyst aun dem vegg.

POLICEMAN —— pawlitzYAHNT
POLICE STATION: pawleeTZAY stahntzyeh

PORCH —— GAHnik
Come, sit on the porch.
Koom, zitz oyfin gahnik

PORRIDGE —— KAHsheh
Make the porridge hot.
Mahch die kahsheh hayss.

POSITION —— SHTEHleh
The position is open.
Die shtehleh iz auffin.

POTATOES —— kahrTAUFlyeh
Potatoes are healthy
Kahrtauflin zahnen gehzundt.

POT ROAST —— RAUSil flaysh

POUCH —— ZEHKIL
I have it in the pouch
Ich haub dos in zehkil

POUND —— FOONT
How much is it a pound?
Veefil iz dos ah foont?

PRAY —— DAHvin
PRAYING: Dahvenin.
PRAYER: Gebeht
BLESSING: Braucheh.

PREPARE —— graytTZU
Prepare to eat.
Grayttzu tzu essehn.

PRESS —— OYSprehsin
Will you press this suit?
Vestu oysprehsin dehm kaustyoom
PRESSED: Oysgehprehst

PRETTY —— SHAYN
She's a pretty girl
Zie'z ah shayneh maydil

PRICE —— PRYZ
What's the price?
Viefil iz die pryz
or
Viefil kohst dos?

PRINTER —— DROOkehr
Who is the printer of this book?
Vehr iz dehr drookehr foon dem booch?

PRIVATE —— preeVAHT
I want a private room.
Ich vill ah preevahten tzimehr.

PROFIT —— RAYvach
This is a good profit.
Dos iz ah gooter rayvach.

PROGRAM —— PRAUgrahm
This is a long program.
Dos iz ah lahnger praugrahm.

PROMISE —— TZUzaugin

PROSTITUTE —— KOORveh or ZHOYneh

PROVOKE —— OYfryhitzn
Don't provoke him.
Tzeryhtz emh nisht.

PRUNES —— FLOYmen

PUBLIC —— EHFINtlehkeh

PUDDING —— KOOgil
Noodle pudding.
Laukshen koogil

PULL —— SHLEPP
Pull this for me.
Shlepp dos fahr mir.

PURPLE —— LEELyah or POORpil

PURSE —— BYtil
He stole her purse.
Ehr haut gehgahnvit eer bytil.

PUSH —— SHTOOP
Don't push.
Shtoop nisht.

PUT —— LAYG
Put it on the bed.
Layg dos oyfin bett.

Q

QUARTER —— FEHRtil
Four quarters make a dollar.
Feer fehrtlech mahcht ah tollehr

QUESTION —— FRAHgeh
Ask me a question.
Frehgg mich ah frahgeh
ASK: Frehgg.

QUICK —— GEECH or SHNEHL
He's very quick.
Ehrz zayer shnehl

QUIET —— SHTILL
Be very quiet.
Zyg zayer shtill
QUIETNESS: Shtillkyte.

QUITE —— ZAYEHR (also means) Very
I am quite satisfied.
Ich bin zayehr tzufriddin.
He is very good.
Ehr iz zayer goot.

QUILT —— PEHRehneh
The quilt is warm.
Die pehrehneh iz vahrehm.

R

RADIO —— RAHDyaw
Play the radio.
Shpill die rahdyaw.

RADISHES —— REHtechehr
I'll have some radishes.
Ich'll hauben ah shtikl rehtech

RAG —— SHMAHteh
It's only a rag.
Ess iz naur ah shmahteh.

RAIN —— REHgin
It'll rain tomorrow.
Ess vett rehgehnen maurgin

RAISIN —— RAUzshinkeh
Raisins and almonds.
Rauzshinkiz un mahndlin

RATE —— CAUST
What is the rate?
Veefil caust dos?

RAZOR —— GAULmesser
I need a razor.
Ich darff ah gaulmesser.

READ —— LEHZ or LAYN
Read the book.
Lehz dehm booch
READING: Lehzenin or Laynin

READY —— GRAYT
I am ready.
Ich bin grayt.

RECEIVE —— KRIG
I receive it today.
Ich krig dos hyhnt.
RECEIVED: Gehkraugen

RED —— ROYT
She's wearing a red dress.
Zee traukt ah royteh klayd.

REFRESHMENT —— EEberbyssin
I only want a small snack.
Ich vill naur ah bysse

REGARDS —— ah GROOS
Regards to your mother.
Ah groos tzu dyn mahmmeh.

REGULATE —— rehgooLEERT
Regulate the clock
Rehgooleert dem zaygehr.

RELATIVE —— KAUrev or mishPAUcheh
She is my relative.
Zee iz myn kaurev
RELATIONS: Mishpaucheh

RELIEVE —— fahrLYCHtehrin
I need something to relieve me.
Ich darff eppes mich tzu fahrlychtehrin.

REMAIN —— BLYBE
Remain here.
Blybe daw.
REMAINED: Gehblibbin

REMEMBER —— gehDENK
I don't remember.
Ich gehdenk nisht.
What do you think?
Voss deynkstu?
REMEMBERED: Gehdenkt.

RENT —— DEERehgelt
Did you pay the rent?
Haust tu bahtzault die deerehgelt?

REPAIR —— fahrECHTin
Did you repair it?
Haustu dos fahrrecht?

REPUTATION —— SHEM
He has a good reputation.
Ehr haut ah gooten shem.

RESPONSIBLE —— fahRANT vohrtlech
He's responsible
Ehrz fahrantvohrtlech.

RESTAURANT —— restawRAHN
Where is a good restaurant?
Voo iz ah gootehr restawrahn?

RETAIL —— lahKAUDim or ENTZL
Don't buy at retail.
Koyf nisht oyf entzel.

RETURN —— OOMkehrin
They have to return.
Zay darffin zich oomkehrin.
Bring back the money.
Brayng tzurick die gelt.

RIB —— RIP
He has a broken rib.
Ehr haut ah tzubraucheneh rip.

RICE —— RYHZ
Rice pudding.
Ryhzkoogil

RIDE —— FAUR
Don't ride with him.
Faur nisht mitt ehm.
RODE: Gefaurin
RIDING: Faurihn

RIGHT —— gehRECHT
You are right.
Du bist gehrect.
The right man.
Dehr richtehcher mahn.

RING —— FINgehril
A gold ring.
Ah gaulden fingehril.

ROAD —— VEGG (also means) Way.
Is it a good road?
Iz dos a gooter vegg?
Show me the way.
Tzyg meer die vegg.

ROB —— GAHNveh
Don't rob him.
Gahnveh nisht foon ehm.
ROBBED: Gehgahnveht
ROBBING: Gahnvehnen

ROBE —— CHAHlaht
She's wearing a robe.
Zee traukt ah chahlaht

ROLL —— BOOLkeh
I like this roll
I glych die boolkeh.

ROOF —— DAHCH
This is a high roof.
Dos iz ah haycher dahch.

ROOM —— TZImehr
I want a good room.
Ich vill ah gooten tzimehr.

ROPE —— SHTRIK
It's a strong rope.
Dos iz ah shtahrker shtrik

RUBBERS —— kahLAWshin

RUN —— LAYF
Run away.
Layf ahvek.
RUNNING: Layfin
HAD RUN: Haut gelaufin.

RUPTURE —— KILLeh
He has a rupture.
Eht haut ah killeh.

RYE —— KAWrin
Rye bread.
Kawrinbrayt.

S

SALAD —— SAHLAHT
This is a good salad.
Dos iz ah goóter sahlaht.

SALAMI —— VOORSHT
The salami is bad.
Der voorsht iz nisht goot.
GARLIC SALAMI: K'naubel voorsht.

SALARY —— SHREErehs
I get my salary on Mondays.
Ich krig myn shreerehs yehdin Mauntik.

SALMON —— LOX
SALT —— ZAHLTZ
Salt and pepper
Zahltz un feffehr

SANDWICH —— SENDvitsh.
I'll have a cheese sandwich.
Ich'll hauben ah kehz sendvitsh.

SARDINE —— sahrDEENkiz
SAVE —— RAHtehveh.
Save her.
Rahtehveh zee.

SAY —— ZAUG
What are you saying?
Vauss zaugstu?
Say it again.
Zaug dos nauch ahmaul.

SCARF —— SHAHRfil or SHAHL
Wear a green scarf.
Traug ah grinneh shahrfil.

SCISSORS —— DIE SHEHRRLECH
A pair of scissors.
Ah paur shehrrlech.

SCREW —— SHROYF
It needs a screw.
Dos darff ah shroyf

SEASON —— SEHzaun or Tzyht

SEAT —— SITZort
You can have my seat.
Du kenst hauben myn sitzort.

SECOND —— TZVAYteh
The second time.
Dos tzvayteh mauhl.

SEE —— ZEH
See all the dogs.
Zeh alleh hiint.
SEEN: Gehzehn
What do you see?
Vos zehstu?

SEEDS —— KIMmehl
Bread with seeds.
Brayt mitt kimmehl.

SELL —— FAHRkayf
Sell me the house.
Fahrkayf meer dos hoyz
SOLD: Fahrkayft.
SELLING: Fahrkayfin.

SEND —— SHICK
Send me the bill.
Shick meer dem cheshbin.
SENT: Geshickt.
WILL SEND: Vell shicken.

SHAVE —— AWPgawlin
I need a shave.
Ich darff sich awpgawlin.

SHINE —— AWPpootzin or GALNTZ
Shine my shoes.
Pootz aup myneh shich.

SHIP (v) —— SHICK
Ship it tomorrow.
Shick ess morgen.

SHIRT —— HEMD
Your shirt is dirtz.
Dyn hemd iz shmootzik.

SHOE —— SHOOCH
The left shoe hurts.
Dehr leenkeh shooch toot vay.
SHOES: Shich.

SHOP —— IYNkoyfin
She's going shopping.
Zie gayt iynkoyfin.

SHORT —— KOORTZ
It's a short rope.
Dos iz ah koortzer shtrik.

SHOULD —— ZAUL or VAULT
He should go.
Ehr zaul gayn.
We should go.
Meer zaulin gayn.

SHOULDER —— AHKsil
His shoulder hurts.
Zyn ahksil toot vay.

SHOW (v) —— TZYHGG or VYHST
Show me the way
Tzyhgg meer dem vegg
Show me how.
Vyhst meer vie.

SHOWER —— SHPRITZ
I'm going to take a shower.
Ich gay nehmen ah shpritz.

SIDE —— ZYTE
He's holding his side.
Ehr hahlt zich byh dehr zyte

SIGN —— OONtehrshribin or Shribe oontehr.

Sign your name.
Shribe zich oonter.
SIGNATURE: Oontehrshrift.

SILK —— ZYHD

SILVER —— ZILBER
A silver vase.
Ah zilberneh vahzeh.

SINGLE —— AYNTZikeh

SISTER —— SHVESTehr
She is my sister.
Zee iz myn shvestehr.

SIT —— ZITZ
Sit down.
Zitz zich ahvek.
SITTING: Zitzin
SAT: ZETZT.

SIZE —— MAUS
What is your size?
Vaus iz dyhn maus?

SKIN —— HOYT
Her skin is red.
Eehr hoyt iz royt.

SKIRT —— KLAYdil
She has a short skirt.
Err klaydil iz koortz

SLEEP —— SHLAUF
Sleep a little.
Shlauf ah bissil.
SLEPT: Gehshlaufin

SLOWLY —— PahMEHlech
Do it slowly.
Tu dos pahmehlech.

SMALL —— KLAYN
It's a small dog.
Dos iz ah klayner hoont.

SOAP —— ZAYFF
Give me the soap.
Gibb meer die sayff.

SOCKS —— skahrPEHtin
He's wearing blue socks.
Ehr traukt blaueh skahrpehtin.

SODA —— SAWdeh
Whiskey and soda.
Shnahpps mitt sawdeh.

SOFT —— VAYCH
The plums are soft.
Die floymin sahnehn vaych.
SOFTER: Vaychehr
SOFTEST: Vaychist

SOME —— ah BISSIL
Give me some.
Gibb meer ah bissil.
SOMETHING: Eppis
SOME ONE: Ehmitzin

SON —— ZOON
He is my son.
Ehr iz myhn zoon.
SONS: Zihn

SOON —— BAHLT
He'll be here soon.
Ehr vett daw bahlt zyhn.

SORRY —— bahDOYrin (implies 'Regret')
I am sorry.
Ich bahdoyr
fahrDREESIN: (implies 'mild anger')
Leidin: (implies 'sympathy)

SOUL —— niSHAWmeh

SOUP —— ZOOP

SOUR —— ZOYehr
The milk is sour.
Di milch iz zoyehr.
SOUR CREAM: SMEHTe-neh

SOUTH —— DAUrem

SPEAK —— REHD
Speak to me.
Rehd tzu meer.
SPOKE: Reht

SPELLING —— OYSlayg

SPINACH —— shpeeNAHT
I don't like spinach
Ich gliych nisht shpeenaht.

SPINE —— ROOKinbayn
He broke his spine.
Ehr haut tzubrauchehn ziyn rookinbayn.

SPLIT —— SHPALTIN
The melon split in half
Der mehlawn haut geshpaultin in hahlb.
BURST: Plotz

SPOON —— LEHfil
This is a soup spoon.
Daus iz ah zoop lehfil.

SPRAIN —— OYSlinkoong

STAIN —— FLEK
His shirt has a stain.
Zyne hemd haut ah flek.

STAIRS —— TREP
I'm going upstairs.
Ich gay oybin

STAND —— SHTAY
Stand up.
Shtay oyf
Let it stand.
Lauz dos shtayn.

STAMP —— MAHRkehs
Give me five stamps.
Gibb meer finif mahrkehs.

STARCH —— KRAUCHmahl

STARS —— SHTEHRrin
There are many stars in the sky.
Ess zennen daw ah sahch shtehrrin in himmil.

START —— FAHNG awn.
Start the motor of the car.
Fahngawn dem oytaw.

STATEMENT —— OYStzoog
This is the weekly statement.
Daus iz dehr vauchndikir oys-tzoog.

STATION —— VAUKzahl
We're coming to the station.
Meer koomin tzu dem vauk-zahl
DEPOT: Stantzyeh

STAY —— BLYBE
Stay here.
Blybe daw.
STAYED: Gehblibbin

STEW —— GOOlahsh
Hungarian stew
Hoongehrehshen goolahsh.

STICK (n) —— SHTEHKin
It's a big stick.
Daus iz ah grayser shtehkin

STILL —— NAUCH (also means) Yet.
How many are still to come?
Viefil nauch vellin koomen?

STOCKINGS —— ZAUKIN
She's wearing red stockings.
Zie traukt rayteh zaukin.

STOMACH —— MAUgin or Boych
I have a stomach ache.
Ich haub ah boychvaytaug

STONE —— SHTAYN
Don't throw the stone.
Varff nit dehm shtayn.
STONES: Shtaynehr

STOP —— OYFhehrin
You have to stop running.
Du moost oyfhehrin tzu lay-fin.

STORE —— KRAUM
Where is the milk store?
Voo iz dehr milchkraum?

STRING —— SHTRIKIL
The string is too weak.
Dos shtrikil iz tzu shvahch.
ROPE: Shtrick

STROKE —— SHLAHK
He had a stroke.
Ehr haut gehhaht ah shlahk.

STRONG —— SHTAHRK
He is very strong.
Ehr iz zayer shtahrk.

STUCK —— GeSHTAUchin

STUDY —— LEHRNen
He's studying.
Ehr lehrnt
STUDENT: Tahlmud

STUFF —— gehFILL
STUFFED FISH: Gehfilteh fish.

SUGAR —— TZUkehr
Sugar and salt.
Tzukehr un zahltz

SUIT —— KAUSTyoom
He's wearing a blue suit.
Ehr traukt ah blauen kaustyoom.

SUMMER —— ZOOMehr
It is hot in the summer.
Ess iz hays in zoomehr.

SUN —— ZOON
The sun is high.
Die zoon iz hoych.

SUPPER —— VEHchehreh
The supper is good.
Die vehchehreh iz goot.

SWEATER —— SVEHtehr.
The sweater looks good.
Dehr svehtehr kookt goot.

SWEET —— ZEES
You are very sweet.
Du bist zayer zees.

T

TABLE —— TISH
Put the food on the table.
Layg dos essin oyfin tish.

TAILOR —— SHNYdehr
He's a good tailor.
Ehr iz ah gooter shnydehr.

TAKE —— NEHM
Take a little.
Nehm ah bissil
TAKEN: Haut gehnoomen
TOOK: Gehnoomen

TAXI —— TAHKsee
Take a taxi.
Nehm ah tahksee.

TEA —— TAY
A glass of tea.
Ah glauz tay.

TEACHER —— LEHRehr
TEACH: Lehrnen
TAUGHT: Gelehrint

TELL —— ZAUG
Tell me.
Zaug meer.
TOLD: Haut gehzaugt
TELLING: Zaugen

THAN —— AYdehr
Better than nothing.
Bessehr aydehr gornisht.

THANKS —— ah DAHNK

THAT —— YEHder or Dauss
That person.
Yehnehr mensh.
What is that?
Vaus iz daws?

THERE —— DAURtin
Go over there.
Gay daurtin

THESE —— DAUSS or DEE
These are no good.
Dee zahnehn nisht goot.

THICK —— GRAUB or DIK
A thick slice of bread.
Ah graub shtik broyt.

THIEF —— GAHniff
He's a thief.
Ehrz ah gahniff.

THING —— ZAHCH
What is this thing?
Vaus iz die zahch.
THINGS: Zahchin

THIN —— DIN
She's very thin.
Zie iz zayer din.
THINNER: Dinnehr

THIRD —— DRITtehn
The third time.
Dehr drittehn maul

THIRSTY —— DAURshtik
I'm very thirsty.
Ich bin zayer daurshtik.

THIS —— DAUS
This is the last time.
Daus iz dehr lesteh maul.

THREE —— DRIYH
Three times three are nine.
Driyh maul driyh iz niyn

THROAT —— HAHLDZ
My throat is dry.
Myn hahldz iz trookin

THUMB —— GRAWber fingehr

TICKET —— beeLEHT
I'll take two tickets.
Ich'll nehmmen tzvay beeleh-tin.

TIGHT —— SHTYFT
TIGHTEN: Fahrshtyftin

TIME —— TZYHT
It is time.
Ess iz thyht.
What time is it?
Viefil iz dehr zaygehr?

TO —— TZU
Go to the house.
Gay tzu die hoiz.

TOO —— TZU
Too much.
Tzu feehl.

TODAY —— HYHNT
Today is Sunday.
Hyhnt iz Zoontik

TOE —— Dehr fingehr foon foos.

TOMATO —— PAUMidaur
A red tomato
Ah rayter paumidaur.

TOMORROW —— MAURgin
Tomorrow is Monday.
Maurgin iz Mauntik.

TONGUE —— TZOONG
Your tongue is white.
Dyhn tzoong is vyhss.

TOOTH —— TZAWN
His tooth is broken
Zyhn tzawn iz tzubrauchin.
TEETH: TZAYN

TOP —— OYbin
On top of the house.
Oybin oyf dem hoyz.

TOUGH —— HART
He's very tough
Ehrz zayer hart.

TOWEL —— HAHNtahch
The towel is dirty.
Dehr hahntahch iz shmootzik.

TOWN —— SHTET'L
It's a small town.
Dos iz ah klayn shtet'l.
LARGE TOWN: SHTAUT

TRAVEL —— FAWR
He travels a great deal.
Ehr fawrt ah sahch.

TRUST —— TZUTroy

TURN —— DRAY
Turn around.
Dray sich ahroom

TWICE —— TZVAY MAUL. (Two times)

TWIN —— TZVILing.

U

UMBRELLA —— SHEErim
Have you an umbrella?
Haust du ah sheerim?

UNDER —— OONtehr
Under the bed.
Oontehr dehm bett.

UNDERSHIRT —— OONtehrhemd

UNDERWEAR —— OONtehrvesh

UNDERSTAND —— FAHRshtay.
I understand.
Ich fahrshtay.
WE UNDERSTAND: Meer fahrshtayin.

UNTIL —— BIZ
I'll wait until tomorrow.
Ich'll vahrtin biz morgin.

UPPER —— AYbersht

UPSTAIRS ——OYbin

US —— OONDZ
Did you see us?
Haustu oondz gezehnz?

V

VEGETABLES —— GREENZ
I only eat vegetables.
Ich ess naur greenz.

VERY —— ZAYEHR
I'm very satisfied.
Ich bin zayehr tzufriddin.

VEST —— VEStil
The vest is small.
Dehr vestil iz klayn

VIA —— DOORCH
Go via New York.
Gay doorch Noo Yaurk.

VINEGAR —— ESSik
The vinegar is sour.
Der essik iz zoyehr.

VIRUS —— VEErus
He has a virus.
Ehr haut ah veerus.

VISA —— VEEzeh
I have a visa.
Ich haub ah veezeh.

VISIT —— bahZOOCHin
We'll visit the ruins.
Meer vellin bahzoochin die roynen.

VOMIT —— OYSbrechin

VULGAR —— PRAUST.
He's very vulgar.
Ehrz zayehr praust.

W

WAGE —— LOYN
Do you work for a wage?
Ahrbitztu fahr ah loyn?

WAIT —— VAHRT
Wait a minute.
Vahrt ah minoot.

WAITER —— KELnehr
He's a good waiter.
Ehrz ah gooter kelnehr.

WALK —— GAY
Walk with me.
Gay mitt meer.
WALKED: Gehgahngin

WALL —— VAHNT
It's a high wall.
Daus iz ah hoycheh vahnt.

WALNUTS —— VELTshener Nis

WANT —— VIL
I want to go.
Ich vil gayn.
What do you want?
Vaus vilstu?

WARM —— VAHRehm
It's a warm day.
Ess iz ah vahremer taug.

WASH —— VAHSH
Wash your face.
Vahsh dyhn paunim.

WATCH —— ZAYgehr
It's a gold watch.
Daus iz ah goldener zaygehr.

WATER —— VAHsehr
Give me a drink of water.
Gibb meer ah troonk vahsehr.

WAY —— VEGG
Where is the way?
Voo iz dehr vegg?

WEAK —— SHVAHCH
She is weak.
Zee iz shvahch.

WEDDING —— CHAHseneh
This is her wedding.
Daus iz yeehr chahseneh.

WEEK —— VAUCH
Seven days make a week.
Zibbin teg mahcht ah vauch

WELL —— GOOT
Well done.
Goot gehtaun.

WHAT —— VIE or VOS
What do you want?
Vos vilstu?
What way are you going?
Vie gaystu?

WHEN —— VEN
When are you going?
Ven gaystu?

WHERE —— VOO
Where are you going?
Voo gaystu?

WHICH —— VELchehr
Which way are you going?
Oyf velchehn vegg gaystu?

WHILE —— VYHleh
I'm going to wait awhile.
Ich vell vahrten ah vyhleh.

WHITE —— VYHSS
I have a white horse.
Ich haub ah vyhsseh fehrd.

WHO —— VEHR
Who are you?
Vehr bistu?

WHOLE —— GAHNtzeh
I want a whole loaf of bread.
Ich vill ah gahntzeh broyt.

WHOM —— VEHmehn
Whom are you going with?
Mitt vehmehn gaystu?

WHY —— FAHRvauss
Why have you come?
Fahrvauss bisstu gahkoomen?

WIDE —— BRAYT
It is very wide.
Ess iz zayehr brayt.

WIFE —— VYHB
This is my wife.
Zee iz myn vyhb

WILL YOU —— VESTU
Will you come?
Vestu koomen?

WITH —— MITT
Come with me.
Koom mitt meer.

WITHOUT —— UHN
He's coming without shoes.
Ehr koomt uhn shich.

WOOD —— HAWLTZ
He's chopping wood.
Ehr hahkt hawltz.
A wooden house.
Ah hiltzerneh hoyz.

WOOL —— VAWL
A woolen dress.
Ah vawleneh klayd.

WORK —— AHRbet
I'm working today.
Ich ahrbet hyhnt.
WORKER: Ahrbehtehr

WORSE —— EHRgehr
He is worse than she is.
Ehr iz ehrgehr vee zee iz.

WRITE —— SHRyhb
Can you write in Yiddish?
Kenstu shryhbin in Yiddish?
WRITER: Shryhbehr.

X

X-RAYS —— RENTgenshtrahlin
His X-rays are good.
Zyne rentgenshtrahlin zahnen goot.

Y

YARD —— YAHRD
I'll take one yard.
Ich'll nehmen ayn yahrd.

YEAR —— YAWR
She is one year old.
Zee iz ayn yawr ahlt.

YELLOW —— GEHL
Her dress is yellow.
Eehr klayd iz gehl.

YES —— YAW
No is not yes and yes is not no.
Nayn iz nisht yaw und yaw iz nisht nayn.

YESTERDAY —— NECHtin
He came yesterday.
Ehr iz gehkoomen nechtin

YET —— NAUCH
He hasn't come yet.
Ehr iz nauch nit gehkoomen.

YOKEL —— KOONilemmil or Zshlaub
He's a yokel.
Ehrz ah koonilemmil.

YOU —— DU or IR
You have said nothing.
Du haust gornisht gehzaukt.
What do you want?
Vos vilt ir?

YOUNG —— YOONG
It is good to be young.
Ess iz goot tzu zyhn yoong.
YOUNG MAN: YOONGER-MAHN
BOY: Yeengil

YOUR —— EYEHR or DYHN or EYEHREH
Your pants are too short.
Dyhn hayzin zahnen tzu koortz.
They are your relatives.
Zay zahnen eyehr mishpau-cheh.

Z

ZIPPER —— BLITZshlehsil
The zipper is broken.
Dos blitzshlehsil iz tzubrau-chin.

BIBLIOGRAPHY

The following books are those from which much of the information has been referred to in compiling the numerous facts in this encyclopedia. Many are currently available in local book stores and all will assist those who desire to probe more deeply into any of the subjects covered in the preceding text.

Abrahams Israel; ''By-Paths in Hebraic Bookland''
Blackman Philip; ''The Mishnah''
Berliner Abraham; ''Migdal Hanaeel''
Bentzen, Aage; ''Introduction to the Old Testament''
Bridger, David and Wolk Samuel; ''The New Jewish Encyclopedia''
Baer, Yitzhak; ''A History of the Jews in Christian Spain''
Bentwich, Norman; ''The Jews in Our Time''
Cohen, Dr. A.; ''Everyman's Talmud''
Deutsch, Emanuel; ''The Talmud''
Dimont, Max A.; ''Jews, God and History''
Dubnow, Simon; ''A History of the Jews in Russia and Poland''
Edelman, Lily; ''The Jewish Heritage Reader''
Eichrodt, Walter; ''Theology of the Old Testament''
Elbogen, Ismar; ''A Century of Jewish Life.''
Fein, Harry H.; ''Gems of Hebrew Verse''
Friedman, Lee M.; ''Pilgrims in a New Land''
Friedman Lee M.; ''Jewish Pioneers and Patriots''
Finn, James; ''The Jews in China''
Glazer, Nathan; ''American Judaism''
Goldin, Judah; ''The Living Talmud''
Goodman, Paul; ''History of the Jews''
Graetz, Heinrich; ''Popular History of the Jews''
Ginzberg, Louis; ''Students, Scholars and Saints''
Grayzel, Solomon; ''A History of the Contemporary Jews''
Halevi, Judah ben Samuel; ''Ha-Kuzari''

Harris, Maurice H.; "Hebraic Literature"
Hirsch, Samson Rephael; "The Pentateuch"
Halper, Ben Zion; "Post Biblical Hebrew Literature"
Handlin, Oscar; "Adventure in Freedom"
Herberg, Will; "Judaism and Modern Man"
Holde, Artur; "Jews in Music"
Irwin, William A.; "The Old Testament
Jacobs, Louis; "Seeker of Unity"
Jacobs, Joseph: "Jewish Contributions to Civilization"
Kertzer, Rabbi Morris; "What is a Jew?"
Kravitz, Nathaniel; "3000 Years of Hebrew Literature"
Kohler, Ludwig; "Old Testament Theology"
Kadushin, Max; "The Rabbinic Mind"
Kaplan, Mordecai M.; "Judaism as a Civilization"
Katsh, Abraham; "Judaism in Islam"
Kisch, Guido; "The Jews in Medieval Germany"
Korn Bertram W.; "American Jewry in the Civil War"
Learsi, Rufus; "Israel: A History of the Jewish People"
Liber, Maurice; "Rashi"
May, Herbert G.; "Oxford Bible Atlas"
Marcus, Jacob Rader; "The Jews in the Medieval World"
Minkin, Jacob S.; "The World of Moses Maimonides"
Nahman, Moses ben; "Commentary of Genesis"
Neumann, Abraham; "The Jews in Spain"
Pheiffer, Robert H.; "Introduction to the Old Testament"
Pederson, Johs; "Israel: Its Life and Culture"
Roth, Cecil; "The Jewish Contribution to Civilization"
Rabinowicz, Harry M.; "A Guide to Hassidism"
Reitlinger, Gerald; "The Final Solution"
Roback, A.A.; "Jewish Influences in Modern Thought"
Schwarz, Leo. W.; "A Golden Treasury of Jewish Literature"
Spiegel, Shalom; "Hebrew Reborn"
Steinberg, Milton; "Basic Judaism"
Sykes, Christopher; "Crossroads to Israel"
Wise, Stephen; "Challenging Years"
Wallis, Louis; "The Bible and Modern Belief"
Wolk, Herman; "This Is My God"

INDEX

A.

B.